WALKS AND SCRAMBLES IN NORWAY

WALKS AND SCRAMBLES IN NORWAY

by

Anthony Dyer, John Baddeley and Ian H. Robertson

with contributions from
Tony Howard, Espen Nordahl, Egil Birkemoe, Arnt Flatmo,
Vibeke Steen, Krystina Lotoczko, Denis Wilson and Ann Quirk

Maps by John Baddeley and Alison Haywood

Edited by Anthony Dyer, John Baddeley and Ian H. Robertson

RippING YARNS.COM

Published in 2006 by Ripping Yarns.com, an imprint of
Rockbuy Limited, Findon, Aberdeenshire, Scotland
Website: www.RippingYarns.com

First Edition 2006

British Library Cataloguing in Publication Data
Data Available

ISBN 1-904466-25-7

Printed by
Bell & Bain Limited, Glasgow

Distributed by Cordee, 3a de Montfort St, Leicester, England

Front cover: Kyrkja from Langvasshøe *Anthony Dyer*
Back cover: Approaching the South Top of Jiehkkivárri *John Baddeley*
Frontispiece: Falketind *Ann Baddeley*
Front endpaper: Uranostinden *John Baddeley*
Rear endpaper: Moskenesøya, Lofoten *Ian H. Robertson*

CONTENTS

APPENDICES

MOUNTAIN AREAS OF NORWAY

A Telemark (1)
B Hardangervidda (2,3)
C Folgefonna (4)
D Naerøyfjord (5)
E Jotunheimen (6-14)
F Hurrungane (15-17)
G Jostedalsbreen (18-20)
H Rondane (21,22)
I Dovrefjell (23,24)
J Sunnmøre (25-28)
K Tafjord (29)
L Romsdal (30-33)
M Trollheimen (34)
N Bodø (35)
O Narvik (36-38)
P Lofoten Islands (39-47)
Q Senja (48)
R Troms (49)
S Lyngen (50-53)

The mountain areas of Norway that are covered by this book are shown above. The numbers in the legend refer to the chapters and routes in this book.

Kolåstinden from Kvanndalen   *John Baddeley*

Introduction

*Norway is a country where you can still do "first ascents"
on mountains that have been climbed before.*
Ove Skjerven (writer & mountaineer)

Loftoten Peaks above the Raftsund   Ian H. Robertson

Norway is a long thin, coastal country in the north of Europe with a mountainous spine that stretches 1700k.n along its length. Over 70% of Norway's land is classed as mountainous and the country has one of the most indented coasts in the world with over 25000 km of coastline. It also has one of the most enlightened pieces of land access legislation in the World. Known as "Allemannsretten" it guarantees virtually unrestricted public access to the outdoors. Combine these facts with Norway having one of the lowest population densities in Europe and you have a country that offers more than a lifetime of opportunities for both hillwalker and mountaineer.

Norway has a blend of terrain that will appeal to all tastes; from hillwalkers used to the more gentle areas of the British mountains, to serious alpinists who want countless mountains, both easy and technical, awaiting exploration. The visitor is, however, likely to be struck by the way that Norwegian mountains don't appear vastly different from those in Britain, merely having a compressed horizontal scale and an extended vertical one. This familiar feeling is largely a result of the Norwegian mountains having a broadly similar underlying geology and geological history to those of Britain. A band of Caledonian geology runs up the length of Norway, giving rocks related to the mica schists of the central Scottish Highlands. This is flanked by areas of familiar volcanic rocks such as gabbro (Skye Cuillin) and granites (Glen Etive).

Within the south of Norway, much of the landscape is composed of large swathes of high plateaux punctuated by numerous deep valleys and fjords. The northwestern part of southern Norway has a large concentration of slender summits, ranging from easy to technical. They are much akin to quality Alpine summits, but on a scale that would not be out of place in Scotland. The western part of southern Norway contains mainland Europe's largest glacier: The Jostedalsbreen. The central part of Southern Norway has the highest and most celebrated mountain range in Norway: Jotunheimen. This area contains the largest concentration of 2000m peaks in Norway and has a wide variety of summits from alpine to plateau, and even some icecaps.

While it would be easy to fill many guidebooks with 'he superb mountain areas of the south of Norway, to say nothing of Northern Norway would be a travesty. Most English-language guidebooks pay only lip service to the summits close to and within the Arctic Circle. This region of Norway has an intense concentration of summits along its coast from Brønnøysund in the south to Alta in the north – a distance of about 600 kilometres. The scenic and technical variety of adjacent peaks is stunning and offers opportunities for all abilities and tastes. It is the home of Norway's national mountain – Stetind, as well as one of the most famous and stunning island chains in the world – the Lofoten Islands. Northern Norway is also home to the second-largest icecap in Norway – Vestre Svartisen as well as numerous other large icecaps. The general lie of the land in the north is lower than that in southern Norway, with most of the higher ground lying across the border within Sweden. Being closer to the coast, most of the valleys have altitudes below 300m, while peaks typically reach 1000–1500m.

One of the biggest distinguishing features between the Scottish Highlands and Norway is the vegetation. Norway's vegetation has suffered much less from the effects of overgrazing, animal browsing and deforestation. Thus while many plant communities in each country may be broadly comparable, in Norway they are likely to be more lush. Interestingly, they also often occur at higher altitudes than in Britain, despite the more northerly latitude. For example, in the eastern Dovrefjell the treeline extends up to 1000m, whilst some of the valleys have farmland with populations of luxuriant meadow plants that would not be out of place in lowland England, but at altitudes of 600–700m.

In the mountains, at lower altitudes, natural conifer forests provide thick cover for the undergrowth of shrubs beneath. At higher altitudes and on the coast these pine forests give way to more open birch forests, which grade into more arctic-alpine communities. These often have a rich variety of the more familiar dwarf shrubs, grasses, sedges and mosses, plus many more of the attractive flowering plants often very rare in the flora of Britain uplands (*e.g. Diapensia lapponica*, one of Britain's rarest plants but common in Norway, see picture).

Diapensia lapponica   *John Baddeley*

Norway has spectacular summits at relatively low altitudes – in certain areas such as Lofoten or Hurrungane it is possible to do Alpine-style peaks and still return to your lodgings or car in the evening. In other areas, day visitors will barely scrape the surface of what can be visited on foot.

In the more remote regions, many mountains require a round trip of several days from the road if you wish to reach their summits. Compared with what are considered remote areas in Central Europe, Norway's wilderness areas are an order of magnitude greater in extent. Finding solitude, in its totality, is not difficult and yet in many of the more popular areas, networks of paths and huts maintained by local mountain touring organisations make mountain walking accessible to people in a manner that is not too intrusive on the wilderness.

It is a country that has plenty of room for everyone. Unlike the Alps, man-made intrusions, commercialism and regulations are rare out in the mountains. While antennas, high voltage power lines and bulldozed tracks are occasionally found out in the mountains, their extent is nowhere near as horrific as the commercial exploitations found in the Alps and increasingly in the more remote areas of uplands in Britain. Norway would be very difficult to crowd even if many guidebooks publicised the beauty of its mountains.

Notes on the Use of this Guide

Walking

Mountain walking in Norway is generally more demanding and serious than it is in Britain. One reason for this is that paths are fewer and of poorer-quality than on British mountains or in the Alps. While many T-marked paths are shown on maps, these often turn out just to be a marked route, rather than a constructed path. Another factor is that the underfoot conditions are often quite difficult.

Lower down, forests provide branches and thick vegetation to slow you down, while the roots do their best to increase your chances of tripping or slipping. Although not always easy to find, it is usually worth spending some time trying to locate the start of any path that may be present. Higher up, the terrain at first becomes boggy, which presents familiar problems, then is largely devoid of significant vegetation. Progress across these areas, with a mixture of usually loose and unstable slabs, stones and extensive boulder fields, is tiresome at best, and requires considerable care, especially if they are wet. Higher still, snow is often encountered. While many of the delays encountered in snow travel will be familiar, special note should be taken of the extra time needed to deal both with deep, thawing snow early in the season, and with roped glacier travel. One further factor to consider is the frequent need for what are, by British standards, fairly major stream crossings, especially during times of major snow-melt (see Safety Notes for more information on this).

The commonly used Naismith's Rule (5km/hour plus 1 hour for every 600m ascent), derived in the Scottish Highlands, is an impossible figure to stick to in most mountain areas of Norway. As such, you should plan your walks to allow a lot more time for difficult terrain. When walking through thick forests or across boulder fields, your walking speed would be closer to 2–3km/hour. It is only in the tundra zone that your walking speed is likely to be closer to what you are used to. For this reason, the book includes the author's judgement of the time needed to complete each walk by a reasonably fit and experienced hillwalker. Whilst the times given take the terrain into account, note that the times are for fine, dry conditions with, where appropriate, a "typical" amount of snow cover. Apart from several routes that are established ski tours, we have not attempted to indicate winter routes. Many, but by no means all, routes in the book would be suitable for winter ascents but the reader is left to make their own judgements about such ascents.

Scrambling and Climbing Grades

In common with more recent practice in British guidebooks, we have extended the scope of this scrambling guide to include easier rock climbs (up to Diff). There are also three routes that require technical climbing skills to reach the summits, although they also provide very good scrambling excursions for most of their length. Scrambling grades given in this book have been equated with the three-point scale commonly used for British mountain areas. Here they are given adjectival descriptions, to avoid confusion with the numerical UIAA climbing pitch grading system. Examples of each grade from North Wales, The Lake District and Scotland are given for comparative purposes, but see Safety Notes.

Easy Scrambles (UK Grade 1). A simple route that will be achievable by most experienced hillwalkers. Mainly steep, rough walking but with short passages where hands will be needed. Any exposure will be confined to the easiest sections and the exact route is likely to be variable. (North Ridge of Tryfan; Jack's Rake, Pavey Ark; The Horns, Beinn Alligin)

Intermediate Scrambles (UK Grade 2). More sustained scrambling, with some exposure. The harder sections are likely to be short and not particularly exposed, but holds may be small and you may have to think about how you use them. Individual sections, but rarely the whole route, may be difficult to escape from once committed. Many people may require a rope on short sections, particularly in descent or in poor conditions. (North East Ridge of Y Garn; Cam Crag Ridge, Langstrath; Forcan Ridge of The Saddle).

Hard Scrambles (UK Grade 3). Sustained scrambling with some short sections of more difficult moves, where there may be limited holds that have to be used in the correct sequence. Some parts of the route may have considerable exposure and will often equate with "Moderate" rock climbs. Many parties will use a rope and a small amount of protection on some sections of these routes. (The Chasm, Glyder Fach; Slab & Notch, Pillar Rock; Curved Ridge, Buachaille Etive Mor).

Routes harder than this are given climbing grades, in both the Norwegian (equivalent to UIAA overall grade for easier routes) and British systems. While direct conversions are always difficult, a broad comparison table of climbing grades is given.

Norwegian/UIAA*	UK
I	Easy (moderate scramble)
II	Mod – Diff
III	Diff – Vdiff
IV	Vdiff – S
V	S – VS

Note: some areas (notably Romsdal) use climbing grades in Arabic numerals. We have retained local practice for this book. For the lower grades covered in this guide, these are roughly equivalent to the grades in Roman numerals.

Included Maps

Sketch maps are included for all of the routes in this book. They show the approximate lines of the routes, and are intended to give readers an appreciation of what is involved in a given outing before they purchase the appropriate detailed map. The information on the sketch maps has been compiled from out-of-copyright base maps in conjunction with observations and GPS recordings by the authors on the ground. The positions of crags and other features should therefore be regarded as diagrammatic only, and some actual features may be omitted, exaggerated or shifted for clarity. These maps must **not** be used for navigational purposes: the appropriate Statens Kartverk (or other) large-scale, authoritative topographic maps are listed in each chapter and you need to take these with you on the hill. Web and conventional sources of these products are given in Appendix D.

Warning and Disclaimer

Readers are reminded that climbing, hill walking and mountaineering are activities with a danger of personal injury or death. Participants in these activities should be aware of and accept these risks and be responsible for their own actions and involvement.

Additionally, readers should be made aware that there are additional hazards in the Norse mountains that are not present in British upland areas or some Alpine areas. Please refer to Appendix G for further safety notes and Appendices E and F for details on weather and equipment.

Whilst the authors have made every effort to ensure that the information in this guidebook is as accurate as possible, please be aware that scrambling routes can be changed by rockfall, and glaciers can move or shrink; so the depiction of a route in this guidebook is no guarantee that it will be in the same condition when you visit it. Also, despite our best efforts to be consistent, individual perceptions of routes and difficulties differ, so readers should be prepared to use a considerable amount of personal judgement on all ascents.

"Hill-sense" and experience are as important today as they were in the day of the early pioneers. Ripping Yarns.com and the authors can accept no responsibility for anyone having a mishap through reading this book, directly or indirectly.

1. Gaustatoppen

Anthony Dyer

Gaustatoppen   *Leif-Dan Birkemoe*

Grading: Easy path ascending moderate rocky slopes. Narrow summit ridge. Time: 4–5 hours Overall distance and ascent: 10km, 720m	Access to starting point: From Highway 37, head 3km east out of Rjukan and turn right onto a tarmac road that zigzags up Vestfjorddalen. Start at the car park by Heddersvatn. Maps: Statens Kartverk 1:100 000 Turkart "Hardangervidda"
Best enjoyed: During a period of high visibility to appreciate its status of having Norway's most extensive view.	

Route summary:
A return walk from Heddersvatn car park to Gausatoppen and back. Follow the marked path west-northwest up moderate slopes to the broad south ridge of Gaustatoppen. Continue up the ridge to Gaustatoppen turisthutte and beyond on a narrow ridge to the summit. Return by the same route.

The summit ridge of Gaustatoppen   Anthony Dyer

Rjukan is a bustling town sitting at the bottom of a deep valley off the southern edge of the Hardangervidda plateau. Above the southern side of this valley sits the summit of Gaustatoppen. At 1882m, this summit rises head and shoulders above all other summits within an 80km radius. Because of its relative ease of access from Oslo, it is a popular summit.

The view from the summit is said to encompass an area that is 50 000 sq km making it the most extensive viewpoint in Norway. It may surprise you that the highest mountain in Norway, Galdhøpiggen (2469m) doesn't hold this title, but the proximity of other nearby high summits decreases the viewing area seen from its summit. Galdhøpiggen has a viewing area of 35 000 sq km.

Gaustatoppen is an easy summit for a day. The mountain top itself has a pyramidal profile when seen from the north and a more gentle concave profile when seen from the east. It is made more distinctive by having an antenna enclosed within a cylindrical tower that can be seen many kilometres away.

The walk starts from a car park on its eastern slopes by Heddersvatn lake. The well worn path soon leaves the vegetated slopes for the barren quartzite rocky slopes for the remaining ascent. Quartzite is a very light coloured rock, and forms a complete contrast to the dark gabbro rocks seen further north in the Jotunheim National Park.

8

The path ascends up the summit slopes beside the ski tows to the hut and accompanying military antenna. Beyond the hut, the summit ridge narrows considerably and progress is quite tough up and over many large boulders to get to the summit itself. The walk returns the same way, but a variation can be made by descending the steeper western side of Gaustatoppen to the end of a motor track at Selstalli (2.5hrs, 4.5km).

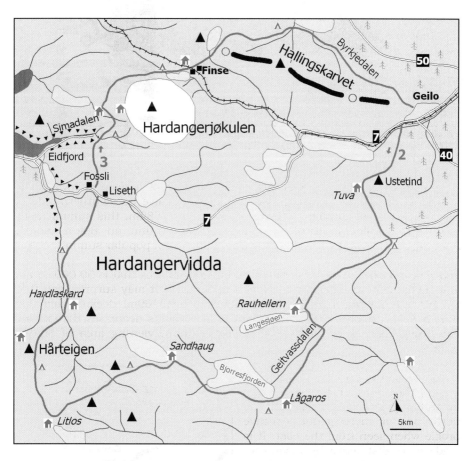

Map for routes 2 and 3

2. Backpacking Across Hardangervidda

Anthony Dyer

Hårteigen seen from the south   *Anthony Dyer*

Grading: Easy Walking over heather and moss. *Time: 6½ days* *Daily distance, ascent and time:* *Day 1: 24km, 680m ascent, 10 hours* *Day 2: 20km, 380m ascent, 7 hours* *Day 3: 22km, 440m ascent, 8 hours* *Day 4: 28km, 200m ascent, 8 hours* *Day 5: 27km, 540m ascent, 10 hours* *Day 6: 22km, 400m ascent, 8 hours* *Day 7: 12km, 520m ascent, 4 hours*	*Access to starting point: From highway 7, the starting point for the walk is 4km west of Geilo at Tuftelia.* *Maps: Statens Kartverk 1:100 000 Turkart "Hardangervidda"*
Best enjoyed: Alone – to fully appreciate the remoteness of the landscape.	

Route summary:
A linear walk from Tuftelia (near Geilo) to Liseth. From Tuftealia, head south via Tuva hut to camp at a major river confluence 2.5km southwest of Åan hut. Day 2: Head southwest towards Rauhellern Hut via the Geitsjøen lake. Camp 2km short of Rauhellern Hut at the end of Langesjøen. Day 3: Head south to Lågaros hut and camp 2km west of the hut at lake "1225m". Day 4: Continue west to Sandhaug hut and on to Besså hut. Camp 2km southwest of Besså at a lake close to the 1300m contour. Day 5: Continue southwest to Litlos before heading north to camp 3km south of Hårteigen. Day 6 & 7: Continue north to the shoulder of Hårteigen and continue to walk northwards past the Hadlaskard and Hedlo huts before heading northeast to highway 7 near Liseth.

Lågliberget and the river Lågen in eastern Hardangervidda   *Anthony Dyer*

The Hardangervidda is Europe's largest mountain plateau. From west to east, this plateau stretches for 85km between the two nearest road points. From north to south, the nearest roads sit 40km apart from one another. This is Norway's largest untracked wilderness area and to put this into context, it would require an area equivalent to 4½ UK Ordnance Survey 1:50 000 Landranger maps to provide complete coverage of this plateau. Another way of comprehending this scale of wilderness is to imagine walking across the Highlands of Scotland from Braemar to Fort William without crossing a single road or railway!

In terms of relief, the plateau exhibits different characteristics. The eastern half of the plateau gently undulates with summits rising up 200m from the lie of the land at 1100m. The eastern plateau is strewn with lakes everywhere and some stretch out for many kilometres. To the west, the wilderness is more rugged with summits rising up 300–500m from the valleys and some of these summits host a number of small glaciers.

The crown of the Hardangervidda plateau is without a doubt the summit of Hårteigen at 1690m. Hårteigen isn't, however, the highest point but it is the most shapely and distinctive summit that also happens to be centrally placed on the plateau. The title of "highest summit" belongs to the mountain of Sandfloegga at 1721m located in the southwest corner of Hardangervidda.

In terms of backpacking, the Hardangervidda plateau has an extensive network of paths linking many DNT huts together. Navigation and route finding is generally easy along these paths although they do occasionally thin out and disappear for temporary periods. Most paths have bridges crossing the streams and rivers although early in the summer season, some of the smaller bridges may not be in place while the annual spring thaw is in progress. These summer bridges are marked on the Statens Kartwerk 1:100 000 map.

This walk describes a route that starts in Geilo to the northeast and takes you straight into the heart of the plateau before emerging into fjord country in the northwest of the wilderness. The route is described as taking 7 days but due to poor weather, I took 8 days to complete the route.

The walk starts at the Tuftelia hotel, 4km west of Geilo town centre. A dirt track takes you southwards to Tuftebrui where the Usteåne river is crossed before a narrow path takes you steeply up a forested spur to the edge of the moorland above. The forest gives way to waist high birches on quite marshy land. This is the boundary between the valley forest and the upland tundra of the plateau. Ahead the path climbs slowly until you pass underneath some high voltage power lines where the slope steepens up, taking you to the summit of Ustetind (1376m).

The view from Ustetind gives the first glimpse into the vastness of the plateau that you will walk through. Far to the south, the pyramid of Gaustatoppen (1882m) can just about be seen 70km away. Gaustatoppen is just a few kilometres south of the southern end of the Hardangervidda plateau. From Ustetind descend west and follow the path heading toward Tuva hut. The hut marks the end of a public motor track and can be quite busy at weekends.

From Tuva, head south, weaving amongst some small lakes and ascend another slope before leaving the marked path at Bjordalsstølan. Descend a thin path serving some private huts. As you descend back into the forest, the path becomes quite tough as you battle through the trees, however this only lasts a short distance before you arrive at another DNT path. Follow the Heinelvi river 2km east, to a major confluence with the Lågen river. Cross a bridge and find an idyllic camping spot on the spit of land between the two rivers.

The next day start the major walk southwest deep into Hardangervidda. A good path follows the north bank of the Lågen river through the forest which steadily thins out to open moorland. You pass beneath a distinct 150m tall crag known as Lågliberget. I've thought of this valley profile with the crag as being a gateway offering passage into wilderness beyond. Soon after this crag, you round a slope above Geitsjøen where the vastness of your walk is presented before you. Your camping spot for tonight still looks a huge distance away.

Langesjøen and the distant Rauhellern hut   *Anthony Dyer*

Around the northeast side of Geitsjøen, the path thins out for 300m amongst low birch and I found that progress was quite tough. The path reforms and provides easy continuing passage for the remaining distance. Camp at the bridge before Langesjøen on the south bank of the river Djupa. The views here are quite extensive with glimpses of the 1900m Hallingskarvet massif seen to the north.

The next day begins by proceeding in a southeastern direction rising up the slopes of Reinavasshovda (1345m). The path then descends into Geitvassdalen where a large suspension footbridge gives access to the south bank of the river.

Here the path follows the river up quite a distinct valley. Although the summits either side only rise some 150m above the path, they feel much higher than they actually are. The path follows the valley for 4km before branching off to cross a few small saddles. Suprisingly you reach a vehicle track that penetrates this far into an otherwise unspoilt wilderness. It's around this track that the westward view opens up again to reveal a vast flat basin hosting lake Bjorresfjorden which seems to stretch on to the horizon.

The path continues south rising up a small slope towards the DNT hut of Lågaros. The hut sits 60m above the flat basin to the west and despite the low relative elevation, it feels rather exposed to the elements. I certainly wouldn't want to be here in a thunderstorm. A good camping opportunity exists 2km west along the path to Sandhaug where a small stream near a lake at 1225m offers water and relative comfort on a thicker carpet of heather.

A long footbridge in Geitvassdalen   Anthony Dyer

On the fourth day, you observe the beginnings of the transition between west and east. The path to Sandhaug briefly departs from Bjorresfjorden to circumvent the south side of a hill before returning to walk on a southern slope above Bjorresfjorden. The view ahead extends 10km to Sandhaug and beyond. What you notice is a band of relatively steep hills to the southwest of the river basin that you are walking in. This band of hills marks the boundary between east and west Hardangervidda.

The DNT hut of Sandhaug marks a junction between five paths. The southern path towards Besså is the path required and this goes up to the slopes of the hills once seen in the distance. On a clear day, the Hardangerjøkulen icecap can be seen 40km to the north across the Nordmannslågen lake. On the day I saw this view, the air was of a clarity that could never be achieved in England.

From Besså, take the path signposted to Litlos and begin the ascent into the rougher hills of the west. 2km southwest of Besså, a fine lake at 1302m provides a reasonable camping opportunity before the vegetation thins out too much.

Bjorresfjorden in central Hardangervidda   *Anthony Dyer*

It may be interesting to know that at this point, the wilderness to the south is completely devoid of any coherent path network. With the exception of local paths serving private huts, you could walk south across untracked country for 40km without crossing any paths. What's more is the fact that this country is very difficult to access and even dangerous to cross on account of some voluminous unbridged rivers such as the rivers Songa and Kvenno.

The fifth day takes you further west into rougher country. Beyond the camping spot, the path continues upwards and as it does so, the vegetation rapidly thins out to reveal a barren land of rock and earth. A saddle is crossed at 1400m and the westward view reveals the remaining portion of the plateau as it stretches out for 40km before ending at the cliffs above Sørfjorden. Immediately ahead, many small knobbled peaks vie for your attention especially around the lake of Skadvatn. I've likened these small mountains to the view of the Langdale pikes as seen from Stickle Tarn in the English Lake District. As you walk past the small mountain of Holken, a shortcut can be taken to the northbound path going from Litlos to Hårteigen. It cuts off a kilometre for those not wanting to stop at the Litlos hut.

The westward journey now ends and is replaced with the journey northwards back to the road and civilisation. The terrain and relief becomes a confused twisted mess. In thick mist, and without the path, navigation here could not be described as "easy". Many micro-features exist and it leaves you wanting something better than the 20m contour intervals on Norwegian Turkart maps.

Besså hut, Nordmannslågen lake and the distant Hardangerjøkulen   Anthony Dyer

Your first view of Hårteigen can be seen after rounding a ridge 3km north of Litlos where the way ahead is seen to undulate across thinly covered hillslopes. Closer to Hårteigen, camping opportunities on thin moss can be had at Sandvatnet (1363m).

On the sixth day, the walk continues north and ascends onto the eastern shoulder below Hårteigen. The view to the north suddenly bursts into view but with the end still a very long distance away. If you want to ascend Hårteigen (500m distant, 200m ascent), the way up is steep and involves easy scrambling assisted by fixed ropes in places.

The main backpacking walk skirts Hårteigen and continues to the hut of Hardlaskard. It begins by descending steeply down luxuriant vegetation. At times, this vegetation can be quite thick and it does slow down your progress on the rough narrow path. Once you reach Hardlaskard, the northward path frequently goes along broad bedrock slabs that provide excellent progress when they are dry but can be treacherous in places when wet due to slippery lichen.

The path continues down the valley of the river Veig and climbs some spurs to avoid cliffs abutting onto the riverside. Continue past Hedlo hut and on northwards to a small bridge crossing a stream. Here a single camping spot is available amongst all the thick vegetation.

Day seven finalises the journey through the wilderness. The final day is a small walk, taking half a day to return to the main road. The walk begins by climbing high above the valley where you see the river Veig disappear, plunging many hundreds of metres down to a valley just above sea level.

The south face of Hårteigen   *Anthony Dyer*

The path then drops into the high valley of Berastøldalen before climbing up the eastern slopes of Hallingehaugane (1300m) along slabby bedrock.

After 2km of moorland walking, you finally descend on bedrock into the forest and cross the huge river of Bjoreio (bridged) and reach highway 7 at Liseth. After seven days, you have walked right into the heart of the Hardangervidda, and even in a one-week trip, there was only a scarce opportunity to climb many summits. In fact, seven days is hardly any time to fully explore the Hardangervidda and more than one visit is required. The next walk detailed starts at Fossli, just one kilometre down the road and explores a mountainous area that is very different to the one just covered.

The map for this route is on page 9.

3. Round the Hardangerjøkulen and Hallingskarvet

Anthony Dyer

Rembesdalskåki – a glacier tongue flowing off Hardangerjøkulen   Anthony Dyer

Grading: Smooth bedrock slabs, short snowfields (some steep) some extensive boulder fields and some long periods of easy walking on trodden footpaths. Time: 4 days Daily distance, ascent and time: Day 1: 15km, 840m, 6 hours Day 2: 23km, 830m, 10 hours Day 3: 22km, 700m, 9 hours Day 4: 34km, 350m, 12 hours	Access to starting point: The starting point is on a short road just off highway 7, 22km east of Eidfjord at the Fossli Hotel. Maps: Statens Kartverk 1:50 0000 Turkart "Finse" & "Hallingskarvet"
Best enjoyed: After a period of heavy rain to see the mighty Fossli waterfall	

Route summary:
A linear walk from Fossli to Geilo. Day 1: From Fossli, head north to a path junction high above Simadalen. Turn east and camp 3km further east just off the path. Day 2: Continue east then northwest towards the hut of Rembesdalseter. Continue west, then north, then east round Hardangerjøkulen. Camp 3km short of Finse. Day 3: Continue east to Finse and beyond on the path to Raggsteindelen. Camp in Raggsteindalen 4km short of the road at Strandavatnet. Day 4: Continue east on the south side of Strandavatnet before heading SE on a path signposted to Geilo. Descend past the Geilo Ski centre to Geilo.

Fossli plunging 200m seen from the Fossli Hotel   Anthony Dyer

After the Hardangervidda, this walk is a complete contrast in scenery. Gone is the vast comparatively gentle plateau and here comes a combination of deep valleys cutting in from the fjords, and heavily glaciated scenery influenced by the Hardangerjøkulen icecap.

The Hardangerjøkulen icecap rises to a height of over 1840m and extends 10km east-west and north-south. It throws out many glacier tongues and this walk passes close to one of the most impressive tongues called Rembesdalskåki.

The Hallingskarvet group has its highest summit at 1933m. The character of these mountains is reminiscent to the plateaux that exist in the Scottish Cairngorms. They throw out quite impressive northern corries which host a number of lakes. This massif is split into two mountains separated by a high pass known as Folarskarvet (1610m). The main difference with the Cairngorms is the presence of fragmented permanent snowfields and some small glaciers in its northern corries.

The walk lasts four days and it completes a circuit started on the previous walk back to the town of Geilo. The route circumvents the Hardangerjøkulen icecap and the Hallingskarvet mountains and provides plenty of scope for you to explore the nearby summits. The settlement of Finse lies in the middle of this walk and hosts a train station serving the main railway line between Oslo and Bergen.

The river Bjoreio flowing towards Eidfjord   Anthony Dyer

The walk begins at the Fossli Hotel. A concrete wall here is all that separates you from the 300m drop on the other side. Looking over the wall, you see the mighty river Bjoreio plunge 200m into this deep valley and release a plume of mist that rises far above your head.

The path heads northwards through birch forest and on up to the mountain moorland, reaching a saddle 2km east of the summit of Storelshaug (1485m). The path then drops steadily down a shallow rocky valley along bedrock in places. The path reaches the lip of a grander valley called Simadalen. Here the muddy path drops steeply down to a broad heathery platform before a colossal vertical drop right down into Simadalen.

Simadalen is a deep U shaped valley that is 1000m deep, 2.5km wide at the rim and 500m wide at the bottom. There are many smooth crags, some over 600m high, that would be hugely popular if they existed in the British Isles.

At the heathery platform, a path junction is met where a turn to the east is made. The heathery platform extends out to become part of an impressive hanging valley known as Skykkjedal which is rimmed by 200m high cliffs. The steep nose of a ridge known as Smørbotnkulten provides passage through these cliffs. From the north side of this ridge, glimpses can be had over a 400m high vertical drop into Simadalen. Higher up the ridge some small grassy basins with minor streams provide ample opportunity for camping before the vegetation thins out completely.

Simadalen extending out towards Simadalsfjorden   *Anthony Dyer*

On the next day, the walk makes a transition from the deep fjord valleys of the west to the glaciated scenery of the icecap. The path continues up yesterdays ridge where it becomes more rocky. The ridge broadens out and reaches another path junction where you pick up a path that heads northwest.

You now descend 200m into a valley that has been carved out by the receding but heavily crevassed Rembesdalskåki glacier. Although the descent looks easy on the map, the path zigzags down bare bedrock slabs that can be quite treacherous when wet. The path descends weaknesses in each crag where you can descend to the next slab. In dry weather this descent should be easy.

At the bottom of the valley, you cross the rapid river by a bridge and then traverse steep grassy slopes above the lake of Rebesdalsvatnet to get to the hut of Rembesdalseter. Beyond you head north but not before heading west to avoid the cliffs that rise up behind the hut. As you ascend you leave the green pastures by the hut behind and venture into a barren landscape with many knolls and tarns. Here it can be quite confusing in mist if you venture off the path.

The view ahead gradually opens out as you gain height. A formidable river is crossed by quite an impressive bridge. The two summits of Luranuten (1637m) and Ramnabergnuten (1729m) would be quite achievable from the bridge were it not for the river, lake Nutvatnet and an abutting glacier barring access to the easy slopes beyond.

The north side of the Hardangerjøkulen icecap   Anthony Dyer

The path continues past the lake of Ramnabergvatnet where a river can be seen at the far end tumbling out of the glacier above the lake. Beyond, the path rises slowly near to a point where an antenna can be seen. The terrain takes you across thin black moss and this makes progress quite easy.

Beyond the antenna, the descent to Finse starts. The path is rough & rocky and negotiates some short steep icy snow slopes. At the bottom of the valley, a bridge crosses the river Ustekveikja and numerous camping spots can be found by this river.

The third day of the walk sees a brief return to civilisation before venturing back into the mountains. From the camping spot, the path meets a popular track known as Rallarvegen. Finse is popular with school and outdoor pursuit courses. It's quite common to see large walking and cycling groups along this track. Finse itself is a compact place with the railway station very much at the hub of all activity. The railway museum is quite an interesting attraction for those with time to spare. Basic food supplies can be purchased here before continuing to Hallingskarvet.

The path climbs gently northeast out of Finse. The views back to the icecap are spectacular. Soon the vegetation disappears around the 1500m contour. The Hallingskarvet massif is hidden from view on this section of the path due to the rather knobbly nature of the ground. The terrain becomes quite tough once you rise up above Flakavatnet with extensive boulder fields slowing you down.

The Hardangerjøkulen icecap seen from the slopes above Finse   Anthony Dyer

The highest point of the entire walk is here at 1620m. Ahead, the path crosses a permanent snowfield which is marked on the map. It's a flat snowfield but it has occasional small visible cracks which are not very deep – about 2–3 metres deep and 30–50 centimetres wide. After the snowfield, the path continues past a deep cut in a valley before opening out to a gently undulating plateau with extensive northerly views.

It is here, on the north side of the Hallingskarvet that you are presented with a series of north facing crags and corries harbouring small glaciers. (This is the Hallingskarvet!) The slopes rise up further behind this steep frontage and still hide the full scale of this mountain group. Some of these glaciers are not on the map, but are quite sizable.

Slowly the path descends into the valley of Raggsteindalen where some camping opportunities present themselves next to the vigorous Raggsteindøla river. If you wish to climb the summit of the Hallingskarvet at Folarskardnuten (1933m), you need to descend to the road to cross the river. The ascent of this mountain looks like a challenging excursion (9km, 930m ascent from the road) which I was unfortunately unable to achieve due to rapidly deteriorating weather.

Hallingskarvet summits seen from the forest near Strandavatnet   *Anthony Dyer*

The route continues along the gravel road along the south side of Strandavatnet the next day. At the southern end of this large lake, a path sets off south-eastwards from the road and makes its way to Geilo. Initially the path ascends through a birch forest, but this soon gives way to vegetated moorland. The path continues along Byrkjedalen amongst boggy ground and plenty of thick shrubs.

A path junction is reached at the watershed. Our path turns right at this junction and continues south-eastwards below some of the most impressive corries in the Hallingskarvet. The cliffs around here rise up very steeply for 400m. A large river is crossed but, contrary to the map, there is no bridge. During a period of prolonged heavy rain, I found the river could be crossed, but not without getting wet up to my knees.

The path continues down to Budalen where a track and some huts are reached. Here, the mountains of the Hallingskarvet are more behind you than beside you. Stride out southeast, leaving the track, across bare open moorland to a cluster of summerhouses served by bulldozed tracks. Soon, you follow the paths down into Geilo by the ski-centre where the walk is concluded.

The map for this route is on page 9.

4. Ulvanosa

Arnt Flatmo

Ulvanosa seen from the valley of Uskedalen   *Arnt Flatmo*

Grading: Technically easy terrain. The route to the summits is marked with Red "T" markers. Be aware of loose boulders above 800m. *Time: 7–8 hours* *Overall distance and ascent:* *12km, 1350m*	*Access to starting point: From Bergen, take route 48 (or ferry) to Rosendal, then south to Uskedal. The Uskedalen trailhead is located on the right hand side, 3.7km from highway 48 ("Musland" exit). A bridge across the river marks the start of the route.* *Maps: Statens Kartverk 1:50 000 sheet 1214-I*

Best enjoyed: The route is more enjoyable in summer, when the rock and boulders are dry. A clear horizon will let you take in the views of the beautiful Hardangerfjord, Folgefonna glacier and Rosendal "Alps".

Route summary:
Follow a forest road to its end, then the marked Ulvanosa path. Follow the marked route to Geitadalstind. Scramble down the ridge to the saddle or follow the flanking path. Follow the ridge up to Ulvanosa. Return by the marked T route which avoids reascending to Geitadalstind.

Geitadalstind in spring   Petter Bjørstad

After moving to Bergen in 1998, I discovered Ulvanosa on my very first hike to Mt. Ulriken. 64km to the southwest, I saw two giant, snow-covered, twin peaks that dominated the southern horizon. I was swept away by this majestic appearance, and promised myself that one day I would be standing on top of these beautiful peaks.

The Ulvanosa (*Wolf's nose*) massif is located above Uskedalen valley in Hordaland fylke (county). Just north of the mountain lies Hardangerfjorden, the second longest fjord in Norway. Ulvanosa is the name of a mountain massif, which consists of several tops and named points. Høgeteen is the highest top on this massif, at an elevation of 1246m. Still, many refer to this top as Ulvanosa.

Geitadalstind is the most characteristic top on this massif, with a distinct alpine profile. The top does not have a map height, but the height is probably in the range 1210-1215m. When translated directly into English, the name means something like "Goat Valley Peak". People in Uskedalen call this peak "nåså" (the nose). People living on the south side of the mountain refer to the Høgeteen high point as "Katthuså". It is very common that people on different sides of the mountain, use different names.

Ulvanosa connects to another characteristic mountain – Englafjell (Angels' mountain, 1200m) through the Fagerdalsskardet pass (approx. 710m). Seen from the north, these two mountains appear as twin peaks, completely dominating their local region. Together with the Rosendal "Alps" a bit to the northeast, Ulvanosa and Englafjell form a mountain region that is unique in Hordaland fylke. Some of the Rosendal mountains require exposed scrambling on the very easiest routes.

26

Geitadalstind seen from Ulvanosa   *Arnt Flatmo*

Ulvanosa is well known by Norwegian climbers. Amongst the popular walls are Øktertindveggen, Aksloveggen, Geitadalstindveggen and Vetletindveggen. A number of routes have been done in these walls, ranging from 4 to 7 on the Norwegian climbing scale. Uskedalen does not have a long climbing history. Although local enthusiasts had been known to climb a number of routes from early on, the climbing community did not discover Uskedalen until late in the 1980's.

The easiest hiking routes from the north and south offer no technical challenges to the average walker, other than safely manoeuvring across small boulders that tend to move on contact. The trail to both summits is marked with the letter "T" painted in red on rocks.

From the bridge (80m elevation), follow a forest road to its end (1.3km), and you will see the "Ulvanosa" trail-sign. Follow the forest path upward (red T markers) As you approach Veslanosa (540m), you get Geitadalstind in clear view up to your left. Ulvanosa lies beyond, and can not yet be seen. The T trail forks at 630m elevation. Take the left path towards Geitadalstind. The path is no longer visible at this elevation, but the route is marked. Proceed up Geitadalstind's northwest ridge. You may either follow the high ridge, which gets gradually more exposed the higher you climb, or stay right of the high ridge, where there is no exposure.

Ulvanosa seen from Geitadalstind Arnt Flatmo

On the summit of Geitadalstind, a majestic panorama appears in front of you. You've probably already noticed the Rosendal Alps and the Folgefonna glacier further northeast, but now you also have the wild and steep Ulvanosa's west face below your feet. Proceed over to Geitadalstind's unnamed south top, and you have the Ulvanosa high point in clear view.

From the south top, the eager scrambler may attempt a direct approach from Geitadalstind down to the Geitadalstind-Ulvanosa saddle. This is a steep and exposed hard scramble. A much safer route is to proceed down Geitadalstind's southwest ridge until you join a T route at 1140m elevation. Follow the T route towards the saddle mentioned above, and follow the high ridge up to the Ulvanosa summit cairn. Upon your return, follow the lower T route that takes you below Geitadalstind (no vertical gain on the return route) and continues towards the trail fork where you turned left on your way up.

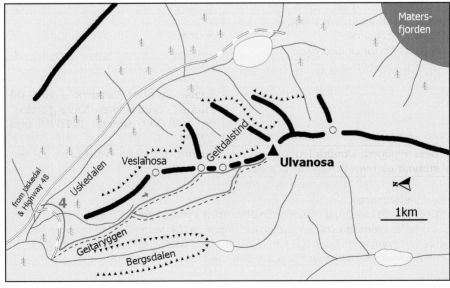

5. Storebreen and the Nærøyfjord

Ian H. Robertson

Storebreen towering above the Nærøyfjord   *www.fjords.com*

Grading: Rough walking over narrow steep paths, followed by a stony plateau. A good introduction to Norwegian mountain walking. Time: 6–8 hours Overall distance and ascent: 13km, 1300 m	Access to starting point: Take the E16 (car or bus service) from Flåm towards Gudvangen. After the first tunnel, leave the E16 and take the no-through road 601 to Undredal. The path starts near the houses at Langhuso ¼km from the E16.
	Maps: Statens Kartverk 1:100 000 Turkart "Stølsheimen–Nærøyfjorden" or 1:50 000 sheets 1416-IV and 1316-I.
Best enjoyed: Jonadalen is enjoyable in any weather. Navigation on the summit plateau is difficult in mist.	

Route summary:
Starting at Langhuso, follow the DNT trail up Jonadalen. At the upper corrie, follow the cairned path up the scree slopes to the plateau. Once on the plateau, take a compass bearing for the top of Storebreen – the summit is not immediately visible from the path. Descend by the ascent route.

The mountain scenery around the head of the Sognefjord is world famous, and rightfully so. The two most spectacular parts are side-branches off the main Sognefjord, these are the Nærøyfjord and the Aurlandsfjord. It is worth giving up a day on the hills for a ferry trip along these two fjords – and I can think of no better compliment.

However, grand as the scenery is, it would be an unusual mountaineer who didn't wonder what the mountain summits were like towering above the ferryboat. This route up Storebreen takes you to the hinterland between the two fjords mentioned above and is a splendid walk through varied scenery and terrain.

A suitable base is the village of Flåm at the head of the Aurlandsfjord. This is a reasonable drive from Bergen for those arriving on the Saturday afternoon ferry; it is also accessible via the Flåmsbann railway from Finse or by hydrofoil up the fjord. All three of these approaches are spectacular.

The glaciated valleys that carve through the mountains are incredibly steep, so the hills are difficult to access. From Gudvangen at the head of the Nærøyfjord, Storebreen and its satellites look impregnable – and they probably are from this direction. However, one chink in Storebreen's armour is the steep glen of Jonadalen.

Formerly, Jonadalen would have been accessed by boat, however now two road tunnels on the E16 connect Gudvangen to Flåm. When driving from one to the other, you briefly "pop" out into the open air in Undredalen. Turn off the E16 here on route 601. Parking is found not far from the E16 junction on the right, those without cars can reach the start of the walk by bus.

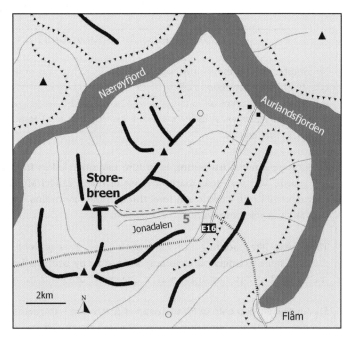

As well as providing a practicable way up Storebreen, approaching from this side also has the advantage that you can motor to a height of 350m; useful as Storebreen is

1662m above sea level. The path starts near the houses at Langhuso, a few metres down Undredalen.

A marked DNT trail winds its way from Langhuso through the birch woods and soon gains height as you climb into Jonadalen. The views continually unfold and you will soon be out of the trees.

Just above the tree line are the remains of a sæter (or shieling). This seasonal high living has gone out of favour since the Second World War, although you may find a few sheep grazing in the grassy alp that forms the higher part of the corrie. At the top of Jonadalen, there are two small lochans and a receding glacier.

Leaving the corrie, the DNT path zigzags its way onto the plateau. To get to the summit of Storebreen you have to leave the marked route and head across the tops. The top is bouldery and stony and precise navigation is difficult. To the northeast of the summit is a small, spectacularly steep glaciated corrie, which is a considerable contrast to the flat plateau.

The author did Storebreen as a medium day walk – bad weather forced an early return down Jonadalen; but in good weather this walk could easily be extended. The highest top on the plateau is Stiganosi (1761m) and this could be included in a high level walk.

For those who want a multi-day walk, the path can be followed south from Storebreen over the plateau then descending to the hut at Grindaflethytta. From here, other paths lead either back to Langhuso, to Stalheim or to Flåm.

Other Outdoor Activities around Flåm

No chapter on the mountains around Flåm would complete without a mention of a couple of other attractions of the area. The Flåmsbann railway winds it way steeply inland from sea level to Finse at a height of 1222m. It is one of the World's most spectacular railways. A landrover track and cycle track ("Rallervegen") runs parallel to the railway tracks.

A highly recommended outing is to hire mountain bikes from Flåm, load them on the guards' van and disembark at Finse or (more easily) Myrdal. You then have an easy downhill ride back to sea level through the mountains. Utter masochists or the very fit can cycle both ways.

Those who like paddling can hire sea kayaks. It is possible to paddle along the Aurlandsfjord to Stigen, a farm only accessible by boat, and ascend Stiganosi from the north. The views are spectacular. See www.fjords.com for more information.

Finally the station café in Flåm deserves a mention – the pizzas are huge! One pizza is large enough for two people, even after a hungry day on the mountains. Shared between two, it is one of the better value meals to be had in Norway.

6. Backpacking in Western and Central Jotunheimen

Anthony Dyer

Hurrungane seen from Urdadalen   Anthony Dyer

Grading: Moderate backpacking tour on well-worn paths, rocky high up. *Time: 6 days* *Daily distance, ascent & time:* *Day 1: 15km, 830m, 7 hours* *Day 2: 10km, 250m, 4 hours* *Day 3: 17km, 400m, 6 hours* *Day 4: 15km, 450m, 8 hours* *Day 5: 15km, 300m, 5 hours* *Day 6: 17km, 520m, 6 hours*	*Access to starting point: From Lom, take highway 55 southwest to Leirdalen where a private toll road is followed south to Leirvassbu.* *Maps: Statens Kartverk 1:50 000 Turkarts "Jotunheimen Vest" and "Jotunheimen Aust".*
Best enjoyed: Any time from mid July until early September when the snow has receded far enough not to cause difficulties.	

Route summary:
A circular walk from Leirvassbu Hotel. From the hotel follow a marked path south to Olavsbu hut with a detour up to Skardalstinden (2100m). On Day 2, follow a path south of Olavsbu to a crossroad on a saddle above Snøholsvatnet. Turn northwest and camp north of the lakes of Mjølkedalstjørni. On Day 3, continue on the westward path down Skogadalen to Utledalen before heading southeast up Urdadalen and camp. On Day 4, carry on along the path southeast to Urdadalsvatnet and onwards to Fondsbu hut. On Day 5, take the path northeast to Gjendebu and finally on Day 6, take the northwest path back to Leirvassbu.

The view east from Skarddalstinden to Skarddalseggje   Anthony Dyer

The Jotunheim National Park has by far the greatest collection of 2000m peaks in Norway. Well over 200 summits breach the 2000m contour, many of which provide spectacular serrated ridges and sheer cliffs plunging hundreds of metres to glaciers below. This is quite understandably the most popular National Park in Norway.

The National Park sits right on the watershed that separates rivers draining into the western fjords, from the rivers that ultimately drain into the south eastern fjords near Oslo. The western half of Jotunheimen receives notably more precipitation than the east, as is seen by the fact that in the west some of the glaciers drop down below 1300m, whilst to the east they barely reach down to 1700m. The west is also more rugged, with the spectacular Hurrungane mountain range rising up from the deep valley of Utledalen. Elsewhere in Jotunheimen, the valleys drop down to altitudes that vary between 1000m to 1300m. While the mountains are the highest in Norway, frequently the relative height of the mountains above their valleys is similar to that in the western highlands of Scotland.

The National Park itself is quite small being roughly 25km north to south and 60km east to west. The actual area of the mountain range of Jotunheimen is about one third larger by area and is bound to the south by Lakes Tyin and Bygdin, to the east by Highway 51, to the north by highways 15 & 55 and to the west by the road linking Turtagrø with Øvre Årdal.

Backpacking in Jotunheimen is well catered for with marked trails and large accommodating huts run by DNT and others. Most paths are very easy but

Midtre Høgvagltindan seen from above Raudalsbandet   *Anthony Dyer*

many of the higher valleys involve prolonged boulder hops and very occasionally you'll find sections that are quite steep with fixed ropes to provide assistance.

The route described takes in a six-day, anti-clockwise tour of the mountains from Leirvassbu in the north to the top end of Utledalen in the west through to Fondsbu in the south before continuing to Lake Gjende in the east and finally back to Leirvassbu. When combined with some mountain ascents it could easily form the backbone of a two-week trip.

On the first day, the path remains above the 1400m contour for the entire duration. Vegetation is at best quite thin in the valley sections. From Leirvassbu, a track is followed south for the first kilometre along the shore of Leirvatnet. Where the track turns west, follow the path branching off south to the saddle at Høgvaglen. You now continue on the path southeast down the very attractive valley of Høgvaglurde to a junction beyond a lake called Nedre Høgvagltjønnen.

The way down Høgvaglurde is dominated by the beautiful pyramidal summit of Skardalstinden (2100m). This mountain makes a great short detour from the main path to Olavsbu. From the path junction, follow the signposted path south to Olavsbu. The path ascends steeply up to the saddle of Raudalsbandet. From Raudalsbandet, Skardalstinden is a three hour round trip up its easy southwest ridge.

Beyond, the path to Olavsbu opens out into Raudalen. The westward view down this valley is one of the best valley views the author has seen in all of

Looking down Raudalen with Vestre Raudalstind (2157m) on the right   Anthony Dyer

Jotunheimen.   The hut of Olavsbu (DNT) at 1420m is located halfway between the northern and southern access points for Jotunheimen.   It's surrounded by four beautiful mountains including Austre Raudalstind (2086m), Store Raudalseggje (2168m), Snøholstinden (Sjogholstind on some maps) (2141m) and Mjølkedalstinden (2138m), and makes an ideal base for several days of peakbagging.

The second day continues the cross-country tour south on the path signposted to Fondsbu. After passing through a field of huge boulders, the path ascends to the 1600m contour before descending to the upper lake of Snøholsvatnet. From this lake, Snøholstinden may well yield an easy route up the summit's western slopes to gain access to the south ridge. If you have time and weather on your side, it would be well worth investigating a route onto this summit. The northwest ridge up to Snøholstinden, however, is the normal route but at times this ridge is said to be quite exposed.

The path rises up to a saddle just above upper Snøholsvatnet where a path crossroad is met. Follow the path northwest down to Øvre Mjølkedalen. Two lakes are passed, collectively called Mjølkedalstjørni. As the valley turns west, camping opportunities can be had.   A second summit worth investigation sits south of this camping spot. Storegut (1968m) offers a 3km long broad ridge to its summit. It should provide excellent views west to Uranostinden (2157m) and Mjølkedalsbreen.

The third day continues on the path west down towards the upper reaches of Utledalen. The valley descends in a series of abrupt steps interspersed with

Snøholstinden seen from Raudalen near Olavsbu Hut   *Anthony Dyer*

long flat pastures down to the treeline where the name of the valley changes to Skogadalen.

At the end of Skogadalen, where the valley opens out into Utledalen, stands the hut of Skogadalsbøen (DNT). This is a good base if you want to head further east for a day to climb Fannaråken, or campsites can be found about 1km north of the hut. Utledalen drains southwestwards in an extremely deep gorge down to Årdalsvatnet which is 3m above sea level. Utledalen also hosts Norways tallest single waterfall, Vettifossen, which has a vertical unbroken drop of 289m. Across Utledalen, is the mighty Hurrungane mountain range. This is the most alpine mountain range in the whole of Jotunheimen with a web of knife edge ridges towering many hundreds of metres above wild glaciers and corries.

Follow the path south until you reach a path junction after 500m. Take the upper path which contours round the mountain slope and into the valley of Urdadalen. You soon ascend out of the forest as the path turns east to continue a steady ascent up to the limit of vegetation. Here you can find numerous camping opportunities which afford grand views back west to Hurrungane and east to Slingsbytinden (2020m) and Uranostinden.

The fourth day of walking continues southeast up to the saddle of Urdadalsbandet and south following the west shore of Urdadalsvatnet. Progress along this shore is slow and rough going across large boulder fields. This terrain continues to Kvitevatnet and east right up to the final descent

Camping high up in Urdadalen beneath Uranostinden   *Anthony Dyer*

down to the hut of Fondsbu. South of Urdalsvatnet, the view opens out to take in Falketind (2068m). As you progress east, the profile of Uranostinden changes to present the mountain as a knife edge ridge. Further information on Falketind and Uranostinden can be found in chapters 13 and 14.

Beyond Kvitevatnet, the path heads east undulating somewhat across boulder strewn moorland. At this point of the journey, the southern view opens out to reveal many kilometres of extensive plateau and rolling summits. The path eventually leaves the moorland and descends down a shallow valley to the main road leading to Fondsbu (DNT) on the western shore of Bygdin.

Bygdin is the largest lake in Jotunheimen. At 1058m, it forms a natural southern boundary for the mountain range. South of Bygdin, the terrain is much more gentle. A boat service operates along the length of the lake between Fondsbu and Bygdin calling at Torfinnsbu.

The fifth day of walking heads east along the north shore of Bygdin before striking north across open moorland and then northeast toward Gjendebu. Progress along this section is quite easy, being mostly vegetated. At Fondsbu, follow a series of tracks initially along the shore of Bygdin before picking up a path that continues along the north shore of Bygdin for 3km. Here, the path ascends diagonally up the steep slope to meet the river Høystakka at the top.   Cross the bridge (summer only) and continue north

Uranostind on the left above Uranosbreen　　　　　　　　　　　　　　　Anthony Dyer

across high moorland. This moorland separates the southeastern Jotunheim mountain ranges from the central ranges. The high point of the day is reached at 1372m before the steady descent down to Gjendebu.

The path continues northeast from the high point down into Vesledalen and the tree line. After another 2km, you arrive at Gjendbu (DNT). One summit worth investigating is Gjendetunga (1516m). From Gjendebu, an unmarked path proceeds west to the summit where you get a view looking east right down the western half of lake Gjende. Further information on Gjende and its surroundings can be found in chapter 11.

The final day follows a path northwest from Gjendebu back to Leirvassbu. The path walks up Stordalen to start with, gently at first and then ascending more steeply at Hellerfossen. Beyond Hellerfossen, the views open out taking in Semeltinden (2236m) to the north, Visbretinden (2234m) to the northwest and Skardalseggje (2159m) to the west. The path continues west-northwest towards Langvatnet.

At Langvatnet, the view will be familiar, ahead is the valley of Høgvaghurde, where you were on the first day. Progress along Langvatnet is easy across the thin vegetation. At the end of Langevatnet, a path junction is met where you then continue to follow the path from the first day back to Leirvassbu.

Falketind seen from the east near Kvitevatnet   *Anthony Dyer*

The walk lasts six days, but in those six days you will see most of the mountain ranges that make up Jotunheimen. After completing the walk, you'll no doubt be persuaded to come and visit Jotunheimen many more times in the future.

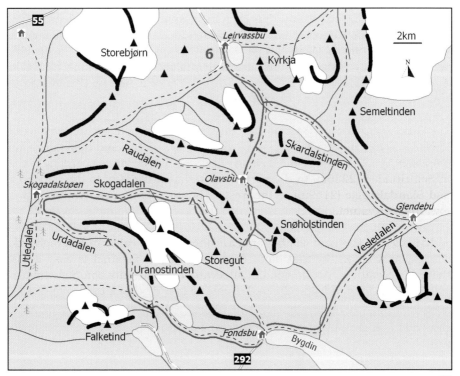

7. Galdhøpiggen – Norway's Highest Mountain

Ian H. Robertson

Crossing the glacier at Svellnose   *Ian. H. Robertson*

Grading: Technically easy, but take care on the crossing of the glacier at Svellnose. An ice axe is recommended. Time: 6–8 hours Overall distance and ascent: 11 km, 1300m	Access to starting point: From highway 55 (Sognefjell road) take the minor road to Spiterstulen. Maps: Statens Kartverk 1:50 000 Turkart "Jotenheimen Vest"
Best enjoyed: Keep for a clear day when the views make all the effort worthwhile. Start early or late to avoid the crowds.	

Route summary:
From the road-end at Spiterstulen, cross the river over the bridge and take the obvious steep path up the hill (DNT trail for Galdhøpiggen). At the signposted junction of two paths, take the left path for the summit (the right hand path contours round to Juvasshytta). Follow the path until the grass (and the path!) give way to boulders. The way is now marked by a series of red T markers over the boulders until the ridge line is gained. Continue to follow the obvious trail until the first top of Svellnose is reached. Now descend to the glacier and cross this with care. After one more top (Keilhaus Topp) the summit is finally in view and a last pull will give you the summit hut and one of the best views anywhere.

The view from the summit   Ian H. Robertson

Galdhøpiggen was not always the highest mountain in Norway – before its icecap receded, Glittertind used to have that honour. But in these days of global warming and climate change, Galdhøpiggen's 2469m summit is now loftier.

There are two popular ways to the top: one is the path from Spiterstulen. This often over-crowded hut is at 1200m, so you will have a 1269m ascent in front of you. Some tourist/walking maps of Norway have times marked on the popular trails. For Galdhøpiggen, the times quoted are 4 hours up and 2 down, but more of this later.

If you think that the approach to Kyrkja is incredibly bouldery, Galdhøpiggen will give you second thoughts. From the plateau edge at 1800m the path peters out, and the way is stepping from boulder to boulder. These vary from the size of footballs to the size of car engines; it is impossible to get into any kind of rhythm. However, the boulders are stable, the passage of many feet has seen to that.

Fortunately, the views get ever more splendid as you gain height – it will take your mind off the underfoot surface. If you are lucky you may also get to see a reindeer at the halfway plateau – they tend to stand around in snowfields during hot weather to cool down.

The crossing of a part of glacier at Svellnose will give some relief from the stones. This section must not be taken lightly. Although there will be a well-worn path and you will probably see some Norwegian kids scampering across here in trainers, a slip would result in an unstoppable slide. This author would certainly recommend an ice-axe. Soon you will be at the summit and the view over the seemingly endless Norse ice fields will be compensation for the ardour of the walk – see the photograph above.

In the other direction you can look down onto the Styggebrean glacier – it looks very tempting from up here. But first you have to get back down to Spiterstulen.

In the appendix in the 2003 edition of Slingsby's book, mountain guide David Durkan had urged some caution on using the path times marked on the maps, stating "Be warned: the Norwegians have long long legs, and the times given do not allow for rests."

It took the author 4½ hours to get to the top, which isn't too bad compared to the map time of 4 hours. However, a long steep descent of over 1000m on boulders is always going to be a slow business, certainly if you want to avoid crocking your knees for the remainder of the holiday. It took the author 3½ hours to descend from Galdhøpiggen. As well as long legs, I deduced that Norwegians must have titanium knees, carbon fibre calves and run down boulder-fields for fun.

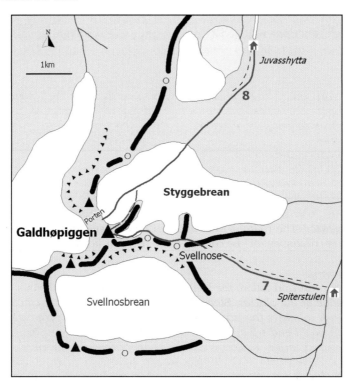

8. Styggebrean – "the Dangerous Glacier"
Ian H. Robertson

On Styggebrean, Galdhøppigen to the left   Ian H. Robertson

Grading: An easy and enjoyable glacier romp. Ice axes, crampons, rope and prussic loops are essential. Time: 6 hours Overall distance and ascent: 13 km, 700m (to Galdhøpiggen) or 13km, 400 m (to Porten)	Access to starting point: From highway 55 (Sognefjell road) take the toll road to Juvashytta (signposted somerski centre) Maps: Statens Kartverk 1:50 000 Turkart "Jotenheimen Vest"
Best enjoyed: Keep for a clear day when the views make all the effort worthwhile. Start early or late if you do not want to follow a long roped team over the glacier. The route is best avoided on a misty day, when navigation through the crevasses will be considerably more difficult.	

Route summary:
Park near the hut and follow the lochan round and then the obvious path. Rope up at the edge of the glacier. Steer right first of all to avoid the crevasses, then steer left back towards the ridge coming down from Galdhøppigen. If you steer left too soon you'll end up in a big crevasse field! For Galdhøppigen, follow the slightly exposed ridge to the summit. To continue the glacier walk, head towards the Porten with care. Watch out for signs of hidden crevasses – this part of the glacier can be snow covered. If in doubt, sign up to join a roped party at Juvasshytta.

Prusik loops at the ready on Styggebrean   *Ian H. Robertson*

If the thought of the view from Galdhøpiggen appeals but the toil up 1269m of boulders does not, then a more enjoyable approach to Norway's highest mountain is over Styggebrean – the "Dangerous Glacier". As the name suggests, this will involve some glacier work and you must be equipped with ice axe, crampons and Prusik loops – and know how to use them. Alternatively you can sign up with one of the roped parties from Juvasshytta.

This is a shorter way to Galdhøpiggen than the path from Spiterstulen, and has the advantage that you can drive up to a height of 1800m! On the other hand, you have to cross Styggebrean. Warning signs that show some poor sod jammed in a crevasse (head down) indicate clearly that the glacier is not to be taken lightly.

Having taken ice axes, crampons, rope and kitchen sink with us to Norway, Krys and I were quite keen to use them and Styggebrean seemed like a sporting day out. (NB I am not masochistic enough to go up to the summit of Galdhøpiggen two days running, we just went to the "Porten" – the col at the top of the glacier).

On this particular day, most of the glacier was "dry", i.e. snow free, however the upper part was snow covered and so we roped up and got the ice axes and Prusik loops out. It was excellent fun and good practice. We also saw about 50 lemmings (dead ones) in the middle of the glacier.

If I was to recommend a way up Galdhøpiggen to someone, this would be streets ahead of the Spiterstulen route – but you need to know what you are doing on the glacier and how to cross crevasses safely.

9. Glittertinden

Egil Birkemoe

The summit of Glittertinden from the east   *Egil Birkemoe*

Grading: Mainly rough hill walking but it includes some snow/ice and a glacier crossing. Some easy scrambling. Time: 2 days Daily distance, ascent and time: Day 1 15km, 1350m, 7 hours Day 2 16km, 300m, 5 hours	Access to starting point: From Spiterstulen, at the end of a private road south from road 55 between Lom and Luster. Maps: Statens Kartverk 1:50 000 Turkart "Jotunheimen Aust"
Best enjoyed: August, with minimum snow cover.	

Route summary:
Day 1: From Spiterstulen, go 1km back down the road and take the marked path to the north east signposted to Glitterheim and Glittertinden. After another 3km the path divides. Ascend in a north easterly direction and keep on the northern-most path following Steindalselvi. After about 6km there is a steep ascent including some easy scrambling, then follow the path, later turning into snow fields and a glacier to the summit. Descend by following the path east to the hut of Glitterheim. Day 2: Return to Spiterstulen following the marked path through Veodalen.

The ascent of Glittertinden, with Galdhøpiggen in the background   *Egil Birkemoe*

Glittertinden is Norway's second highest mountain at 2452m, only surpassed by Galdhøpiggen at 2469m. However as Glittertinden has a permanent ice cap some additional, but variable, metres must be added to its height and for many years it was considered as the highest point in Norway. On the 1998 map the height is set at 2472m, making it higher than Galdhøpiggen. According to the locals at Glitterheim, there have been below-average winter snowfalls since then, and Glittertinden has been regarded as lower than Galdhøpiggen. However, in the winter 2004/2005 the snow gained height and Glittertinden is most likely the highest peak in 2005. Official measurements have not been made in recent years, which leaves the discussion open. The dedicated peak-bagger is advised to climb both while in the area, just in case. The route described here makes a traverse of the mountain from west to east, returning the following day through valleys. This makes the most of the area and gives you the chance to stay in two of Norway's more historic mountain huts.

From Spiterstulen follow the road north 1km and take the well-marked path signposted to Glitterheim and Glittertinden. The ascent starts when you leave the road and takes you to the first plateau at 1500m. During the climb take some breaks to enjoy the views across the green, vegetated valley of Visdalen, where Galdhøpiggen becomes more visible as you ascend. When reaching the ridge where the path levels out under Skauthøe, the path divides before starting to go up again. The path to Glittertinden goes north east and is clearly marked.

Approaching the summit of Glittertinden   *Egil Birkemoe*

Continue towards the next steep ascent ahead, making some stops to look at Veobreen and its surrounding mountains to the south. Cross the Staindalselve and fill up your water bottles, as this is your last chance for a refill before the summit. The steep ascent starts here, including some easy rock scrambling, and takes you from 1700m to 2100m before it levels out. During the ascent make several stops and enjoy the magnificent view of Galdhøpiggen with surrounding mountains and glacier, as well as Veobreen glacier with its many peaks. The higher part of this ascent is a good spot for a lunch, where it will probably be less windy than further up.

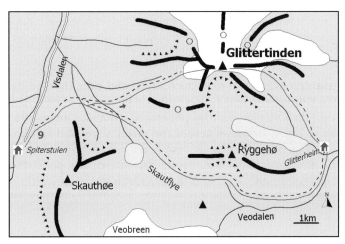

Looking up the Veo river to Voebreen   *Egil Birkemoe*

The final 350m of ascent is not as steep: head first across boulder fields before you finally reach the snow-cap and glacier covering the top. In some years the blue of the glacier is visible and the local view is that no glacier equipment is needed [although the editors know of at least one incident of a person falling into a crevasse near the summit]. Do however keep left, close to the vertical drop to the north, as there are crevasses further to your right on the slope down south from the summit. The ridge is usually corniced so keep some metres away from the northern edge. Navigation on this section is tricky and people have fallen off, so if in thick weather and without the usually obvious path you may have to turn back before the summit. The final steps to the summit are almost flat and give a pleasant walk with an opening view to the east, where the mountains are less rugged. Return can be made by the same route, but it is recommended that you continue to Glitterheim. This hut is located just beneath the east side of Glittertinden. A return to Spiterstulen can be made the next day without much ascent.

Descend to Glitterheim across snow in an easterly direction. The opening picture of this chapter shows Glittertinden from the east, with its characteristic icecap. Follow the footsteps or take a bearing to Point 2274m, where you leave the glacier and continue down in a south easterly direction, following the path to Glitterheim at 1384m. Glitterheim is operated by DNT and offers good food and a relaxing atmosphere. It has been operated by three generations of one family over almost 100 years, making it one of the more classic DNT cabins. From Glitterheim it is possible to take daytrips to many of the nearby mountains.

The return from Glitterheim to Spiterstulen is best done on the marked path starting to the southeast along the Veo river. From the path you have a great view of Veobreen ahead as the path turns to west. Five kilometres from Glitterheim the path turns to northeast away from Veobreen. A steep ascent of 150m to Veslgluptjønnen takes you to the highest point of the path and over into the Skautflye valley. This leads back down to the fork in the path where you began the ascent of Glittertinden the day before. From there, follow the marked path back to Spiterstulen.

Another classic outing in Jotunheimen –   *John Baddeley*
on the East Ridge of Store Bukkholstind

10. *Kyrkja and Visbretinden*

Ian H. Robertson & John Baddeley

Kyrkja – the cathedral   *John Baddeley*

Grading: Mainly rough walking over rocky ground and boulder fields. The summit tower of Kyrkja is an airy but easy scramble. Optional ascent of Visbretinden involves intermediate scrambling. Time: 10 hours (6 hours Kyrkja only) Overall distance and ascent: 13km, 1400m (8km, 700m for Kyrkja only)	Access to starting point: From highway 55 (Sognefjell road) take the private toll road to Leirvassbu. Maps: Statens Kartverk 1:50 000 Turkart "Jotenheimen Vest"
Best enjoyed: On a dry day when the boulder fields and scrambling sections will be dry and non-greasy.	

Route summary:
For the direct ascent to Kyrkja: from the road-end at Leirvassbu, follow a track then a path southeast along the shores of the Leirvatnet to Høgvaglen col at 1518m. Follow the developing path through the rocks to the minor top at 1843m. Descend to the col at 1755m. Ascend north through steepening boulder fields to a section of easy scrambling up the summit tower. To descend, reverse this scramble, then follow the ascent route back to Leirvassbu.

*To include Visbretinden, from Leirvassbu follow the path around the north side
of Leirvatnet to the lake of Kyrkjetjørni. Scramble up northwest ridge of
Visbretinden, easy at first and intermediate near summit. Descend southwest
to col 1958m and ascend Langvasshøe (2030m). Follow the broad ridge of
Kyrkje-oksle to northwest over loose boulders to col at 1755m, south of Kyrkja.
Ascend and descend Kyrkja as described above.*

Kyrkja from Langvasshøe   *Anthony Dyer*

The Jotunheim, the "home of the giants", is probably Norway's most popular
area, and rightfully so. Valley level here is about 1400m and there are
glaciated peaks less than 1000m above. Valley level in the Jotunheim is
considered by some to be comparable in character to hut level in the Alps,
but without the altitude problems. To get the best out of the Jotunheim you
should take a tent and go into the interior, but there are some excellent
peaks which are also accessible as day walks.

One of the best is Kyrkja – the cathedral. It is a short walk from the roadhead (and hut) at Leirvassbu. In high summer it can be ascended without
going over any snow or ice, so it makes for a day with a comparatively light
rucksack. The inclusion of Kyrkja's taller neighbour, Visbretinden, turns the
route into a full mountain day out, with much more scrambling.

The usual ascent route up Kyrkja is easier than it looks, despite the
mountain's spectacular appearance. It is a boulder scramble onto the col at
1755m, between Kyrkja and its neighbouring peak (point 1843m) to its
south, and then more boulders to the foot of the final summit tower.

The scramble leading to the summit of Kyrkja   *Anthony Dyer*

This final tower looks quite intimidating at first glance, but is a straightforward easy scramble. The easiest line follows the lighter rocks, where the thick black lichen crust has been worn away. There is one tricky move (at the bottom for a change) – and that move has a hidden undercut bombproof handhold if you look for it. Overall, it is perhaps comparable in scrambling grade with Bristly Ridge on the Glyders. Remember though that you will need to reverse the scramble to descend.

The summit though is very different from Glyder Fach. It is a small summit, and you feel on top of the world. The views from Kyrkja are also immense. Whilst the Norse ice fields are impressive, the mountain that draws the eye is the neighbouring peak of Visbretinden. It is an irresistible challenge and its ascent as part of a longer circuit is highly recommended.

~

An alternative to the ascent of Kyrkja described above is to combine it in a circuit, ascending Visbretinden by its northwest ridge and then heading to Kyrkja via Langvasshøe. This gives a route of great variety and interest throughout. The ascent of Visbretinden has the feel of real exploratory mountaineering, without being unduly difficult or committing. Finishing on the summit of Kyrkja, if possible near midnight around midsummer, is a perfect finale.

Visbretinden from the north   *John Baddeley*

The approach can be from either Leirvassbu to the west or Spiterstulen to the north, although the latter is considerably longer (add 12km, 300m). Both are straightforward, on T-marked paths. There are superb views of Kyrkja from either approach, which should be enough to whet anyone's appetite. For now though, concentrate on Visbretinden, best seen on the approach from the north. From here it has one of the classical mountain forms; a central summit with two long, sweeping ridges falling from it encircling a small, crevassed glacier. The scene could be compared to a much more extreme version of the Scottish Ben Lui.

The ascent begins from the east end of Kyrkjetjørni, where there are potential campsites. Aim for the bottom of the northwest ridge of Visbretinden across steepening boulder fields. Bands of glacial slabs cut across the direct route but the degree of difficulty these present is largely a matter of choice, as the mood takes you. The ridge becomes better defined with less choice of route as height is gained, and affords good views of the glacier. At about 2000m the ridge flattens and has several small pinnacles that must be negotiated before you can tackle the final steep section to the summit. Up to now there has been nothing more than easy scrambling, with situations that are impressive but not particularly exposed. This final ascent has some intermediate sections that are harder and steeper.

The rock quality is reasonable but as with all the routes in this book, even ones like this in popular areas, you should use much more caution than on a

On Visbretinden looking towards Kyrkja   *John Baddeley*

typical British mountain scramble. It may be possible to avoid this section by a traverse south but this is across very steep boulders so on balance it is probably best to stick to the ridge.

The summit (2234m) appears suddenly and is marked by a small cairn. There is an extensive panorama of peaks of the Northwestern Jotunheim. Most arresting is the view to the north across the deep trench of Visdalen, to the sharp peaks and expansive glaciers of the Galdhøpiggen massif. In the opposite direction is the major valley of Storådalen, forming a principal through-route between Leirvassbu and Gjendebu, at the head of lake Gjende. Beyond this are glimpses of the bulky mountains of the Southeast Jotunheim (see Chapter 11).

To continue to Kyrkja, head down the steep SW side of Visbretinden. This is very bouldery and loose in places, so care is necessary. From col at 1958m make the short, easy ascent of Langvasshøe (2030m). Although this mountain is often classed as a 2000m peak in its own right, the situation is such that it feels like a minor spur of Visbretinden. Now turn northwest and follow the broad, bouldery ridge around to join the route described above at peak 1843m for the ascent of Kyrkja.

Descend from Kyrkja as described above if returning to Leirvassbu. If heading north, descend northeast into the corrie from col 1755. High in this corrie is a large snowfield that can ease passage over areas of steep loose boulders.

Vestre Raudalstind seen from Kyrkja   Anthony Dyer

This descent route can be icy, so at least an ice axe should be carried if you plan to use this route. Descend by the north edge of this snowfield, then go down to the west shore of Kyrkjetjørni and follow this back to the marked path.

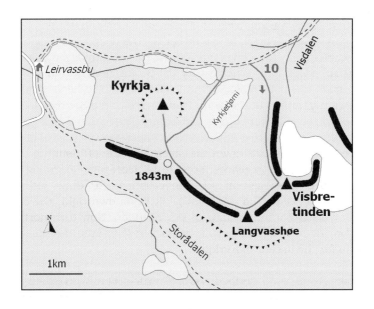

11. Gjende, Besseggen and Besshøe

Anthony Dyer

Besseggen and Bessvatnet   *Anthony Dyer*

Grading: Rough and bouldery with very easy scrambling on Besseggen. *Time: 2 days* *Daily distance, ascent and time:* *Day 1: 12km, 800m, 6 hours* *Day 2: 16km, 900m, 8 hours*	*Access to starting point: From Fagernes, take highway 51 north to Maurvangen and turn left onto a short side road to Gjendesheim.* *Maps: Statens Kartverk 1:50 000 Turkart "Jotunheimen Aust"*
Best enjoyed: In August or early September.	

Route summary:
A circular walk starting and ending at Gjendesheim. On the first day the route starts on a westward marked path crossing Veslfjellet. This path descends the mountain via the narrow western ridge of Besseggen down to the saddle between Bessvatnet and Gjende. The route then leaves the path to head northeast along the north shore of Bessvatnet to camp by the Grotåe stream. The next day, head up to Besshøe via the Brue ridge on the south side of Besshøbrean. Return to the camping spot and then continue east along the Bessvatnet shore to its eastern end where a marked path is picked up heading south back to Gjendesheim.

Knutshøe seen across Lake Gjende   *Anthony Dyer*

Lake Gjende lies at the eastern end of Jotunheimen National Park. The lake is designated as a UNESCO World Heritage Site and that makes it one of the most important lakes in the world. It certainly isn't difficult to appreciate some of the reasons why. The lake lies east-west and is 20km long and 1km wide. The lake has a milky green colour due to the glacial rivers feeding it with rock flour. On either side of the lake sit steep mountain slopes, glaciers, thundering mountain streams and impressive summits, many of which exceed 2000m in height.

No paths traverse the full length of the lake's south shore. A combination of steep ground, big rivers and thick forest all act as an effective deterrent for an enjoyable exploration of this side. The north side of the lake, however is well served with popular mountain paths. It is the north side of Gjende that this walk covers.

The walk starts from Gjendesheim hut at the eastern end of the lake near the edge of the National Park. The hut is a popular place complete with a large pay and display car park and other tourist facilities. Two marked paths head off to Memurubu – a hut half way along lake Gjende. One path sticks to the lake shore while the other goes high up over the mountain plateau. The upper path is the one to follow.

Gjende seen from the saddle with Bessvatnet Anthony Dyer

The path initially heads north out of Gjendesheim, through the woodland and out onto the mountain moorland above. Soon a path junction is reached where the left branch is taken. The path continues up steeper slopes to reach the upper slopes leading to the Veslfjellet mountain plateau. The vegetation disappears here and the path turns west to head up bouldery slopes up to the broad mountain plateau of Veslfjellet (1743m).

The summit lies at the far end of the plateau where the view suddenly opens up to reveal the rest of Jotunheimen. Soon after leaving the summit, the ridge tapers away to become narrow and scrambly. It is not too dissimilar in difficulty to Striding Edge in the English Lake District. The route is popular, almost as popular as Striding Edge itself. The views across Gjende are majestic as is the view of tomorrow's summit, Besshøe (2258m).

At the bottom of Besseggen, you reach the saddle between Bessvatnet and Gjende. The saddle is dramatic in that Bessvatnet sits just a few metres below the saddle, while Gjende sits 400m below; down steep, near vertical cliffs. At this saddle you depart from the path to head northeast along the shore of Bessvatnet. Above you sit some of Besshøe's southeast facing crags which thrust out in between steep scree gullies. Soon you reach a series of minor streams (not marked on the map) near a major stream called Grotåe. The streams all provide camping opportunities on sloping ground.

Besshøe and Bessvatnet   *Anthony Dyer*

The next day, an ascent of Besshøe is made. The easiest way up is to stay on the west side of stream Grotåe until it disappears into the glacial moraine. The terrain becomes much rougher now that the vegetation has disappeared. An ascent aiming for the Brue ridge should be made taking care not to get too close to Besshøebrean where the ground is composed of large loose cumbersome boulders. If you trend to the south side of the broad ridge, you will find easier ground.

Higher up, the ridge remains broad but gains definition with a steep corrie to the left above Bessvatnet and cliff to the right above Besshøebrean. The ground higher up makes for easier progress on bedrock rather than loose moraine. The ridge merges into the broad summit slopes and soon you reach the large summit cairn. Not far away, a huge cliff plunges down 800m to lake Russvatnet. It goes without saying that the views from Besshøe are tremendous.

Return the way you went up and then continue east along the Bessvatnet shore on gentle slopes. The vegetation is luxuriant around Bessvatnet, but not so as hinder progress. At the eastern end of Bessvatnet, a path is taken south to Gjendesheim. 500m south of the lake there is a junction, take the left fork. The path steadily descends down through thicker vegetation and eventually woodland back into Gjendesheim.

The map for this route is on page 65.

12. Leirungsdalen, Tjønnholstinden and Svartdalen

Anthony Dyer

Leirungsdalen with Munken Mugna on the left   Anthony Dyer

Grading: Extensive rough and rocky ground with one occasion of easy scrambling Time: 2 ½ days Daily distance, ascent and time: Day 1: 12km, 350m, 4 hours Day 2: 14km, 1300m, 10 hours Day 3: 14km, 750m, 8 hours	Access to starting point: From Fagernes, take highway 51 north to Maurvangen and turn left onto a short side road to Gjendesheim. Maps: Statens Kartverk 1:50 000 Turkart "Jotunheimen Aust"
Best enjoyed: In fine weather, late in the summer when the snow has receded.	

Route summary:
A linear walk starting in Gjendesheim and ending at Gjendebu. On the first day, cross the river Sjoa with the boat service. Follow the path south towards Leirungsdalen where a bridge is crossed and the river is followed up Leirungsdalen. A good camping spot is found just below the 1300m contour. The next day, the route heads northwest off track for the summit of Tjønnholstinden. From the summit, the walk continues west and then south to the subsidiary summit of Tjønnholsoksle before descending south to Leirungsdalen to regain the path. The path heads west to Svartdalen where some camping is possible. On the final day head northwest up Svartdalen and then ascend the north ridge of Nørdre Svartdalspiggane before returning to the path and descending down to Gjendebu.

Kalvehøgde seen from the slopes below Tjønnholsoksle   Anthony Dyer

The south side of Gjende contains a fine range of mountains which host impressive corries, glaciers and alpine ridges. A volumous river called Leirungsåe flows into the south side of Gjende. This river flows down a wide valley that cuts right into this mountain range. The valley is called Leirungsdalen and a large number of peaks encircle this valley giving it a wild character despite being less than 10km from the road.

As well as exploring the two valleys of Leirungsdalen and Svartdalen, this walk also climbs the summits of Tjønnholstinden (2334m) and Nørdre Svartdalspiggane (2137m). Despite the proximity to the popular Gjendesheim hut, the valley is relatively quiet and this is probably due to the long distance needed to walk from Gjendesheim to the next nearest hut at Torfinnsbu via this valley.

The walk starts by crossing the river Sjoa at Gjendesheim where it forms the outlet to lake Gjende. This river is huge, and cannot possibly be waded. For a nominal sum of money, a boat service is provided by the hut to take you across to the start of the path. People coming the other way can summon the boat service with a bell on the far side of the river.

The path starts through thick vegetation as it heads south passing by lake Nedre Leirungen and continues roughly parallel with highway 51. At a path junction, the path turns west down into Leirunsdalen where a bridge is used to cross the river Leirungsåe. Here the valley is broad and shallow with expansive marshes near to the river.

Looking north along Svartdalen   *Anthony Dyer*

The path heads southwest and departs from the river to keep a good distance above the marshes. Where the path rejoins to follow the river, the valley closes in and it is here that the wild mountains of Leirungsdalen present themselves. About 30 minutes later, some good camping ground can be had among some old stone circles.

The next day is a full mountain walking day up to Tjønnholstinden. When I did this summit I made many wrong turns that cost me a lot of time. The way to the summit is all off track and begins by ascending the easy heather clad slopes northwest to rockier ground above. Wherever possible it is advisable to trend more to the west than the north. There is much loose glacial moraine here. A small glacier abutting onto the south side of Steinflybrean needs to be circumvented on its western side. If you try for the ridge of rock in between the two glaciers, you will certainly slow to a crawl as you try to negotiate house sized boulders of dubious stability. The western side of this glacier is good bedrock and is easy to walk on.

This bedrock takes you onto the final summit slopes leading up to Tjønnholstinden. Make a rising diagonal traverse to gain the broad western summit ridge of Tjønnholstinden. I made the mistake of heading straight up to the eastern ridge only to be confronted with an exposed ridge demanding some short climbing pitches. The views on the top are as expected, spectacular. To the north, a cliff face drops near vertically for 300m to the glacier below, while the westward ridge leads the eye towards the alpine ridges of Skavflyløytinden (2250m).

Nørdre Svartdalspiggane seen from Gjende   *Anthony Dyer*

The route continues west towards the saddle with the subsidiary summit of Tjønnholsoksle (2145m). There are numerous rocksteps along the western ridge of Tjønnholstinden and these are avoided by trending a little to the north along this otherwise broad ridge. The route heads south and ascends Tjønnholsoksle before descending steep bouldery slopes down to the corrie in which Skavflyløyftbrean sits. Beneath this glacier, the vegetation slowly returns by the time you reach the 1600m contour.

You rejoin the path. It now passes beneath the magnificent glaciers of the Kalvehøgde mountain range to the south as it heads west towards the rough and rocky watershed with Svartdalen. The watershed is very barren, being completely devoid of vegetation. The view across to the Svartdalen summits, however, is impressive. The path finally finishes the day by descending steeply down to Svartdalen where some camping on thin vegetation is possible by the lake at 1475m.

On the final day, the route takes you up to the summit of Nørdre Svartdalspiggane before heading down to Gjendebu hut. The path heads northwest beneath the impressive Knutsholstinden (2341m) towards the northern end of Svartdalen before it drops steeply down to Veslådalen.

Just before the drop down to Veslådalen, strike west off towards the bottom of the steep rise to Svartdalspiggen's north ridge. A series of red T's marks the way up to the summit. This route isn't marked on the map. The steepest and most difficult part of the route is getting onto the north ridge itself. Some short easy scrambles are had in places. Once on the ridge, the ascent is straightforward on rough bouldery ground and the red T's guide you up the broad ridge to the summit. The final 50m of ascent is a little steeper, with a simple clamber on solid bedrock. Once on the summit, the southern view opens out to reveal an impressive exposed ridge continuing south to the other summits of the Svartdalspiggane chain.

I returned the same way back to the path before continuing steeply down into Veslådalen where the forest returns. The path continues round the head of Gjende to Gjendebu hut. At Gjendebu, a scheduled passenger ferry service can be taken to get you back to Gjendesheim.

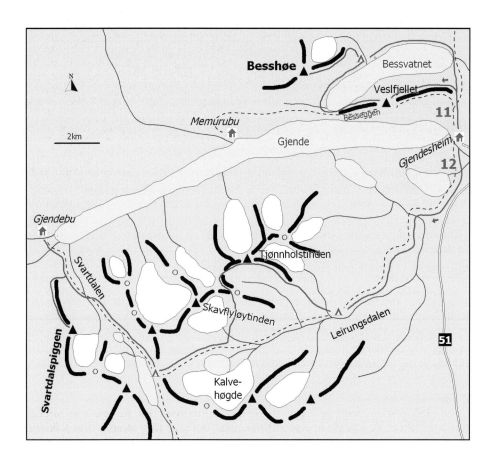

13. Falketind

John Baddeley

Falketind from the east John Baddeley

Grading: A simple mountaineering outing, including a glacier crossing and some easy rock scrambling. Time: 8–10 hours Overall distance and ascent: 16km, 1000m	Access to starting point: Take the minor road up the east side of Lake Tyin to Tyinholmen. From there, take the rough road west to the hut of Koldedalen. Maps: Statens Kartverk 1:50 000 Turkart "Jotunheimen Vest"
Best enjoyed: Mid-season, when snow has melted from rock but still covers crevasses. Morka-Koldedalen can be very dangerous in winter, making this route impracticable.	

Route summary:
From Koldedalen hut, go through Morka-Koldedalen as far as the stream coming from Stølsnosbreen. Ascend the west bank of this stream and follow it until you reach the glacier. Go east up the glacier until you can gain the West Ridge of Falketind, and scramble up this to the summit. Descend the North Ridge, turn west and descend the glacier to rejoin your outwards route. Follow this back to the road.

Steep scrambling up to the glacier   *John Baddeley*

Falketind is one of a small number of peaks whose allure was so great that they were ascended before mountaineering as a sport really began in Norway. In this case it was in 1820, by Christian Boeck and Baltazar Keilhau. In contrast, Slingsby, the "father of Norwegian mountaineering", didn't make his first visit to the country until 1872.

Together with Stølsnostinden, Falketind forms a compact massif in the south western corner of Jotunheimen. From most angles Falketind appears as a spectacular summit. The most imposing view of all is from the east, where the sharply pointed summit stands above long drops into the surrounding valleys. From this angle its form is mirrored by Hjelledalstinden to the south, across Morka-Koldedalen. The route described in this chapter ascends Falketind from the east, although it is also possible to climb it from the west, from a base near the huge waterfall of Vettifossen.

Start at the hut of Koldedalen (Årdal Turlag). It may be possible to drive this far, but the road is sometimes barred or blocked with snow 1.5km further back. Just west of the hut you must cross the braided river outflow from Falkebreen. Continue westwards, into the deep and rocky valley of Morka-Koldedalen. We are not used to thinking of valleys as difficult places to travel but this one is. On both sides, steep rock outcrops drop down into a chain of small lakes. The ground is rough and bouldery, and the line of the traversing path is broken in many places by large slabs and outcrops of rock. Avoiding them necessitates much steep up and down. The whole valley, and especially the north side, below the now towering summit of Falketind, is particularly

The West Ridge of Falketind   *Ann Baddeley*

hazardous in winter and spring due to avalanche risk, when the area is best avoided. Slingsby gives an entertaining account of what he believed to be the first crossing of this valley.

Pass the first lake (1291m) on the north side, generally keeping about 10m above the water. Towards the far end there is a tricky passage across a large snow patch that sits in a shady hollow. This may be quite firm, an ice axe and possibly crampons will be necessary for safe crossing. A slip will result in at least a cold swim, and possibly a lot worse, so take care here. Once across, the vague path continues more easily to the end of this lake and down slightly to the larger lake of Andrevatnet. Again, stick to the north side of this lake on a path of sorts, a short distance above the shore.

When you are just over halfway along the lake it is possible to begin a rising traverse across the hillside above you. Aim to cross the stream coming from Stølsnosbreen about 100m above the lake, then follow the west bank of this stream up moderately steep scree. At about 1400m the angle increases as you encounter a band of slabs. Although they look a little intimidating from below there is nothing harder than easy scrambling up these, but take care as there is plenty of loose rock to dislodge. The slabs could be slippery and quite difficult in the wet.

These slabs end rather suddenly in a pleasant open bowl, through which the stream meanders. Cross the stream at a convenient point, rope up and head up onto the glacier. Keep to the right-hand side as you go up this, gradually curving around to the east. Continue heading due east until you are north of the prominent nose on the West Ridge of Falketind. Turn south, cross from the glacier onto snow fields and scramble easily up onto the West Ridge, from where the views down the 800m drop into Morka-Koldedalen are particularly impressive. The half-kilometre journey along the ridge is pleasant and airy, but not difficult, all the way to the small summit of Falketind (2067m).

Massive drops lie to the south and east, the latter apparently overhanging for a considerable distance. There are fine views of Uranostinden to the east, but it is hard to look anywhere other than north west, towards Hurrungane. This relatively compact group of sharp summits and steep icefalls offer some of the finest mountaineering days out in Norway and are best seen from this angle.

Slingsby said of the view, "*the grimness and sharpness of the peaks coupled with terrific precipices bounding deep and dark defiles, the wild glaciers, cataracts, rivers, forest land, green clearings, and picturesque sæters combine to form a view of exceptional beauty and grandeur*".

Some ascents in Hurrungane are described in chapters 15 to 17, and the area has just had its first English guidebook published (see bibliography).

When you have finished taking in the view, begin your descent down the North Ridge. This is initially quite steep but not difficult. Follow along the crest until it starts to level out and an easy passage can be made westwards onto Stølsnosbreen. Staying well to the south avoids the worst of the crevasses on this glacier, which you continue down until you join your outward route, and follow this back to the road.

It is also possible to carry on along the ridge following on from the North Ridge of Falketind, around Stølsnosbreen, to take in the summit of Stølsnostinden (2074m). This is a fine peak in its own right, and the inclusion of it with Falketind makes for a good, if much longer, day out.

The map for this route is on page 74.

Stølsnostinden from Stølsnosbreen   *John Baddeley*

14. Uranostinden

John Baddeley

Approaching the summit of Uranostinden from the South Ridge   John Baddeley

Grading: A good mountaineering trip with rough walking, a grade II- (UK Mod) ridge climb and a glacier crossing. Time: 6–9 hours Overall distance and ascent: 13km, 1150m	Access to starting point: Take the minor road up the east side of Lake Tyin to Tyinholmen. From there, take rough road west to Raudehaugen. Maps: Statens Kartverk 1:50 000 Turkart "Jotunheimen Vest"
Best enjoyed: Mid-season, when snow has melted from rock but still covers crevasses. Ascent via glacier and north ridge used as a ski route.	

Route summary:
From Raudehaugen, head for the southern end of the South Ridge of Uranostinden. Ascend this, go over the two southern tops and climb the ridge to the summit. Descend north to a col, and then head steeply down eastwards onto Uranosbreen. Go south to the end of the glacier, then back to the starting point.

The summit of Uranostinden from the South Ridge   *John Baddeley*

Approaching Jotunheimen from the south is always an exciting experience. The first good view of the mountains comes at the south end of the large lake of Tyin, where there is a fine panorama of distant peaks seen over the water. One of these catches the eye more than any other, a large and shapely pyramidal peak. This is Uranostinden, first climbed in 1876 by Slingsby and Mohn, on the same trip as they made the first ascent of Store Skagastølstind (see box in chapter 15). The route described here makes a south-north traverse of the peak, and includes an easy climbing ascent of the South

Ridge. Those not wanting to take this line can ascend by the much easier descent route but should note that although not climbing, it does involve a glacier crossing.

Start at Raudehaugen, on the minor road to the hut of Koldedalen (Årdal Turlag), where a large stream comes down to Koldedalsvatnet from the north. How close you can get a vehicle to this point depends on snow cover. Frequently, snowdrifts block the road until into July, so bear this in mind. A telephone call to the DNT hut at Fondsbu (see accommodation appendix for DNT link) might be a good way to check the access situation. Cross the bridge and take the path on the west side of the stream northwards for 2km, until it forks, and follow the right branch down to the outflow of Urdadalsvatnet. Now quit the path and take the best line north up increasingly steep and rocky ground towards the prominent South Ridge of Uranostinden. The ridge becomes better defined as height is gained, and is composed mainly of large boulders of rough gabbro, covered with very hard crusty lichen. Some small sections of easy scrambling, in particular a short, narrow length of ridge, present themselves higher up, until the ridge levels out as you reach the South Eastern Top (2048m). On the final approach to this top you get the first good views of the main summit, which appears both impressive and daunting. Head northwards along the narrow and well-defined, although not difficult ridge: make a short descent, go over the small rise of the South Top (2037m) and continue until you reach the base of the final ascent.

Ahead lies the most difficult section of the ridge and many will want to rope-up here. Although the technicalities on this climb of about 150m are not great (Grade II-, UK Mod), in places the exposure is intense. It is broadly comparable with the North Ridge of Clach Glas, on the Isle of Skye. Begin by going up a short, narrow ridge, and then make a short traverse left over large drops until it is possible to ascend a well-marked chimney back onto the ridge. Follow the crest from here, where a less steep section of ridge gradually narrows. The most exposed part is an inclined slab at the end of this section, about 8m long, which tips away steeply to the right and ends abruptly with a large drop to the glacier hundreds of metres below. Traverse this slab on a system of small cracks for the feet and using the knife-edged top of the slab as handholds. This is no place for a slip, and it is worth considering placing some protection, if only for the benefit of your second. A long pendulum fall might leave you hanging free over the end of the slab. At the end of the slab is a short and slightly tricky corner. Climb this on the left-hand side and then regroup, before continuing up the rest of the easier but spectacular ridge to the tall, thin cairn on the narrow summit ridge of Uranostinden (2157m).

Exposed climbing on the South Ridge   *John Baddeley*

The views from the summit are impressive in all directions. Back south is the fine profile of the South Ridge, backed by the blue expanse of Tyin and endless rolling hills, with Gaustatoppen obvious on a clear day. East are the bulky, rounded hills of the eastern Jotunheim, while to the north the heavily glaciated massif of Galdhøpiggen is the most prominent sight in a sea of peaks.

Start your descent by heading north down a gradually broadening snow ridge. This leads out onto a glacier and if it is snowy you may not be able to spot the transition, so you may want to rope up before leaving the summit. Where the angle of the ridge eases into a col your route lies down to the east.

There is often a sizeable cornice on the edge, so choose your place of departure from the col with care. It may appear tempting to continue into the large glacial col several hundred metres further north east. Beware that this route will take you into an area of often huge crevasses, largest nearer to Urdaknatten. Those feeling like some more peak bagging can continue north west from the col up to the minor top of Slingsbytinden (2026m).

The steep descent from the col (large crevasses possible) establishes you on the Uranosbreen. Although this glacier is gently sloping, it has lots of small crevasses so care is needed if it has snow cover. Go down this, staying on its western half until the ice ends in a pile of moraines. Exiting the glacier may be easiest at the eastern end of the small lake (1518m). From there it is a short distance westwards to rejoin your outward route, which is followed back to the road.

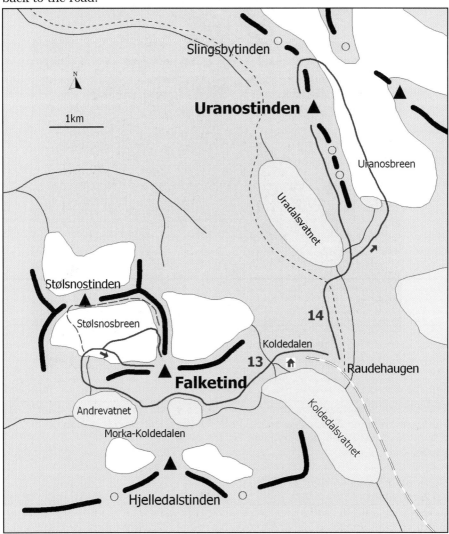

15. Beneath the Shadow of Storen

Ian H. Robertson

"Slingsby" at Bandet, below Storen   *Krystina Lotoczko*

Grading: A simple walk as far as the lake of Fremste Skarstølsvatnet. The final section to Bandet crosses a crevassed glacier. *Time: 6 hours* *Overall distance and ascent:* *12km, 900m*	*Access to starting point: Start at Turtagrø Hotell on highway 55.* *Map: Statens Kartverk 1:50 000 Turkart "Jotunheimen Vest"*

Best enjoyed: The paths are viable under any conditions, but this is a walk that is best left for a good day for the views. Navigation on the glacier in mist is for experts only.

Route summary:
From Turtagrø follow the marked path southeast to the Tindeklubbhytta.
Continue on the marked route over the edge of the boulder field to the
Skardstølsbreen glacier. Cross the glacier with care and climb to the col at
Bandet. Return by the same route.

Store Skagastølstind, more commonly known as Storen, is the most famous
peak in Norwegian mountaineering. Its ascent involves rock climbing to grade
V and is for experienced climbers and mountaineers only; however the walk
to the col of Skardstølsbandet ("Bandet") is straightforward and is in fact one
of the best walks in the Hurrungane.

To get to Bandet, you will
need to cross the glacier of
Skardstølsbreen for which
full glacier travel equipment
is required. However, even if
snow and ice is not your
scene, the walk up the
Skardstølsbotn to the lake of
Fremste Skardstølsvatnet is
still highly recommended – it
is without doubt one of the
most beautiful little lakes in
Norway.

Start at Turtagrø hotel
(914m) and follow the
marked path southeast. After
a couple of hours of effort
you will reach the private
climbing club hut. The view
north to the ice cap of the
Jostedalsbreen is outstanding, but the best is yet to
come.

Fremste Skardstølsvatnet   Ian H. Robertson

Follow the path over the boulder field along the east shores of Fremste
Skardstølsvatnet, one of the most beautiful lochans that the author has seen.
At the edge of the Skardstølsbreen glacier, you will need to stop and put on
ice axes and crampons. There is at least one deep crevasse to be crossed en
route to Bandet, so you will need full glacier equipment to tackle the glacier.

Before too long, you will reach the col at Bandet (1758m). The small DNT hut
here is popular with climbers awaiting a break in the weather to climb
Storen, which towers above the col at a height of 2405m. If you are more a

walker than a climber, this is the end of the road – but the views from Bandet are outstanding.

For those who want more excitement, the climbing routes up Storen are described in James Baxter's excellent "Hurrungane" book.

Dyrhaugstindane from Bandet   *Krystina Lotoczko*

The map for route 15 is on page 82.

The First Ascent of Storen in 1876

The most famous ascent in Norwegian mountaineering took place on 21 July 1876. W.C. "Cecil" Slingsby and his two companions, Emanuel Mohn and Knut Lykken, set off from Vormelid to climb Store Skagastøstind (Storen). Until this day it had been considered "unclimbable".

Slingsby and his companions reached the col below Storen, now called Mohn's skar. At this point, Knut and Mohn declared, "We can now say that it is perfectly impossible."
However, Slingsby decided to give it a try and pushed on alone. Even though the rock was verglassed and was a grade III climb; he made it to the summit, a remarkable achievement for the time.

He built a small cairn on the "unsullied crown of the peerless Skagastøstind" and wedged his handkerchief into the cairn. All Slingsby had to do now was to downclimb back to the col, unroped...

The handkerchief was later seen by telescope from Fortun, thus proving that Storen had indeed been climbed. It remained in place, until the second ascent two years later, when Harold Petersen retrieved it. It is now framed and hangs on the wall of the Tindeklubbhytta below the mountain, the most famous handkerchief in Norwegian climbing.

Slingsby's story remained out-of-print for over sixty years, until his classic *"Norway: the Northern Playground"* was republished in 2003. Apart from the exciting story of the first ascent of Storen, the rest of the book is still a splendid introduction to the Norse mountains. The pictures that accompany this chapter were taken during the book republication celebrations, hosted by Turtagrøs Venner – the friends of Turtagrø – in August 2003.

Mountaineering note:
"Slingsby's Route" up the mountain goes from Mohn's Skar, above Slingsbybreen glacier. This route is very rarely climbed these days – global warming has resulted in Slingsbybreen receding leaving the final approach to Mohn's Skar on smooth unprotectable slabs. The usual way up is from Bandet.

~

Turtagrø Hotel has an extensive mountaineering book library – sadly in 2001 the old wooden hotel burnt down and a collection of over 1500 mountaineering classics went up in smoke. The hotel has since been rebuilt and Turtagrøs Venner have restocked the library. It now possesses one of the best collections of climbing books anywhere in the world. It is well worth a visit, perhaps whilst waiting for the clouds to clear over Storen...

16. Store and Midtre Ringstind

Egil Birkemoe

Store Ringstind seen from the start of the glacier   *Egil Birkemoe*

Grading: A good mountaineering outing, which includes some steep snow/ice, a glacier crossing, and some easy rock scrambling. Glacier equipment essential in summer. Skis recommended in May/June. *Time: 9 hours* *Overall distance and ascent:* *20km, 1400m*	*Access to starting point: From Turtagrø, on road 55 between Lom and Luster.* *Maps: Statens Kartverk 1:50 000 Turkart "Jotunheimen Vest". 1:25 000 map "Hurrungane" is available at Turtagrø.*
Best enjoyed: Early/mid season, which reduces the crevasse danger and gives you one of the best and longest ski descents in Norway.	

Route summary:
From Turtagrø, follow the road to Øvre Årdal for 1.5km, then take the path up the north side of Ringsbotn. Five hundred metres before the head of the valley, take an open snow gully to the left. After 200m of ascent, leave the gully and follow a path to a ridge at the start of the glacier. Go up the glacier on the north side of Midtre Ringstind above the bergschrund, to reach the col between Store and Midtre Ringstind. Climb both mountains from here and return by the same route.

The Summit of Midtre Ringstind, looking towards Store Skagastølstind   Egil Birkemoe

Store and Midtre Ringstind are two of the most spectacular peaks in Hurrungane. They are located in the centre of the area, with excellent views from the summits to Store Skagastølstind, Dyrhaugstindane and Austanbotntindane. The mountains are accessible without technical climbing and can be ascended on foot or, early in the summer, on skis. Store Ringstind is one of the most popular ski routes in the greater Jotunheim area in May/June. The route includes a crossing of the Ringsbre glacier, for which full glacier equipment is required. Turtagrø hotel will have updated information on the current condition of the glacier. The route is described as a day trip from Turtagrø. Alternatively, you can camp on the glacier (with due regard for your choice of site) and have easier access to several other summits in the area.

From Turtagrø, go south west along the road leading to Øvre Årdal while enjoying the view of Skagastølstindane. In good weather you have an excellent view of Store Skagastølstind, indicating why it is regarded the classic mountain in Hurrungane and one of the finest in Norway. After about 1.5km the path to Ringsbotn leaves the road to the south. Follow the path along the north bank of the Ringselvi. The south bank of the river is also possible but it can be difficult to cross further up depending on snow bridges.

When entering Ringsbotn you get the first view of Store Ringstind, soon followed by Midtre Ringstind. Enjoy the views while you go up the valley on the path on the east side of the river. About half a kilometre before the head

Store Austanbotnstind (L) and Store Ringstind (R) from Midtre Ringstind   Egil Birkemoe

of the valley the path makes a steep ascent to the east. Walk up a snow gully, which could be very slippery in wet weather. About half way up the ascent, leave the snow gully on the right and join a path. Depending on season the snow gully may not be possible and you have to follow the slippery path from the valley. Once on the ridge you have access to the Ringsbre glacier, and this is a starting point for other walks on the glacier as well. It is a nice spot for a break to enjoy the view of the valley and Store Ringstind. The first picture in this chapter is taken from this ridge, with the route below Midtre Ringstind visible on the left.

Rope up, go onto the glacier and head north west of Midtre Ringstind, walking between it and the bergschrund to reach the col of Gravdalsskar (1750m) between Midtre and Store Ringstind. Gravdalsskar is the starting point for both summits. From the col the view to the south down Gravdalen and the surrounding Stølsmaradalstinden and Austanbotntindane opens up. This is a nice spot for camping if staying overnight.

Store Ringstind is reached by following the glacier all the way to the top. Keep to the left side of the glacier for the first part to avoid crevasses. Follow the glacier until you leave it about 50 metres from the summit where it ends, and go straight up to the summit of Store Ringstind (2124m). The panorama is stunning in all directions; south west to Austanbotntindane, Stølsmaradalstind to the south east, Store Skagastølstind and Dyrhaugstindane to the north east and Ringsbotn valley and Turtagrø to the north. From the summit, follow your tracks back down to Gravdalsskar. This decent is particularly enjoyable on skis.

Midtre Ringstind is reached from Gravdalsskar by an easy scrambling ascent, keeping to the left (south east) side. Note that Midtre Ringstind is marked as 2284m on some maps, but it is really 2025m. The view is not as open as from Store Ringstind, but there is a great view of Store Ringstind with Austanbotn-tindane in the background. Descend by the same route to Gravdalsskar, then by the ascent route back to Turtagrø.

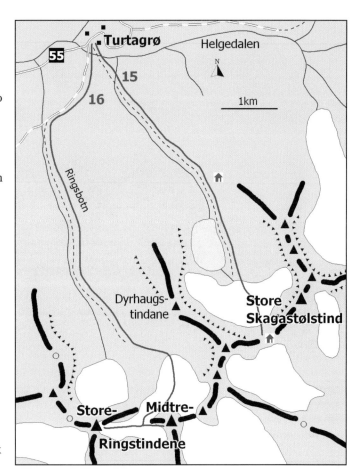

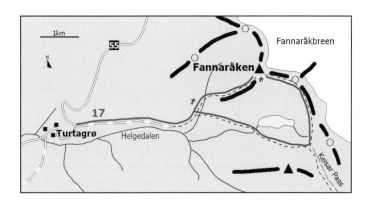

17. Fannaråken

Ian H. Robertson

Fannaråken summit hut   Ian H. Robertson

Grading: A straightforward walk on well marked paths. Time: 8 hours Overall distance and ascent: 18 km, 1100m	Access to starting point: Start at Turtagrø Hotell on highway 55. Map: Statens Kartverk 1:50 000 Turkart "Jotunheimen Vest"
Best enjoyed: The paths are viable under any conditions, but this is a walk that is best left for a good day to savour the extensive summit views.	

Route summary:
Follow the private track up Helgedalen to Ekrehytta. Follow the marked path for Fannaråken. From the summit, head east to Fannaråknosi then southeast along the path to the head of the Keisar Pass. Return along the main track to Ekrehytta and Turtagrø.

The view over Fannaråkbreen towards Galdhøpiggen   Ian H. Robertson

Driving west across the Sognefjell road, it is impossible not to have your eyes drawn to Fannaråken. This is a mountain with one side heavily glaciated. Its ascent from the hotel at Turtagrø is a good walking day out. This route avoids the glacier, so a light rucksack can be carried – in summer, no ice axes or crampons are required.

A pleasant walk up Helgedalen leads to a steep path zigzagging up the west ridge of Fannaråken. Although this mountainside is littered with boulders, the path is surprisingly good and rapid progress can be made.

The summit has the highest mountain hut in Scandinavia, so the sense of desolation apparent from the Sognefjell road is somewhat lacking, but the views are superb. We reached the top at mid-morning and were lucky enough to have a clear view; this is at the western end of the Jotunheim and consequently catches a lot of rain and mist compared to the mountains further east. Another path leads east from the summit to the subsidiary top of Fannaråknosi. From here an easy descent leads to the top of the Keisar Pass.

A well-used cross-country route goes through the Keisar Pass between Turtagrø and the hut at Skogadalsbøen, and this makes a gentle easy descent back to Helgedalen, making a good circular walk.

The map for this route is on page 82.

18. Jostedalsbreen Ski Traverse

Egil Birkemoe & John Baddeley

At the top of Lodalsbrekka, looking to Småttene and Lodalskåpa (R)   Kjell Olav Maldum

Grading: A demanding, multi-day ski camping expedition across a large, crevassed icecap. Escape routes difficult in bad weather.	Access to starting point: Sota Sæter, on the minor road that leaves road 15 at Skjåk.
Time: 4 days Daily distance, ascent and time: Day 1: 25km, 1100m, 12 hours Day 2: 20km, 750m, 8 hours Day 3: 27km, 200m, 8 hours Day 4: 5km, 0m, 2 hours	Maps: Statens Kartverk 1:100 000 Turkarts "Breheimen" and "Jostedalsbreen"

Best enjoyed: On ski in late May or June. Clear, settled weather essential.

Route summary:

A north-south traverse of Jostedalsbreen. Day 1: From Sota Sæter take the usually snowy road on foot to Mysubutta. Go up Mysubuttdalen to Slæom cabin on foot or skis depending on the snow conditions. Cross Kupløyftet and go down to Kupvatnet before ascending Austdalsbreen to the top of Lodalsbrekka. Day 2: Ski down Lodalsbrekka, then up Småttene. Follow the glacier to the highest point, Høgste Breakulen. Day 3: Ski east of Kvitekoll, passing Bings Gryte and over Suphellebreen to Flatbrehytta. Day 4: Ski down to the road at Suphelledalen.

Brenibba (L) and Høgste Breakulen (R) from Lodalskåpa   *James Baxter*

Jostedalsbreen is the largest glacier on mainland Europe. It is an icecap that covers about 487km², with several significant tongues reaching down to lower levels, including several popular tourist attractions such as Briksdalsbreen. The icecap and its immediate surrounds fall within the boundaries of a National Park, which is famous for its wide variety of environments within a short distance of each other. The area is well worth visiting even if only to do relatively easy activities without venturing onto the ice. There is a fascinating variety of geological and geomorphological forms, interesting flora and stunning views. Chapter 19 describes two short walks to the edges of the ice cap, whilst chapter 20 ascends Lodalskåpa, the highest peak in the area.

The route described in this chapter is the sole ski-only route in this book, and is not a walking route. It is included to give non-skiing readers a flavour of the "other side" of the Norwegian mountains, and if done later in June, could easily be combined with a walking tour elsewhere in southern Norway. The traverse is mostly above 1700m and you feel like you are on the roof of Norway, seeing the fjords to the west and Jotunheimen to the south east. The route traverses the icecap from north to south over four days. Accommodation is by camping, making a high degree of fitness essential for its full enjoyment as you will be carrying ski, glacier and winter camping equipment, plus food.

Jostedalsbreen lies between two of the longest fjords in the World, Sognefjorden and Nordfjorden, making it particularly prone to prolonged periods of cloudy weather. However the ideal time to do this route is late May

Looking south along the icecap to Kjenndalskruna   *John Sundt*

or June, when settled, high-pressure conditions tend to prevail. The Jostedalsbre Traverse is a classic route to do during the weekends covering Ascension Day or Whit Sunday as these are public holidays in Norway. If you choose to do the route at these times do not expect to be alone.

Despite the increasing popularity of the traverse, there are several safety points that should be borne in mind. The route is almost all on glacier. While it is difficult to ever recommend unroped glacier travel, this route is unfeasible without substantial sections of it. Thus skiers should be fully aware of the risks they are taking, be highly competent at assessing crevasse hazards, seek current local advice, and rope up if in any doubt. The sections of the route where roped travel is considered essential are indicated. Weather changes on the glacier are common and upon camping in clear weather, ascertain your position, mark it on the map and note compass bearings to escape routes and the next day's course. A GPS can be a great aid to navigation on this route, but do not neglect the paperwork, especially in cold conditions when batteries may fail.

Day 1: This day is the hardest of the trip. It covers a third of the distance and contains most of the ascent, and your pack will be full of food. However, the investment of effort will be repaid during the rest of the trip. The route begins at the cabin of Sota Sæter. To facilitate an early start it is best to stay overnight at the cabin, or in a tent. The cabin is privately owned, but offers

Skiing to Høgste Breakulen   *John Sundt*

a discount for DNT members. Walk about 4km on the road to Mysubutta, which is an alternative place to camp instead of Sota. Follow the path up Mysubuttdalen, cross the river and then keep south west of the river. Depending on snow conditions, ski or walk to Slæom cabin (DNT, unstaffed) about 5km from Musubutta. From here, ski due west up to the highest point of Kupløyftet pass at about 1450m, where you get the first view of Jostedalsbreen. Descend to Kupvatnet, and go out onto Austdalsbreen, which is your first part of Jostedalsbreen. Keep south of Klubben and Stornosa, to reach a campsite immediately before the descent of Lodalsbrekka. From this camp you have a magnificent view of Lodalskåpa and down Erdalsbreen. The picture at the start of this chapter is taken from this campsite. If the weather turns, an escape down Erdalsbreen is a possibility.

Day 2: This day is the most spectacular. Start by descending Lodalsbrekka. Keep on the east side where there are fewer crevasses. Depending on the conditions you may have to rope-up for the descent. From the bottom, where Lodalsbrekka, Strupebreen, and Småttene meet to form Lodalsbreen, you ascend Småttene. This heavily-crevassed icefall definitely needs a rope, and later in the year may be uncrossable. Look for the area of least crevasses and skin up the 600m to Ståleskar. This pass is a place renowned for being sheltered from the wind, and hence is a good place for lunch, and a popular camping site. From here you can make the detour to the summit of Lodalskåpa (see chapter 20) if you feel fit. Carry on to Kjenndalskruna (1830m), which gives you a good view of Lovatnet, almost at sea level, and

Campsite overlooking Fjærlandsfjorden   *Egil Birkemoe*

continue to the highest point of the glacier, Høgste Breakulen (1957m). There is a cairn just past the summit. Camp between Høgste Breakulen and Kvitekulen (1930m), where you will have a good view of Jotunheimen for supper and breakfast. If it is windy, continue to Ramnane for a more sheltered campsite.

Day 3: This is a day to savour, with easy skiing across the high glacial plateau, keeping in mind that almost the entire ascent is behind you. There are great views of glaciers to the west and the peaks of Jotunheimen to your east. Ski north west of Kvitekoll and Ramnane then due south west to Bings Gryte, in about 15km. Bings Gryte is a formation created by the wind on the narrowest point of the glacier. In cloud be sure not to fall into it. Keep heading due south to Suphellebreen, and exit the glacier at Flatbreen, just west of Point 1261m where the real descent starts. A narrow natural half-pipe takes you to Flatbrehytta (DNT, unstaffed) where you can camp, and enjoy the view down Fjærlandsfjorden far below. It is possible to descend to all the way to Fjærland on this day, but the view of the fjord below makes it worth staying high for the last night.

Day 4: Descend Tverrdalen down into Supphelledalen, to the bus stop at Skarestad. At some stage depending on the snow conditions you will finally have to take off skis and continue on foot, undoubtedly tired but happy that you have completed one of the classic ski tours in Europe. An excellent end to the trip is to take a ferry from Fjærland to Flåm and the train back to Oslo, if that is your starting point. While you are waiting for the bus you can visit the glacier museum at the water front, to find out more about this fascinating area.

89

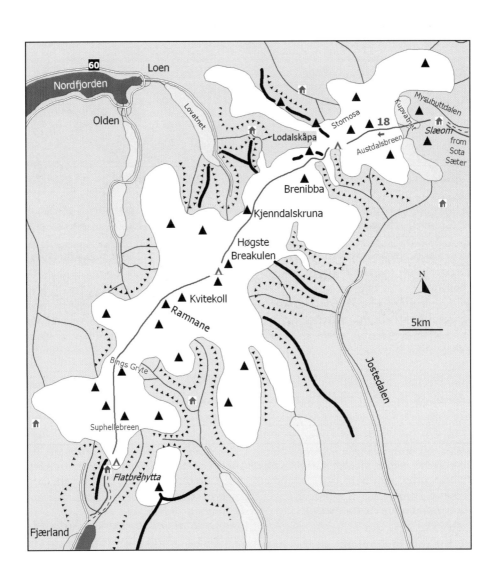

19. To the Edges of the Ice Cap

Ian H. Robertson

Approaching Bødalsbreen　　　　　　　　　　　　　　　*Krystina Lotoczko*

Grading: Two alternative short walks to the edges of the Jostedalsbreen Ice Cap. You will need ice axes, crampons, a rope and prussic loops to have a romp over the ice; otherwise these are straightforward non-technical walks. Time: 4–6 hours each. Bødalsbreen: Overall distance and ascent: 8 km, 600m Flatbrehytta: Overall distance and ascent: 8 km, 800m	Access to starting point: For Bødalsbreen, leave highway 60 and follow the minor road along the Lovatnet. Take the private toll road to Bødalsætra. For Flatbrehytta, leave highway 5 north of Fjærland and take the minor road to Supphella. Start at the car park at GR 825150. Maps: Statens Kartverk 1:100 000 Turkart "Jostedalsbreen", or 1:50 000 sheets 14181V and 13171.

Best enjoyed: The paths are viable under any conditions, but venturing onto the ice is best avoided in mist. Start early on Bødalsbreen to avoid the risk of stonefall.

Route summary:
For Bødalsbreen, cross at a footbridge at Bødalsætra to the south bank of the Bødalselva river. Follow the path southeast. Where the path forks, take the right branch (not for Lodalskåpa!). Avoid the steep ice at the glacier snout by easy-angled snow on the right.

For Flatbrehytta, follow the marked path from the car park up beside the Krokgilja stream. Where the path branches, take the left hand branch. To return from Flatbrehytta, follow the marked path ESE of the hut to return by an alternative path.

Jostedalsbreen is the largest ice cap in Europe. Whilst a full traverse across it (on skis) is for experts only; most walkers or mountaineers should be able to visit the edges of the ice cap. You won't see anything like this in Britain, and one of the two walks below is highly recommended.

The approaches to the edge of Jostedalsbreen are on good paths, but if you have experience of winter walking, taking an ice axe, crampons, rope and prussic loops is recommended – late in the summer after the snow has gone, you can have endless fun cramponing over easy-angled blue ice. It is also a good place to practice crevasse rescue skills in a controlled situation.

The approach from the north (route 19a) is to the glacier tongue of Bødalsbreen. This is a beautiful easy-angled blue glacier, and is in fact everyone's textbook idea of what a glacier should look like. The next valley along has the more famous Briksdalsbreen, but this is very touristy. In amongst the tourist shops in Briksdal there are places where you can hire a glacier guide, useful perhaps if you are inexperienced and want to undertake a bigger trip, maybe even on to Lodalskåpa. Accommodation can be found in Olden and Loen, or at the DNT self-service cabin at Bødalsætra.

The minor road alongside the Lovatnet is one of the most beautiful in Norway, the lake is a bright green colour, caused by the glacier waters flowing into it. However, this peaceful valley has been the scene of two of Norway's most devastating landslides: in 1905, a huge rockfall from Ramnefjellet crashed into the lake, creating a gigantic wave that killed 61 people. In 1936, another even greater landslip occurred from the same mountain and this time 74 people were killed. The lake level rose by 13 metres during this latter event – an incredible height considering that the lake is 10km long.

Assuming that nature is not giving you one of its awesome demonstrations when you are going alongside the Lovatnet, you will eventually come to the tiny hamlet of Bødal. Here a private toll road heads up the dale to Bødalsætra. Car drivers will be able to pay a small fee and drive up, those without their own transport will have an extra 500m of ascent before starting their walk.

From Bødalsætra, look for a bridge that crosses the river. Beware of a false path going along the north bank: this eventually terminates in horrific bush-whacking, followed by a wade through an ice-cold glacier stream to gain the true path.

Eventually you will reach a small delta and the small lochan of Sætrevatnet, an idyllic spot for lunch. The snout of the Bødalsbreen glacier is best avoided, and an easy-angled snow ramp to its right gives an easier way onto the ice. Now it's a case of getting the rope and crampons out and having fun! Return by the same route.

Note: when the author attempted this route, by mid-afternoon stonefall onto the glacier from the crags of Bødalsfjellet was becoming hazardous and forced a retreat. An early start would avoid this problem.

~

Many visitor's first sight of a Norwegian glacier will be on highway 5 north of Fjærland, near the southern edge of Jostedalsbreen. There is a glacier museum at Breheim which is well worth a visit. Incidentally, Fjærland is Norway's book town and has quite a few second-hand bookshops, selling English and German books as well as Norwegian ones. Two good places to spend a rainy afternoon. But back to the mountains.

Two very accessible icefalls are near here. If you stand and watch either the Bøyabreen or Supphellebreen for more than a few minutes, you're almost guaranteed to see an ice cliff (sérac) collapse. It very quickly becomes obvious that a more circuitous route onto the ice cap is required.

A popular way up is to the Flatbrehytta hut on the edge of the ice cap (route 19b). There is a marked trail from the car park, which forks higher up. The left hand branch leads eventually to the hut via a small piece of scrambling, which has a wire rope to hold onto on the steep part. The right hand branch is less steep and gives a good side-on view of the Supphellebreen. You can stand and watch the séracs collapsing... The two combined make a grand circular tour.

From Flatbrehytta, it is easy to access either the easy-angled blue ice (ice axe and crampons essential!) or go and inspect the glacial moraines. If you wanted to venture further onto the snow, you will also need prussic loops and a rope.

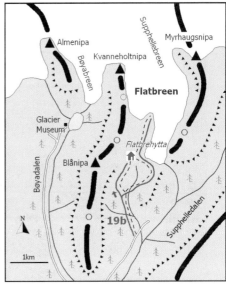

Looking for a safe place to practise crevasse rescue

Krystina Lotoczko

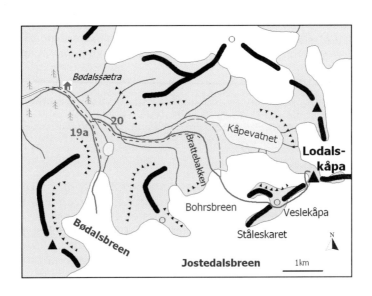

20. Lodalskåpa

Vibeke Steen

The summit of Lodalskåpa from the west   James Baxter

Grading: Complex route finding including glacier crossings and some steep snow/easy rock scrambling (season dependent). Time: 9–12 hours Overall distance and ascent: 18km, 1500m	Access to starting point: Follow a narrow road for 13km along Lovatnet from Loen, then fork left up a rough toll road to a parking place about 300m from Bødalssætra Map: Statens Kartverk 1:50 000 sheet 1418 IV
Best enjoyed: May to September. The later in summer, the greater the possibility of weak snow bridges on Bohrsbreen, but also the easier the final ascent due to less snow/ice cover.	

Route summary:
From Bødalssætra, follow the path along the Bødalselva, and ascend steeply by the waterfall at the end of the valley. Continue on the path by the river from Kåpevatnet, then on the ridge south of this river. A steep ascent south south east takes you to a cairn at the glacier edge. Cross the Bohrs glacier and ascend the ridge leading over Veslekåpa, into the saddle to the south west of Lodalskåpa. From here follow the glacier underneath the western side of the summit into a small notch then ascend steep ground to the summit. Return by the same route.

The approach along the Bødalselva   *James Baxter*

Lodalskåpa is a prominent nunatak standing proud of the northern edge of the great ice sheet of Jostedalsbreen. It lies in an area where the icecap narrows into three steep, heavily crevassed glaciers, Småttene, Strupebreen and Lodalsbrekka, which join to form the Lodalsbre glacier falling into Jostedalen to the east. Many ascents are made as a short diversion to the classic ski traverse of Jostedalsbreen (chapter 18) but the route described here is perhaps the most popular summer route to the summit of Lodalskåpa. Like many mountains that require complex route finding on glaciers, the ascent is not advisable in anything less than fine, settled weather, certainly for the first time.

This route was used on the first ascent by three local farmers from Loen, amongst them Gabriel Rustøen, in 1844. In 1889, Lodalskåpa was climbed from the north east by Slingsby and Hastings, together with an unknown man they met on their way. According to the story, they had to stay overnight on a rock shelf due to bad weather. The unknown man then became hysterical and behaved like that for the next 16 hours.

From Bødalssætra, head south, cross the bridge over the Bødalselva and follow the distinct path along the south side of the river. After the first easy kilometre you meet part of the terminal moraine from Bødalsbreen, which gives you the little extra elevation necessary to get an overview of this glacier, with its wild crevasses. After some undulations there is a second bridge crossing, then keep to the left where the path to the Bødalsbre splits off. The

The summit of Lodalskåpa from the South West Ridge   *James Baxter*

path takes you through birch woods to a steep ascent by a waterfall, which in some parts is steep enough to require easy scrambling. The waterfall thunders down into the cleft on your left hand side and this is a good place for a short rest to enjoy the scene. Another piece of easy scrambling takes you out of the trees onto a flat plateau, giving you excellent view of the steep slope in front leading toward Point 1331m. As you pass along the bare rock slopes you should look out on the ground for sickle-shaped indentations in the rocks (chatter marks) made by glacier movements over thousands of years.

From where the angle of ascent starts increasing again, the path zigzags through a hillside rich in mountain flora. There are also plentiful opportunities to fill up your water-bottles along this part, something that might be difficult as you pass beyond Point 1331m. Heading south east now brings you to the steep slope that well deserves its name of Brattebakken – the steep hill. The path, now based on scree, may be more or less continuous, split up by snow-patches. It may be reasonable insurance to keep your ice-axe to hand for this ascent. After struggling upwards for some 700m, suddenly a pair of cairns appears in front – this is where the Bohrsbre begins. Upon returning from the top it is essential to head off the Bohrsbre at this same point between the cairns.

Deep crevasses hide underneath the harmless looking snow-cover of the Bohrsbre, thus roping-up should be done before embarking on the glacier. Head south east towards a hillside leading up to the ridge that extends from

Lodalskåpa. After less than 1km of glacier crossing, well north of Ståleskaret, walk up the snow-field. This is a short steep ascent at the beginning, then the terrain flattens, but may still offer some hard going if the snow is soft. Continue up the ridge, broad and flat in the beginning, towards Veslekåpa (circa 1980m, not named on the map, a foretop of Lodalskåpa). This can be traversed, or is most easily passed on its south east side. However, before starting the traverse it is worth taking a break here, with a magnificent view of the Jostedalsbre underneath, especially of the heavily-crevassed part of Småttene. Take care while traversing the side of Veslekåpa and the following snow-ridge, if you start sliding it is a long way down... Traversing the snow-ridge leads you on to the saddle between Veslekåpa and Lodalskåpa itself, with the south western edge of Lodalskåpa right in front of you. At this point there is often a huge crevasse in the glacier, be sure to keep well away from its edge. Pass on, to the north side of the saddle, then make a horizontal traverse on top of the steep glacier on the west side of Lodalskåpa until you reach a prominent notch just before a crag projects (the traverse and notch are obvious in the first picture of this chapter). The ascent from this gap is the steepest part of the route, reaching about 50° for the first 20m. The difficulty at this point is highly dependent on the snow conditions. On dry, ice-free ground it is just some easy scrambling, while under snow and ice it may require the use of ice axe, crampons, ice-screws and a rope. After passing the steepest part at the foot of the slope, the way to the top is just scrambling on rocky ground. In some summers it is free of ice and snow all the way to the top, whereas in other years there might be total snow cover even in mid-July.

Two cairns are set up on the top, the second and easternmost one marks the true summit. On a clear day this is the time for harvesting the fruits of your efforts, not only enjoying the satisfaction of reaching the top of this "Queen of Jostedalsbreen", but also the extensive views of large parts of Jostedalsbreen as well as the surrounding mountain areas of Breheimen, Jotunheimen and Hurrungane. On a clear day in the middle of summer one could plan to be at the top as late as ten in the evening – giving you the opportunity to enjoy the sunset from this magnificent viewpoint! A late return to Bødalssætra is well worth it and feasible due to the long, light nights at this time of year.

Return by the same route, except at the cairns after crossing Bohrsbreen, where you should keep a little further to the left. This should bring you down some nice snow-fields, increasing the fun and giving some relief to weary knees. Be aware not to go too far to the left though, as the smooth hillside soon turns into precipitous terrain.

It is also possible to ascend Lodalskåpa from Jostedalen to the east, up Stordalen and Småttene. However, this route is much longer and can only be recommended to strong parties with a high level of glacier experience, and then only early in the season. The snow bridges covering the extensive crevasses of Småttene disappear during the summer and it may become impassable.

21. Up and Over Rondslottet – Rondane National Park

Anthony Dyer

Rondslottet and Storronden seen from Mysuseter   Anthony Dyer

Grading: Some very easy scrambling but generally rough and bouldery. Time: 2 days (+evening approach) Daily distance, ascent and time: Day 1: 10km, 1500m, 9 hours Day 2: 14km, 250m, 5 hours	Access to starting point: From highway E6, take the minor road east from Otta to Mysuseter and then to the car park at the National Park boundary (Spranghaugen). Maps: Statens Kartverk 1:50 000 Turkart "Rondane Nord"
Best enjoyed: Early/Mid June when good quantities of snow linger in the northern and eastern corries and the highest ridges.	

Route summary:

A linear walk from Spranghaugen to Dørålseter. From Spranghaugen, follow the private gravel track northeast to Rondvassbu. On day 1 from Rondvassbu, ascend the marked path up Storronden's broad west ridge. From the summit of Storronden descend north off the ridge (off track) to a weakness in a band of cliffs allowing descent to the saddle with Vinjeronden. Ascend a marked path steeply up Vinjeronden's bouldery ridge and continue on a fine rocky ridge to Rondslottet's summit dome. Descend east down a marked path on Rondslottet's broad eastern slopes into Langglupdalen. On day 2, cross the river and walk west beneath Rondslottet's north face into Bergedalen. Head north to Dørdalen and finish at Dørålseter.

Looking north along Rondvatnet   *Anthony Dyer*

The Rondane National Park forms a compact group of nine summits over 2000m. The National Park has the largest cluster of 2000m summits outside of Jotunheimen and being located in the east of Norway, it receives relatively little precipitation compared with mountains further west. With this in mind, it is possible to walk in Rondane in early June when snow levels are usually not deep enough to make the going too arduous. Walking this early in the season isn't usually possible on high mountains further west as they still have a heavy mantle of snow.

The Rondane mountains are very statuesque, rising above a general plateau that is 1100m high. The summits form three distinct groups with each group being linked by high rocky ridges overlooking huge cliffs and deep corries. The scale of these mountains is roughly similar to the higher mountains in the western highlands of Scotland and they display characteristics that are much akin to Beinn Eighe in Torridon.

This walk describes a linear tour from the southwest of the National Park to the northeast and takes in 3 distinct summits over 2000m including the highest in the national park, Rondslottet, at 2178m. The walk can realistically be done over 2 days as a wild camping tour but it can be completed in one long day if you are fit and travelling light.

Storronden seen from Rondslottet   *Anthony Dyer*

From Rondvassbu, a well worn track heads northeast up the slopes of Storronden where the path splits 1km after leaving Rondvassbu. Keep to the right hand path and ascend the broad west ridge going up to Storronden (2138m). It's a long slog up to the summit but the effort is rewarded with ever improving views north to Rondslottet and the eastern corrie of Vinjeronden.

From Storronden the way down to the saddle before Vinjeronden is not a trivial matter in reduced visibility. There is no marked path to follow and so good navigational & route finding skills are called for. Make a diagonal descent north off the north-northeast summit ridge of Storronden and make your way to a weakness in a band of crags which requires some easy scrambling. Below the crags, the descent continues more easily to the saddle.

The ascent to Vinjeronden (2044m) as seen from Storronden looks steep and difficult but in reality it is quite easy with some impressive glimpses into Storbotn, 400m below. On the summit of Vinjeronden, the largest summit of them all, Rondslottet can be seen 1.5km north along a generally broad ridge with a couple of short scrambly shoulders to ascend.

From the summit of Rondslottet the views in all directions are very extensive. To the east, the rounded summits of Femundsmarka are the only mountain group before the Swedish Border. To the north, the Dovrefjell dominates the view and to the west the serrated peaks of the Jotunheim National Park have drawn your eye to them all day long.

From left to right: Høgronden, Midtronden & Digerronden   *Anthony Dyer*

The path drops east off Rondslottet on steep bouldery ground. The ground is uniform and gradually becomes less steep. The first evidence of vegetation is seen at the 1400m contour and by the time you reach the river Langglupbekken at 1250m, plenty of camping opportunities exist to take advantage of. The next day is a low-level walk beneath Rondslottet's enormous 700m north face. The summits of Høgronden (2118m), Midtronden (2060m) & Digerronden (2016m), however, are well placed for those inclined to do another day of climbing peaks.

The river crossing to the westward path up Langglupdalen is at the confluence between a series of major streams and is easy to cross in dry weather but you're still likely to get your feet wet. Once you are across the streams and ascending the westward path, the vegetation steadily thins out as you reach the top of the pass until it is no more than a thin patchy layer of moss on a field of rocks. The views of Rondslottet's north face however more than make up for the rough path.

The descent down Bergedalen takes you across a wide ancient glacial moraine with curious hollows and humps everywhere. The moraine is also very sterile with little vegetation. The descent into Dørdalen takes you back into the upper domain of trees and the finish at Dørålseter marks the end of a good introductory tour of the Rondane Mountains.

Dørålseter is at the end of a private toll road, those without wheels have an extra 13km of walking east down to highway 27 south of Folldal. Many continuing excursions from Dørålseter are possible including the western Rondane summits or a long walk north across undulating upland fells to the Dovrefjell Mountains.

The map for route 21 is on page 108.

22. A Tour of the Western Rondane Fells and Mountains

Anthony Dyer

Veslemeden and Storsmeden seen from the north   Anthony Dyer

Grading: Occasional very easy scrambling and a mix of mossy fells and bouldery ridges. Mostly off marked paths. Time: 2 days.(+morning exit) Daily distance, ascent & time: Day 1: 22km, 1150m, 11 hours Day 2: 22km, 1250m, 11 hours	Access to starting point: From highway E6, take the minor road from Dovre up Grimsdalen to Grimsdalshytta. Maps: Statens Kartverk 1:50 000 Turkart "Rondane Nord"
Best enjoyed: Early/Mid June to fully appreciate the quietness and remoteness of this wilderness.	

Route summary:
From Grimsdalshytta, take the southwest path that rises above Grimsdalen. Continue southwest on the path over increasingly exposed moors to eventually reach Sletthøe (1577m). Turn off the path and head east crossing the National Park border and descend into the pass of Vasskjelet. Head southeast up a broad knobbly ridge to a larger plateau like ridge before descending into the upper reaches of Bråkdalen for the first camp. Next day head east up to Sagtindan and follow the main ridge south to Bråkdalsbelgen then east to Ljosåbelgen then north up to an unnamed peak "1996m". Head east across to Storsmeden before backtracking to the last saddle and descend south down a marked path via Kåldbekkbotn to Rondvassbu.

High up on remote moors northwest of Rondane   *Anthony Dyer*

This walk provides two challenging days both inside and outside the Rondane National Park and goes to illustrate what can be done when you don't consistently stick to the way-marked paths that are so integral to Norwegian mountain walking culture. The terrain covers both large rolling upland fells and dramatic rocky mountain ridges. Whilst you don't venture far from the road by Norwegian Standards (8km at most), the setting for this walk feels most wild.

The walk starts in the quiet valley of Grimsdalen at Grimsdalshytta. Access is provided by way of an unpaved public road for those with wheels or waymarked paths for those who arrive on foot. At Grimsdalen, as you start at the altitude of 920m, you are just below the tree line. After crossing the river Grimse (bridged), the path heads southwest through the thin forest to the open moorland above. The views down into Grimsdalen are very scenic. In its upper reaches, Grimsdalen becomes a narrower valley with occasional cliffs.

Soon Grimsdalen turns away west leaving the path to cross a marshy undulating plateau until you reach another isolated unpaved road. South of this road, the path slowly gains altitude as you round the shoulder of Hornsjøhøe. The vegetation slowly thins with altitude but never disappears completely. Even on the 1576m summit of Sletthøe there is a thin layer of moss covering the rock underneath with the result that progress across these fells is relatively quick compared with the boulder hops that are typical at this altitude.

Ljosåbelgen, part of the western Rondane range   *Anthony Dyer*

Bråkdalsbelgen seen from Sagtindan   Anthony Dyer

The relief here forms a large undulating plateau with wide remote valleys separating the moorland from the serrated peaks of Rondane. At the summit of Sletthøe turn east and strike off track to aim for the pass of Vasskjelet where another path crosses. From this pass, don't follow the path but instead strike south east up a knobbly subsidiary ridge to eventually reach the broad stony ridge of Gråhøe.

Distances are easily underestimated on this vast plateau and under misty conditions you will need to be sharp on your navigational skills. On the broad plateau-like southwest ridge of Gråhøe, you now descend into the side valley of Vesledalen and follow that down into the upper reaches of Bråkdalen. In this valley there is quite a large river fed by the largest snowfields of Rondane. Early in the season, this river will be dangerous to cross.

Within Bråkdalen the character of the scenery has changed completely. No longer are you striding out across open moors, but you are hemmed into a sterile remote valley. Some camping spots can be found on thin patches of moss. With next day comes an exciting rooftop walk over seldom visited summits in Rondane.

This final day's walk starts by ascending the western shoulder of Sagtindan (1838m) via the Indre Brådalshøe ridge. This is quite a rocky ridge, but progress is fast striding out across what is predominantly bedrock. The southern view opens out with the inviting prospect of ascending the pyramidal profile of Bråkdalsbelgen (1915m) along a broad but dramatically tapered ridge towards its end.

Trolltinden seen from peak "1996m" *Anthony Dyer*

Once on the summit of Sagtindan, the rest of the days walking suddenly comes into view right round to the unnamed peak of 1996m. The other thing that strikes you is the rather large 350m drop into Verkilsdalen.

Continue south easily to Bråkdalsbelgen over and round numerous minor tops. Beyond Bråkdalsbelgen, the terrain becomes much rougher with boulders the size of small cars to negotiate (some of them move!). The ridge east of Ljosåbelgen is quite shapely and a little narrow but it doesn't involve scrambling. Walking north, the unnamed peak "1996m" appears beyond the minor summit of Hoggbeitet. The south ridge of "1996m" appears quite formidable but turns out to be nothing more than a simple clamber up boulders and ledges.

From "1996m", the summit of Storsmeden comes into view, but it's the satellite peak of Trolltinden (2018m) that draws the eye. The Trolltinden ridge is a serious undertaking with requires grade IV climbing for a direct traverse which can be avoided on steep loose ledges. Trolltinden lies about 1.5km out from the main ridge and requires 300m of ascent to reach the summit and 200m ascent to return. Most people will be more inclined to descend to the saddle before Storsmeden (2016m). The ascent of Storsmeden is a steep slog with some easy scrambling closer to the top.

Beyond Storsmeden is Veslemeden (2015m), 1.2km away and requiring 200m of further ascent. The ridge across to Veslemeden is a serious traverse and crosses a series of loose exposed rock-steps that require intermediate scrambling moves. Anyone who wants to avoid the scramble can backtrack to the saddle and pickup the marked DNT path. The descent into Kaldbekkbotn is impressive. The corrie is relatively high and completely devoid of any vegetation. Yet on three sides, the summits tower above you and throw down impressive rocky faces. The path descends out of Kaldbekkbotn and back into the upper reaches of the vegetated landscape.

By the time you reach Rondvassbu, the ground is much more luxuriant with a thicker layer of moss and heather. From Rondvassbu, the summit of Veslemeden can be ascended with ease in a round trip of about four hours. Other destinations await, including the previous walk described. You can finish the walking altogether by following the track southwest towards a private toll road at the National Park Border just north of Mysuseter.

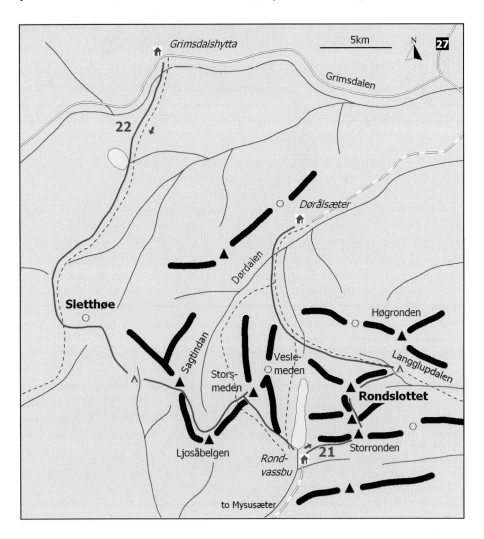

23. Backpacking and Peakbagging Through Dovrefjell

John Baddeley

Typical Dovrefjell scenery – Åmotsdalen from Snøhetta   John Baddeley

Grading: Generally easy walking on well-marked paths. Some river crossings could be difficult or impossible early in the season or after heavy rain.	*Access to starting point: The village of Lesja, on the rail line and the E136 between Dombås and Åndalsnes.*
Time: 3 days, or easily extended. *Daily distance, ascent and times:* *Day 1: 30km, 1400m, 10 hours* *Day 2: 21km, 300m, 6 hours* *Day 3: 16km, 200m, 5 hours*	*Maps: Statens Kartverk 1:100 000 Turkart "Dovrefjell", 1:50 000 Sheet 1519-IV and 1419-I useful for ascents.*

Best enjoyed: Mid to late season, to give chance for the snow to melt off and river levels to drop. Not suitable in winter due to avalanche risk in valleys.

Route summary:

A linear, three-day camping tour from south to north through the heart of the Dovrefjell, designed to be extended to take in many major summits. From the village of Lesja, take the track north to Nysætre and up Skamsdalen. Cross the river Jori north of Lesjøen and head north east through Langvassdalen to Åmoldalshytta. Follow the path north, past Loennechenbua hut and down Skirådalen to Åmotan. Take the track north to the village of Gjøra.

Autumn colour in Dovrefjell - Alpine Bearberry (Arctostaphylos alpinus)   *John Baddeley*

"United and faithful until the mountains of Dovre fall" was the toast raised after the signing of the Norwegian constitution on 17 May 1814 at Eidsvoll. This gives an idea of the place of Dovrefjell in Norwegian hearts, a symbol of national strength and solidarity. Nowadays, a variety of national designations protect much of the area although these are constantly evolving. The Dovre National Park was founded in 1974 and extended to form the Dovrefjell-Sunndalsfjella National Park in 2002. Currently this Park, together with its five adjacent landscape conservation areas and two biotope reservations cover 4365 sq km, some 15% larger than the Cairngorms National Park, Britain's biggest.

Formal designations aside, to the hillwalker the Dovrefjell could be said to form the tract of mountains bounded on the north by the Rv70, to the east by the E6 and to the south by the E136. A western boundary is harder to define but could conveniently be drawn from Aursjøen to Geitådalen. These boundaries ignore the smaller area of the National Park east of the E6. This should not be forgotten for while it lacks the high mountains of the western sector, it is where some of the most interesting flora and fauna are found.

Typical Dovrefjell terrain is reminiscent of much of the central Scottish Highlands with large, U-shaped valleys confined by bulky rounded mountains. Occasionally though these can be steep-sided and some have surprisingly airy, narrow ridges. Climatically if not physically, Dovrefjell sits between the oceanic conditions of the west coast and the continental climate of the Rondane, although conditions vary considerably from east to west across the area, with wetter conditions to the west. It receives enough

Åmotsdalen near Åmotdalshytta   *John Baddeley*

precipitation to sustain some small glaciers, and there is usually enough snowfall to present a significant obstacle to progress on foot early in the season. This makes it a good area for ski touring.

The Dovrefjell is an area of geological contrast. The west is largely dominated by Precambrian bedrock with gneiss and sandstone, which form poor, acidic soils. Further east are found sedimentary and metamorphic rocks such as mica schist. These weather more easily and give fertile soils, which is why the area is known for its rich plant life. Indeed, the mountain flora on Knutshø to the east of Kongsvoll is one of the most diverse in northern Europe. This one site has 170 of the almost 250 species of Scandinavian mountain plants.

There are two plant species endemic to Dovrefjell, *Poa arctica ssp. stricta* and *Taraxacum dovrense*, while *Primula scandinavica* is endemic to Scandinavia. Some other plants that are locally common in Dovrefjell have unusual distributions. *Artemisia norvegica* is also found in Scotland and the Urals, and subspecies of *Papaver radicatum* also occur in the Faeroes, Iceland, Greenland and arctic Canada.

In addition to exceptional botanical richness, Dovrefjell also has a varied and interesting assortment of animals. These include birds such as the golden eagle and gyrfalcon, in addition to more common mountain species like ptarmigan, dotterel and snow bunting. This is the last area in mainland

The descent into Skirådalen   *John Baddeley*

Europe where it is possible to find a mountain ecosystem where wild reindeer, wolverine and arctic fox co-exist. However, without doubt the most spectacular animal to be seen is the musk ox. Extinct in Europe since the last ice age, they were re-introduced between 1947 and 1953 from Greenland. Nowadays a herd of about 140 (in 2004) of these prehistoric-looking beasts roams around the eastern areas of the Dovrefjell. While fascinating to observe, these potentially dangerous animals should not be approached closely, especially if mothers have calves. The recommended minimum distance is 200m, although if the animals start snorting or form a defensive ring it is time to back away.

The through-route described in this chapter has been selected to include many of the main attractions of Dovrefjell. For those in a hurry it could be reduced to two long days and one night (50km, 1300m) with a light pack by arranging transport from Lesja for the first 17km and overnighting in Åmotdalshytta. Many though will want to spend longer amongst the mountains and this route allows for many worthwhile ascents, some listed at the end of the chapter.

Start at the village of Lesja, conveniently situated on the main rail and road routes between Dombås and Åndalsnes. The first part of the route takes a track straight up the steep hillside north from the village. On leaving the forest the gradient soon eases and you get your first good views of the hills to come. After an easy walk of a few kilometres the track heads down towards Nysætre. This section of the walk takes a route that is well used by people driving further up the track to the large lake of Aursjøen. It may be possible to hitch a ride, or alternatively there are taxis available in Lesja if you want to reduce the length of this first day by 17km and 600m. This is an attractive option if you are heading into the area with food for a week or more of peak bagging.

From Nysætre, continue up the steep-sided Skamsdalen to the end of the track. A well-marked path continues from here, gaining height more gradually along the west side of the river Jore. There should be a summer bridge where this path crosses the Tverråe, which flows rapidly down a rocky gorge. Crossing without the bridge in place would be difficult and may be impossible. Another potentially difficult river crossing is soon reached, at the far end of Lesjøen. The path fords the river where it is wide and braided, but although the ford is marked with cairns the best place to cross may lie to either side of this and may be at least knee deep.

Once across the river the path splits. To get to Åmotdalshytta (Kristiansund og Nordmøre Turistforening) with least effort continue north, then northeast around the north side of Drugshøe. To be in the best position for peak bagging, head northeast into Langvassdalen, where there are places to camp

between areas of bog and boulder fields. The path through Langvassdalen is rough going in places but eases slightly as it turns and heads north, down into the open upper reaches of Åmotsdalen at around 1300m altitude. The character of the walk now changes, from being confined in a narrow valley between steep peaks to views of open, rolling hills. The going is easier too, with the tough 800m pull up into Langvassdalen behind you and only relatively gentle gradients to ascend from now on.

The area around Åmotdalshytta is wet and boggy, but this soon changes back to the familiar rocks underfoot as the other side of

The river Svøu at Åmotan   *John Baddeley*

the valley is climbed. The path traverses a shoulder of hillside, with good views south to the Snøhetta group, before dropping down to Urdvassbekken. This stream will probably give you the most difficult fording of the trip. Again, while crossing points are marked the best place will be a matter of judgement. Once across, it is about one hour to the col at just over 1400m that divides the high ground of the central Dovrefjell from that which drops away northwest towards the coast. Just beyond, tucked into the steep hillside and looking out over the lake, is the hut of Loennechenbua (Kristiansund og Nordmøre Turistforening). It would be hard to imagine a better setting for a mountain hut, or a hut more appropriate to its location. It is a small, stone-built cabin, well-equipped with two beds, paraffin stove and lamps and a water bucket.

The path soon becomes very rocky where it clings to the shore of Storvatnet. This section is thankfully quite short and at the end of the lake there are good views of the route ahead and some fine places to camp. After possibly spending many days on the high plateau of Dovrefjell this view of deep-cut, wooded valleys backed by the soaring peaks of Innerdalen almost comes as a shock.

From here, you begin dropping quite quickly into Skirådalen, soon reaching the fresh smell of the open birch woods. The path then becomes a track as it drops down to the confluence of several valleys. This marks the transition from the broad, U-shaped valleys carved by glaciers to a steep sided gorge eroded by the river. From a bend where the track turns sharply north at Jenstad, a zigzag path leads off for the 200m descent of the steep hillside into Åmotan, where the rivers Linndøla, Reppa, Grøvu og Svøu that drain much of the north side of the Dovrefjell converge. Åmotan has been called an "inferno of waterfalls", and standing there amongst it the oxymoron is probably forgivable. Some are cascades, while others fall in single drops of several hundred metres. Britain has nothing like this, and even in this land of big waterfalls the setting is exceptional. The river Grøvu that flows out from the chaos of the waterfalls is also quite tumultuous and attracts kayakers from the more extreme end of the sport.

After getting thoroughly damp at the bottom of the falls, you must now retrace 200 vertical metres up to the track. Then there is a simple walk north of about 5km to the small village of Gjøra in Sunndalen, where you may be grateful to find a small shop. Frequent buses pass through the village, heading either east to the town of Oppdal on the Oslo–Trondheim railway, or west to the town of Sunndalsøra on the coast. Those needing to replenish stocks before the next adventure will find a good variety of accommodation, shops and supermarkets in both places, in addition to helpful Tourist Information offices.

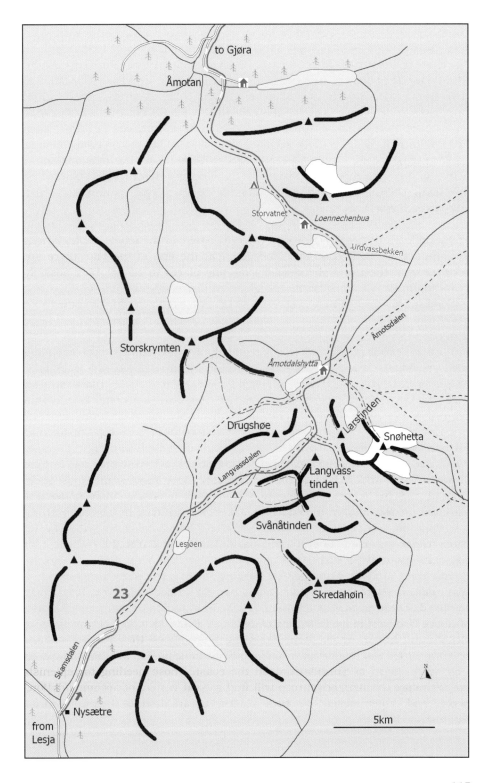

to Gjøra

Åmotan

Storvatnet

Loennechenbua

Urdvassbekken

Åmotsdalen

Storskrymten

Åmotdalshytta

Larstinden

Snøhetta

Drugshøe

Langvassdalen

Langvass-
tinden

Svånåtinden

Lesjøen

23

Skamsdalen

Skredahøin

Nysætre

from
Lesja

N

5km

Store Langvasstinden (L) and Larstinden (R) from Snøhetta　　　　　*John Baddeley*

Mountain ascents that may be made from this route include:

Skredahøin (2004m)
Head south from the southwest end of Langvatnet to Heisavatnet. Go around the north side of this lake to the col between Skredahøin and Svånåtinden. Ascend the north side of Nordre Skredahøin (1943m), then follow the pleasant ridge around to the southeast, over peak 1994m, to the summit.

Store (Øst) Langvasstinden (2085m) and Svånåtinden (2209m)
From the southwest end of Langvatnet, go up the West Ridge of Nordre Svånåtinden (2004m; unnamed on Turkart), or into the corrie to the north of this ridge from halfway along the lake. Gain the summit ridge and head north to Vestre Langvasstinden (2046m). The continuation to the main summit requires 3-4 m of steep downclimbing (Grade III) or an abseil. From there to the summit is narrow and sensational but not difficult. Return by the same route, over Nordre Svånåtinden and continue south along a broadening rock and snow slope to the main summit of Svånåtinden, above spectacular corries to the east. Descend northwest from the summit back to your starting point.

Larstinden (2106m)

One of Norway's more difficult 2000m peaks. Take the path south east from Langvatnet to the col between Langvasstind and Larstind, then head north east up boulder slopes to the highest point on Larseggen (1945m). Traverse along an increasingly narrow ridge to Nordre Larstind (2070m). The difficulties begin south from here with a descent to the col and the climb up the other side (Grade IV) to the higher south summit, in a sensational position. Return by the same route.

Snøhetta (2286m)

The highest peak in Dovrefjell. Follow the marked path up easy stony slopes and snowfields from Åmotdalshytta, by the route described in chapter 24.

Storskrymten (1985m)

This lonely hill in the centre of Dovrefjell provides a fine tramp. From Åmotdalshytta, take the path west to where it forks north of Varden (1438m). Head to the north end of tarn 1420m, then go up the South East Ridge, which is steep in places but not difficult. The return to hut can be varied by descending South East Ridge, then traversing the broad, undulating ridge of Skuleggen.

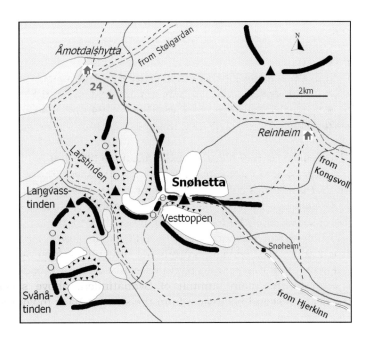

24. Snøhetta

John Baddeley

The Snøhetta group (L) from Nordre Svånåtinden   John Baddeley

Grading: A simple walking ascent by the route described, although an ice axe might be useful. Potential for climbing variation. Time: 5 hours Overall distance and ascent: 13km, 1000m	Access to starting point: Walk in to Åmotdalshytta from E6 (23–26km, 650–800m ascent, depending on route) Maps: Statens Kartverk 1:100 000 Turkart "Dovrefjell", or 1:50 000 Sheet 1519-IV
Best enjoyed: Either on ski, or mid to late season, to give chance for the snow to melt off.	

Route summary:
A circular walk including the summit of one of the most well-known mountains in Norway. On the first day, walk in to Åmotdalshytta from a choice of starting places on the E6 road. From Åmotdalshytta, ascend Snøhetta on a waymarked path up an easy hillside that grades into steeper boulder slopes and snowfields. Descend either by same route or by a choice of descents to the east, back out to the E6.

The Midttoppen to Vesttoppen ridge of Snøhetta   *John Baddeley*

For a long time, Snøhetta was thought to be the highest mountain in Norway. Now, of course, we know that the highest peaks lie within Jotunheimen and Hurrungane, further to the west. Outside of this relatively compact group of peaks though, Snøhetta retains its earlier title. The name translates literally as "snow-hood" and is a particularly apt description of this bulky, complex mountain massif. Snøhetta is the name of the summit at 2286m, but extending to the south west from this is a striking ridge containing the lower tops of Midttoppen, Hettpiggen and Vesttoppen.

The summit of Snøhetta can be approached from a variety of directions, most of them not particularly difficult. The easiest route for those who only want to attain the summit is from the east. From the main E6 road at Hjerkinn, take the track to Snøheim as far as the snow cover allows. Then follow the well-used waymarked track and path to the summit (16km, 820m, 6 hours round trip).

A much better route is from the north. This approach has the advantage of taking the walker into the heart of Dovrefjell and fits well with a longer backpacking trip, such as that described in the previous chapter. As well as significantly increasing your chances of seeing interesting plants and wildlife, it compliments the character of the mountain better than the alterative approaches. On Snøhetta more than on any of the other big Norwegian mountains I was reminded of the words of the great naturalist Adam Watson.

Larstinden from Snøhetta   Ann Baddeley

He wrote of Braeriach in the Scottish Cairngorms that, "[it] *is so big and varied that no one can claim to know it well who has not wandered into every corrie and explored its plateau and flanks without hurry on long summer days"*.

Start the ascent at Åmotdalshytta (Kristiansund og Nordmøre Turistforening). The two most straightforward routes to this hut are on well-marked paths from the E6, which lies to the east. These are either from Kongsvoll up Stroplsjødalen, or from Stølgardan up Åmotsdalen, and both are a good day's walk. Other approaches to the hut are possible from most directions as part of multi-day routes in the area.

The route to the summit from Åmotdalshytta is waymarked but no less interesting for it. After a short, initial bogtrot you get onto more rocky ground that will be with you until covered by snow on the higher slopes. The first excuse for a break in the ascent comes at the lower of the two lakes in the corrie between Snøhetta and Larstinden, which is a short diversion off the path. Until late in the summer this lake is likely to have a reasonable amount of ice covering it and even on a hot day a swim will be short and bracing. The setting is an interesting juxtaposition: there are open views over gently rolling hills to the north and east, while ahead is a huge mountain corrie with the precipitous east face of Larstinden on the right and the pinnacled South West Ridge of Snøhetta on the left, linked by a narrow, curving arete. It is also interesting to note that here you are nearly 300m higher than the highest mountain in Britain, and still have over 600m to ascend.

As you gain height on the path it is worth diverting off to the right at intervals for the view down into the upper corrie, which is especially good from the top of the steep outcrop at around 2100m. Above this, the going can get harder as more snow is encountered, and it is steep enough that you might be glad of an ice axe if it has frozen recently. Eventually you reach the main ridge of the mountain about half kilometre west of the summit. From here you can go left to the summit, or right to Midttoppen (2278m) to get good views of the subsidiary tops of the mountain.

The summit of Snøhetta (2286m) may initially be disappointing due to the presence of a military communications hut, but the exceptional views should soon divert your attention. To the east are the rounded hills and forests leading to the Swedish border, brought to an abrupt end as you look further south by the bulk of the Rondane. To the southwest the views are of the distant but still identifiable peaks of Jotunheimen and, on a very clear day, the unmistakable white flatness of Jostedalsbreen. North of this is Romsdalen, which is not seen to advantage from here. Much closer, to the north and east, are Innerdalen and Trollheimen, both looking worth a visit.

There are two easy descent routes from the summit. You can return to Åmotdalshytta by reversing the ascent route, or alternatively take the path south east (well-marked with large posts) to Snøheim and the main road and rail line. The latter option makes the overall route into a very good two-day tour that is preferable to a quick ascent of the peak from the east.

A much harder alternative takes the South West Ridge of Snøhetta, which turns the route into a real mountaineering adventure. An overview is included but we recommend that you consult a detailed guide before attempting the route. From Midttoppen, head south towards Hettpiggen down a fine ridge with some intermediate scrambling. The ascent to Hettpiggen (2261m) is mainly climbing up to Grade IV in a couple of places, and the descent to the south includes a short abseil (one 50m rope sufficient). After this, the ascent of Vesttoppen (2253m) is easier, with more intermediate, but in places exposed, scrambling. Descents can then be made by a path to Snøheim to the east, or by heading south then north west around the western side of Larstinden to return to Åmotdalshytta.

The map for this route is on page 117.

25. Slogen

John Baddeley

Slogen (L) from Norangsfjorden   *John Baddeley*

Grading: A very steep but straightforward walk to a tiny summit, with sweeping drops on all sides	*Access to starting point: Parking area on road 655 in Norangsdalen, ½km south east of Øye.*
Time: 6–7 hours	*Maps: Statens Kartverk 1:50 000 Turkart "Sunnmørsalpane"*
Overall distance and ascent: 6km, 1600m	
Best enjoyed: On a clear day to appreciate the famous views.	

Route summary:
Uncomplicated but steep ascent of the mountain described by Slingsby as "one of the proudest in Europe". Walk up the path from Øye to join the East Ridge at 1200m. Go steeply up the ridge to the summit, return by the same route.

Slogen from Patchellhytta   *John Baddeley*

> *"The wildest alpine valley I ever saw was not in the Alps, it was the valley Norangsdalen at Sunnmøre, Norway"*
> Slingsby

Norangsdalen is a narrow, almost gorge-like valley that cuts through the 1200 – 1500m high mountains of eastern Sunnmøre. At its eastern end is the village of Hellesylt on the World-famous Geirangerfjord, whilst at its western end, on the shores of Norangsfjorden, sits the village of Øye. This was the base for many of the pioneering ascents in this area and the history is best appreciated by paying a visit to the focus of past activity, the Hotel Union in Øye. This grand old establishment still has the old climbers' book started at the end of the 1800s, which includes entries by Patchell, Slingsby and others.

A fine start to the day's activities would be to spend an hour or so leafing through their exploits whilst attacking a huge breakfast. Local man Jon Klokk first ascended Slogen in 1870, acting on information from Slingsby. After this, most of the early activity on the mountain was by British climbers – Slingsby claimed the formidable-looking North West Ridge, while the redoubtable

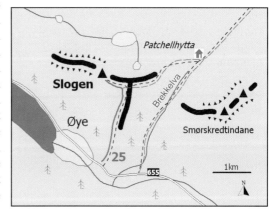

Scots pairing of Harold Raeburn and Willie Ling ascended directly from the fjord in 1903. Their description of the route as difficult and exposed is easily believed.

Feeling sufficiently enthused and infused, you must now struggle out of the hotel and walk south east along the road for ½km, to the point where the path strikes north up the steep hillside. This route is nothing if not direct as it climbs 1200m in 2km, first through birch woods and then across the open hillside until it reaches the East Ridge of Slogen. Here it joins the more leisurely path coming in from Patchellhytta (Ålesund-Sunnmøre Turistforening). This hut, named after the Norwegian mountaineer C.W. Patchell, makes a good base for a few days if you are tempted to try some of the other peaks in the area, most notably Brekketind and Smørskredtindane (both featuring steep glaciers, bergschrunds and Grade II–III rock by their easiest routes). It is also possible to camp in the vicinity of the hut, but not too close.

Once the East Ridge of Slogen has been joined the ascent goes steeply up this with views opening out all the time, especially back down into Norangsdalen. In some places the going is quite rocky and slabby, and there are likely to be areas of snow across the ridge. If these are frozen, they could cause problems without ice axe and crampons. The final section of the ridge is slightly steeper than the rest and requires a little easy scrambling to reach the summit of Slogen (1564m). This tiny, stony eyrie is almost fully occupied by a tall cairn first built by Slingsby in 1884, and he gave probably the best recommendation of the view from Slogen in a letter to Kristofer Randers when he said that, *"you will never see another such view".* Brekketind and Smørskredtindane dominate the near views to the north and east, the upper section of the immense 1500m West Face of Jakta holds the eye to the south, and to the west the bulk of Kolåstinden dominates. When you can tear yourself away, the descent is by the same route and should have you back at the hotel in time for a well-deserved afternoon tea.

High on the East Ridge of Slogen
John Baddeley

26. Råna

John Baddeley

On the South West Ridge of Regndalstindane   John Baddeley

Grading: A varied and interesting mountain ascent including easy scrambling on narrow ridges, steep snowfields and a glacier crossing. Time: 8–9 hours Overall distance and ascent: 18km, 1750m	Access to starting point: The village of Urke, on road 655 on the north side of Norangsfjorden. Maps: Statens Kartverk 1:50 000 Turkart "Sunnmørsalpane"
Best enjoyed: In dry weather, to avoid slippery rock ridges. Dangerous in winter/spring due to high avalanche risk in Urkedalen.	

Route summary:
A circular walk up the highest mountain on the Rånahalvøya peninsular. Start at Urke, follow the path north then northwest to the head of Urkedalen. Ascend Regndalstindane by an easy scramble up the South West Ridge. Descend the North West Ridge, then ascend the broad South Ridge of Råna to the summit. Descend back to the col between Råna and Regndalstindane, and traverse the steep West Face of the latter summit to regain its South West Ridge. Drop steeply south and cross the small glacier to regain the path in Urkedalen.

On the South Ridge of Råna, looking towards Regndalstindane   John Baddeley

If you approach Sunnmøre from the north along Velledalen you will be impressed by the chaotic mass of icefalls on the north east side of the great ridge of mountains running along the spine of Rånahalvøya. The largest of these glaciers, over 2km across, falls from the mountains that are ascended on this route, Råna and Regndalstindane.

From Urke, take the track north into Urkedalen that runs up the west side of the Urkeelva, avoiding the attentions of some over-friendly goats. About 100m after the track crosses the stream, a path branches off left, heading into upper Urkedalen. Follow this path, vague at times but generally well marked with red spots or Ts, right up to the head of the valley at 1100m. The upper section of this path may be obscured by old snow. Avoiding it involves some scrambling around to the sides over damp mossy slabs that are the home of lemmings. When you finally reach the col there is a fine view west down Litledalen and across Hjørundfjorden to Kolåstinden.

Now head up the South West Ridge of Regndalstindane. This begins as a broad, boulder-covered slope but soon becomes narrow and in places exposed. There are sections of easy scrambling and the ridge crest may be snow-covered in places. One short section is harder than the rest and may have a fixed rope in place to give reassurance on an exposed traverse across slabs. Soon after this, there are two large pinnacles on the ridge. Passing them is not difficult, but take note of them for the descent. The final section of the ridge then steepens for the straightforward ascent to the summit of Regndalstindane (1540m).

The summit ridge of Råna in atmospheric conditions   *John Baddeley*

Leave the summit by the easy but well-defined North West Ridge and descend to the col between Regndalstindane and Råna. The character of the mountain now changes as the ridge becomes much broader and boulder covered. Walk easily north up this slope to reach the crenellated summit ridge of Råna. This runs roughly east-west, and the summit is near the eastern end. After the gentle slopes of the final ascent the summit comes as a surprise, being perched on the edge of the very steep rock and glacier slopes of upper Trandalsdalen. The views north are of fjords and islands, with the town of Ålesund clearly visible. This contrasts with the view south, which is dominated by the North East Face of Regndalstindane rising out of the heavily crevassed glacier of upper Regndalen.

The descent begins by retracing your steps south as far as the col with Regndalstindane. From here, traverse horizontally across the North West Face of that mountain. This slope is likely to be icy, is quite steep and is above an even steeper section of the face, so care is necessary. It is possible to avoid this traverse by following the ascent route back over Regndalstindane.

The traverse route regains the South West Ridge of Regndalstindane near the two pinnacles noted on the ascent. Go to the western one of these and then descend south, at first over steep, shattered rocks then across the little bergschrund onto a small glacier. Go down this, at first trending left, then right to avoid the fall line of debris from higher up the mountain. There are small crevasses so glacier equipment is necessary. This glacier can also be followed in ascent but lacks the interest of the ridge route: aim for the two pinnacles, as the glacier is not easily seen from below. Unrope on the moraines at the bottom of the glacier and make a gently falling traverse left, keeping above a band of slabs that runs above the path. At the end of these slabs, drop down to regain the path and follow it back to your starting point at Urke.

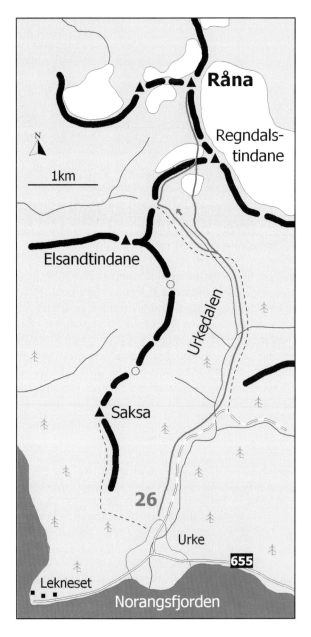

27. Kolåstinden

John Baddeley

The summit of Kolåstinden from the north   *John Baddeley*

Grading: Technically similar to an easy alpine peak, it includes some steep snow/ice, a glacier crossing with a possibly difficult bergschrund, and some easy rock scrambling. Glacier equipment essential in summer. *Time: 7 hours* *Overall distance and ascent:* *10km, 1050m*	*Access to starting point: From Standalshytta, on the rough road between Kolås and Store Standal.* *Maps:* *Statens Kartverk 1:50 000 Turkart "Sunnmørsalpane"*
Best enjoyed: Early/mid season, which makes the bergschrund easier to cross and reduces the crevasse danger. Probably the best easy mountain ski tour in the area.	

Route summary:
From Standalshytta, follow a path through Kvanndalen to the head of the valley. From there, take an open snow gully leading to the lowest point on the ridge to the south. Make a rising traverse on an anticlockwise arc around the upper edge of the glacier to the far end of a bergschrund. Cross this and ascend steep snow then rocks to the summit. Return by the same route.

Kolåstinden from Kvanndalen   *John Baddeley*

Slingsby once wrote:

> *"I know of no alpine environment, be it in Norway, Switzerland or the Alps in general, which possesses such magnificent beauty as that to be found in Sunnmøre. There you will find sceneries of greater richness, greater fertility and of far wilder magnificence. But nowhere will you find such a rich combination of magnificent mountain ranges, delightful foregrounds, narrow fjords and splendid colourfulness throughout the entire landscape as that which you will find in the beauty of Sunnmøre."*

This avid praise was for an area much frequented by the pioneers of Norwegian mountaineering, but often overlooked by modern British visitors in favour of Jotunheimen and Romsdalen. Of all the mountains in Sunnmøre, Kolåstinden is perhaps the most sought after. It offers an inspiring combination of technical variety and scenic interest that is hard to beat; indeed Slingsby called it the "Monarch of Sunnmøre".

The easiest route up Kolåstinden begins at Standalshytta, beside the rough road between Kolås and Store Standal. Ålesund-Sunnmøre Turistforening runs this hut but DNT members can also use it. The summit is visible from outside the hut. It stands at the north end of the pinnacled South West Ridge, and is distinguished by its chisel-like profile rising out of a snowfield. There is, however, no straightforward ascent from the hut without technical climbing.

Crossing the bergschrund below the summit of Kolåstinden　　　　　*John Baddeley*

Our route takes a more circuitous approach, going around to the north side of the mountain to find a relatively easy passage through the ridges and glaciers. A well-marked path traverses across the hillside towards the stream running out of Kvanndalen, through woods of small twisted birch and across rough boulders. This path eventually disgorges into a flatter area of valley south west of the huge, shattered face of Sætretindane. The summit of Kolåstinden is visible high on the left but does not look very significant. What does catch the attention is the front edge of the heavily crevassed glacier as it cascades over steep boilerplate slabs. From here it is easy to imagine how similar features in Britain, as exemplified by those in Coir' a' Ghrunnda of Skye, were formed. Some guidebooks include a direct ascent of the slabs and

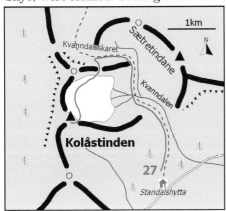

glacier from this point but it certainly doesn't appear a very attractive prospect.

Continue along the path on the marked route through Kvanndalen, past some potential campsites, up and around to the west until you reach the col of Kvanndalsskaret. A ridge of Kolåstinden forms the south side of this pass and the obvious cleft in this ridge, known as Stredet (Grid Ref: 610067), is the next objective. The ascent to this is a steep, north-facing snow gully that is likely to be quite icy and may well need both ice axe and crampons. From Stredet you can see across the glacier to the rocky summit cone, now looking much more pointed. Below it is a large bergschrund that gets smaller further to the left. Take note of this point, as this is where you will cross it later.

Rope up at Stredet, and go out onto the glacier, heading almost straight upwards but trending more towards the summit as you gain height. When you are just below the rocky ridge forming the top rim of the glacier, follow it around towards the summit keeping to the glacier. Alternatively head onto the ridge for some scrambling. This curving route is necessary to avoid the central, more heavily crevassed areas of the glacier.

Continue around below both the summit and the bergschrund until the latter is small enough to be crossed. This can be hard later in the season, as you will have to go further along to cross it, while all the time the glacier steepens. Once across this obstacle, go straight up a steep and possibly icy snow slope for a short distance until you reach the rocks of the summit cone. The glacier gear can be left here for the short, easy scramble up large blocks of rock to the small pointed summit at 1432m.

After recording your visit in the summit logbook, admire the extensive panoramas and the West Face, plunging 1100m into Romsdalen. To the north is the pinnacled massif of the Jønshornet group, while to the east, across Hjørundfjorden, is the impressive ridge of mountains running nearly 20km from Trollkyrkje to Brekketind. This ridge runs down the middle of Rånahalvøya and the ascent of its highest point, Råna, is described in chapter 26. You can also feel satisfied in attaining a summit that eluded Slingsby's attempt at a first ascent. In 1876 he turned back from the upper section of the glacier in thick mist. Your return is by the same route, taking care on the steep icy sections.

On the glacier of Kolåstind

John Baddeley

28. Jønshornet

John Baddeley

Jønshornet (L) from Grønetinden   John Baddeley

Grading: A rough ascent to the highest point of a formidable array of rock spires. Some easy scrambling and one very short section of intermediate scrambling (fixed rope in place). Time: 7 hours Overall distance and ascent: 13km, 1400m	Access to starting point: From Barstadvik on the E39, take the minor road S for 2.5km to Erdalen. Maps: Statens Kartverk 1:50 000 Turkart "Sunnmørsalpane"
Best enjoyed: Later in the season, after snow melt. It would be much more serious in wintry conditions.	

Route summary:
A circular walk and scramble to the summit of Jønshornet, taking in a visit to upper Molladalen. From the end of the minor road at Erdalen follow the main path southeast into upper Molladalen. Contour back around the western shoulder of Nyfjellet to Oksegylvatnet, then go up to the col between Jønshornet and Rametinden. Scramble up the North West ridge of Jønshornet to the summit. Return down this section, then continue north along the ridge and over Rametinden. A gentle descent north west rejoins the minor road about 1km north of the starting point.

Upper Molladalen   *John Baddeley*

The peaks of Sunnmøre are remarkable for their variety. From the very steep, pointed summits of Slogen and Jakta to the bulkier glaciated forms of Kolåstinden and Råna they show extraordinary differences within a small area. This trend is carried on in spades on Jønshornet. Standing near the head of the incredibly rough Molladalen, it is the highest point in an impressive collection of rock spires, ridges and buttresses easily identifiable from afar. Indeed it is well know to local mariners as a key landmark when navigating the waters around Storfjorden, although they know it by the alternative name of Ramoen.

The route starts at Erdalen, for those with their own transport, or walk there from the main road at Barstadvika (adds 5km, 120m to route). Follow the track up the main valley for 1½km to Melbøsætra. You now have a choice of two routes and, while the route described makes the ascent considerably more difficult, it takes in upper Molladalen, which really should be visited whilst in the area. Bear left and take main path into Molladalen. This rises steadily through birch woods above the stream of Molladalselva and gradually steepens as height is gained. At the top of the steepest section of path, it bursts over the edge of the main corrie in Molladalen. A short distance ahead is the lake of Storevatnet and it is worth walking to its edge for a rest and to take in the situation. There are camping possibilities here. In front are the rock spikes of Molladalstindane, leading the eye further up and left to the main peak of Jønshornet although it is hard to identify the summit from here. Then from left to right are the lower peaks of Randers Topp, Mohns Topp and Slingsbys Topp (also called Ytstenestinden).

The view south from the summit of Jønshornet   John Baddeley

Returning to the day's objective, the shores of Storevatnet are 650m below the summit in a horizontal distance of 900m. The ambitious path (marked on the map) that tackles this challenging gradient directly is not recommended due to the loose rock and scree underfoot, and considerable risk of stonefall. A more pleasant alternative is to backtrack from the edge of lake for 300m to grid reference 608119. Then head just north of west on a gently rising traverse onto the west shoulder of Nyfjellet. Follow this broad stony shoulder to a flatter shelf at about 1000m, then leave the ridge and descend slightly to the lake of Oksegylvatnet, which is likely to be ice-covered until late in the season. This section of the route includes some steep contouring across glacial slabs and so should be approached with caution in the wet. If time does not allow a visit to Molladalen it is possible to reach this point directly by taking the path from Melbøsætra alongside the Oksegylelva.

From the outflow of Oksegylvatnet go east up a steep slope to the col between Jønshornet and Rametinden. Then turn south and follow the steep North West Ridge of Jønshornet, which is fairly easy going for most of the way over rough boulders. Approximately half way up this section, the ridge steepens and becomes an intermediate scramble. This was equipped with a fixed rope of dubious quality and even less convincing anchor points. Some will use it, others will prefer not to. Soon after this obstacle, the ridge begins to level out and the crest gives some fine, easy scrambling in superb situations. In fact, the ridge is of such quality that it may well hold your attention right up to the summit cairn at 1419m. Once here the prospect of continuing looks, and is, rather unlikely. Instead you will probably be content, after signing the summit log, to sit in sun and take in the amazing view. To the south and east are the sharp peaks, fjords and glaciers of Sunnmøre, while to the north and west there are the numerous islands in the mouth of Storfjorden and in the distance the town of Ålesund.

There is no easy way to vary the descent as far as the col with Rametinden. From there, you can return down to Oksegylvatnet and take the direct path to Melbøsætra, then return along the track to start point. An alternative, which is not too energetic, is to continue easily north with 100m of ascent to the summit of Rametinden (1198m). From there, a path of sorts heads first west, then north, before finally reaching the road just over 1km north of Erdalen.

Opportunities abound in Molladalen for the adventurous scrambler or climber with a taste for exploration. Both Randers Topp and Mohns Topp may be ascended from Storevatnet via obvious stony gullies that give some intermediate/hard scrambling. Mohns Topp is the location of the famous rock needle Bladet, the icon of Molladalen climbing and a 20m grade V climb. The area between Jønshornet and Randers Topp is the main climbing area with routes generally in the range of grades V to VII. These include long mountaineering lines such as the South and South West Ridges of Jønshornet, and also harder, shorter routes on the lower pinnacles.

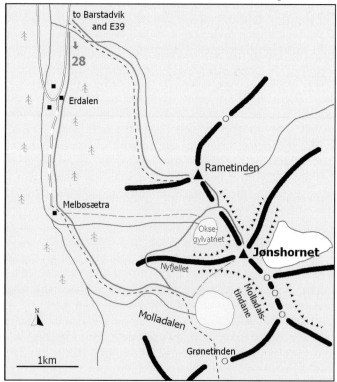

29. A Walk Through the Tafjord Mountains

John Baddeley

From L to R, Karitind, Høgstolen and Pyttegga, seen from the east   John Baddeley

Grading: Easy walking on well-marked paths. Mountain ascents are rough and unmarked. River crossings could be difficult in wet weather. Time: 3 days Daily distance, ascent and time: Day 1: 24km, 650m ascent, 8 hours Day 2: 15km, 1400m ascent, 8 hours Day 3: 25km, 250m ascent, 7 hours	Access to starting point: The hamlet of Bjørnekleive, on the rail line and the E136 between Dombås and Åndalsnes. Maps: Statens Kartverk 1:50 000 Turkart "Tafjordfjella".
Best enjoyed: A good trip at any time of year, although in winter the exit through Veltdalen would be difficult and possibly dangerous.	

Route summary:
A linear, three-day camping or hut tour from east to west through the Tafjord mountains, including ascents of the two highest summits. Take the no-through road/track south west from Bjønnekleiv to the hamlet of Tunga. From there follow the marked path to the hut of Pyttbua or continue to camp in Søre Botnen. Head north west onto the East Ridge of Pyttegga and follow this to the summit. Continue south to Høgstolen, then south east to Karitind. Descend to Veltdalshytta or camp in the area. Head north west down Veltdalen to the roadhead at Furuhaugen and then follow the road to Tafjord.

Karitind from Pyttegga   *John Baddeley*

The mountains of Tafjord lie between Romsdalen and Jostedalsbreen, immediately east of Sunnmøre. In fact in some guides the two areas are combined and called Reinheimen, despite their very different characters. The mountains of Tafjord don't feel as coastal as those in Sunnmøre because the sea is rarely visible and, although the summits of Tafjord are higher, the drops into the valleys are less. They are also not as steep as their western neighbours, but are still generally shapely peaks littered with small glaciers and permanent snowfields. In many ways they are comparable with an area like the Carneddau of North Wales – perhaps less immediately spectacular than nearby areas but in many ways better for it. The walk described in this chapter traverses the area from east to west in three days and ascends the two highest mountains, staying in either mountain huts or wild camping. It could easily be extended by several days to include other peaks and give more time to explore some of the interests in the area.

The starting point will depend on your choice of transport. If using bus then you begin on the E136 just east of the hamlet of Bjørnekleive, whereas the nearest rail station is at Bjorli, further east again. Either of these options leaves you with a long walk up a minor road to a collection of huts at Tunga. A taxi ride is recommended to cut out most of this section of the walk, as even if you have your own transport it will be easier to retrieve when you have completed the route if left near the main road. From Tunga, a marked path of variable quality leads through pleasant birch forest for the first hour. Emerging from the trees at about 1000m, the path borders a narrow, rocky section of stream and you get the first good views of Pyttegga, the highest

Naushornet from the east   *John Baddeley*

mountain in the area and your first summit. Two kilometres further along the path you reach the hut of Pyttbua (Ålesund-Sunnmøre Turistforening), which makes a good place to spend the first night. Alternatively, you can take the path signposted to Veltdalshytta for several hundred metres until it crosses the first river. There may be a bridge in place or it may be necessary to ford the river, bearing in mind that this may not be possible and taking all the usual precautions. Once across, head just south of west into the large corrie of Søre Botnen where there are reasonable campsites by either of its two lakes. The view from this corrie is dominated by the attractive pointed form of Karitind, slightly lower than Pyttegga and the second major summit on this walk.

On the second day, ascend north from Søre Botnen onto the East Ridge of Pyttegga. There is a cairn at the eastern end of this ridge (1511m) that has a fine view of the route so far. The ascent of this ridge is straightforward if rough and rocky, and after about 4km you reach the summit of Pyttegga at 1999m. Almost inevitably, a large cairn was erected in the past to break the 2000m contour, but this is now largely ruined. The north and west faces of the mountain drop very steeply for over 500m, adding to the sense of height and emphasising the views in these directions. The peaks of Sunnmøre are to the west, while to the north the even more distinctive Romsdalen peaks of Bispen, Kongen and Trolltindene are easily seen. To the south lurks the imposing blue and white mass of Jostedalsbreen, in perfect contrast to the gentle, rolling hills and forests that stretch away eastwards.

Returning to the day in hand, leave Pyttegga by the South Ridge to the pass of Søre Skardet. This descent is steep and loose in places but is not difficult if care is taken. There then follows a reascent of about 300m to the intermediate summit of Høgstolen (1953m), before a long, undulating ridge traverse for nearly four kilometres to the south east. Eventually this ends in the graceful summit cone of Karitind (1982m), which is not nearly as sharp as it appears from a distance. The views are similar to those from Pyttegga, but prominent to the south west is the multi-summited Naushornet and the relatively heavily glaciated Torsnos.

From the summit of Karitind there is a choice of two descent routes to the next overnight stop in the vicinity of Veltdalshytta. Go down the bouldery East Ridge, which feels more pronounced that it appears on the map, then follow a broad spur south to the path between Pyttbua and Veltdalshytta. Alternatively, take the more direct South West Ridge for just over 1km, then as it steepens trend around to the south east until it is possible to once more head straight for the hut. From either of these routes it is possible to scout out likely campsites from above, if not staying the night in the hut.

Ten minutes west of Veltdalshytta (ÅST) stands Fieldfarehytta (ÅST). This hut, tucked into a small recess in the rocks (Grid Ref. 324928, unmarked on Turkart), was built by Joachim Rønneberg (who led one part of the heavy water raids in 1943), Olav Aasæther and Birger Strømsheim of the famous Ligne Company. These Norwegians were parachuted into Tafjord in 1944 to disrupt communications in the Romsdalen/Lesja area. This rather ramshackle hut was renovated in 1990 and now provides limited accommodation with four beds, with some of the former atmosphere intact. Staying somewhere like this, with all the comforts afforded by contemporary equipment and an adequate food supply, it is hard to imagine that these men lived here through a year, let alone conducted offensive combat sorties.

In this area of upper Veltdalen you first come across the hydroelectric power schemes that pervade these western mountains of Tafjord. Small grey huts and occasional tunnel outlets are some of the few visual clues and it is quite easy to forget their presence. Appearances, however, belie their extent and you will come across more of the systems later in the walk. For now though you have a choice of routes to follow.

One option is to follow the marked path down Veltdalen. This involves some interesting route finding in places, and includes a short descent down not particularly steep but quite smooth glacial slabs that looks rather unlikely from above. The most exposed sections have fixed cables for reassurance, and some steps and iron pegs are in place. Thereafter the path traverses the steep northern side of Veltdalen for several kilometres until the narrow, V-shaped valley suddenly opens out into a huge bowl of greenery that looks at first almost like the landscaped grounds of some stately house. The scene comes as a surprise after the unrelenting rockiness of the route so far. This bowl is really a large, open corrie and its lush appearance comes mainly from the presence of open birch woodland interspersed with tall groves of pine that surround a sizeable lake. The path soon descends into this area, in the centre of which stands the almost hotel-like hut of Reindalsæter (ÅST), where you may choose to spend the night. If so, there is much of interest in the area. A short walk up the path towards Sæterhorn is worth it for the views back in Reindalen, and for those so inclined much time can be spent botanising at Daurmålshaugen. This area rivals sites such as Knutshø in the Dovrefjell for botanical interest but is much less well known, especially outside Norway.

Reindalen   *John Baddeley*

An alternative route from Veldalshytta is to take a slightly more circuitous path to Reindalsæter that heads east and gains nearly 400m of altitude to the col between Naushornet and Torsnos. It then descends north west to Reindalsæter, down a valley that has seven corries between its head and the fjord, which seems quite remarkable. For those in search of an energetic diversion, both of these mountains may be climbed from this path. From the small lake at the bottom of the Langfonna glacier, head north and up a steep snow slope to a broad, plateau-like col between three of the tops of Naushornet. The main summit (1895m) is several hundred metres to the northeast. To climb Torsnos (1975m), either the North East or North West Ridges that encircle Langfonna may be taken. They are both reported to have steep sections of scrambling but have not been checked by the author.

Following the path west from Reindalsæter a steep descent leads down into a much smaller corrie containing the lake of Sildevatnet. With some imagination and a waterproof groundsheet this area can provide some beautiful places to camp for the night. The path continues down to the shores of the larger Sakrisvatnet, where a bridge crosses the large waterfalls of Reindalsfossen, as yet untamed by hydropower schemes. From there, there is a pleasant, undulating walk along the wooded south shores of the lake for just over two kilometres to the roadhead at Furuhaugen. Soon after reaching the road you arrive at the dam of Sakariasdammen, which at 95m is one of the highest in Europe. There are currently (2005) ambitious plans for a curved hotel on top of the dam and a transparent art gallery spanning the gorge below it. A further six kilometres down the quiet, winding road brings you into the village of Tafjord, where facilities include a small but well-stocked shop, a campsite with cabins, a museum in the old power station and a 25m open-air swimming pool. An infrequent bus service, which can be avoided by good opportunities for hitching, will get you to Sylte for connections north to the railhead at Åndalsnes in Romsdalen, or south if you want to tackle the Jostedalsbre.

The Tafjord Tsunami

Early in the morning of 7th April 1934 there was a huge rockfall from the side of the mountain of Langhammaren on the north side of Tafjord. An estimated 7 million tons of rock cascaded down into the fjord below, creating a huge tsunami that was funnelled up the ever-narrowing fjord. By the time it reached the village of Tafjord at the head of the fjord it was 64m high. There was widespread destruction of property and 34 people were killed.

Today when you visit the village you can look for the transition from the older houses further inland to the newer houses lower down and closer to the fjord, which were built to replace those swept away. It is a surprising distance inland. The wave also travelled westwards out of the fjord and here it struck the village of Fjørå, where another 17 people lost their lives. There are sobering photographs on display in Tafjord of what remains one of Norway's biggest natural disasters.

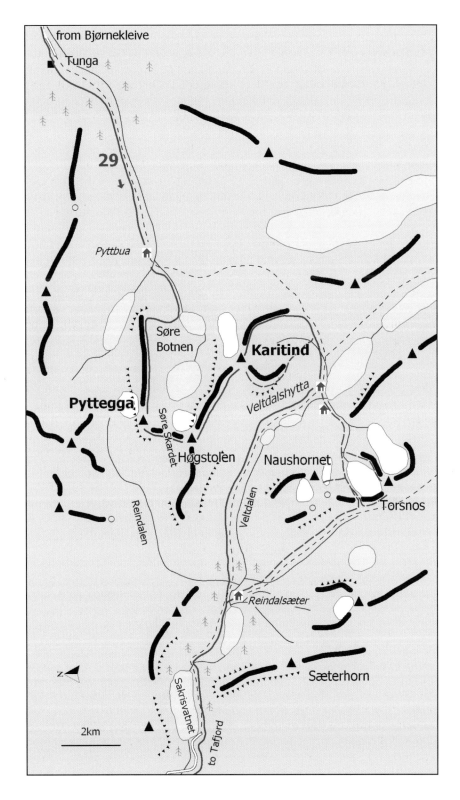

from Bjørnekleive

Tunga

29

Pyttbua

Søre
Botnen

Karitind

Veltdalshytta

Pyttegga

Søre Skardet

Høgstolen

Naushornet

Torsnos

Reindalen

Veltdalen

Reindalsæter

Z

Sakrisvatnet

to Tafjord

Sæterhorn

2km

30. Breitind

Ian H. Robertson

On Breitind, looking northwest to the Trolltindan — Krystina Lotoczko

Grading: An easy walk and easy scramble to a magnificent viewpoint. Ice axes and crampons should be carried for the summit snowfield. Time: 6 hours Overall distance and ascent: 10 km, 1000m	Access to starting point: From Stigrøra, on Fv 63 at the top of Trollstigen. Maps: Statens Kartverk 1:80 000 Turkart "Romsdalen", or 1:50 000 sheets 1319-I & 1319-IV.

Best enjoyed: The scramble would be practicable under most conditions, but the route is best enjoyed on a clear day.

Vehicular access note: The Trollstigen road to the starting point is not officially opened until 5th of June each year, later on a snowy year.   If the road is not open, this route is 16km with 1750m ascent.

Route summary:
From the large car park at the top of the Trollstigen road take a faint path east towards the open corrie of Stigbotnen. Ascend northeast from the lake in this corrie up scree and then snow to the foot of the west ridge of Breitind. Scramble up the blocky ridge to the summit snowfield. From here it is a walk to the summit. Return by the same route.

Looking from the top to Breitind's summit snowfield.   *Ian H. Robertson*
Storgrovfjellet is to the right with Kongen in the middle distance.

The mountains around Romsdal are some of the most spectacular in Europe: the Troll Wall is the continent's highest sheer rock face. Although famous as a rock-climber's paradise, there is also much to interest the walker and scrambler. The chapters in this book give four fabulous outings of varying grades.

Three of the routes (Breitind, To the Top of the Troll Wall and Bispen) start at 750m near the top of the Trollstigen road. This is a place where having a car is a big advantage to the mountaineer. The road with its numerous hairpins is a spectacular drive, but note that is closed until early summer.

The highest summit between Isterdalen and Romsdal is Breitind. It is one of the less steep mountains in the area and should be a practicable proposition for most hillwalkers and scramblers. Breitind is slightly higher than the more spectacular summits that surround it and is an excellent viewpoint. Keep it for a clear day to make the most of it.

As for the walk to the Top of the Troll Wall, start at the car park and café at Stigrøra at the top of the Trollstigen road (750m). The path can either be gained by a little tricky scramble on some slabs near the car park or an easier path – you walk round to the right of the steps at the viewing point.

Follow the path into the corrie of Stigbotnen and climb up either scree or snow slopes (depending on the season) to the foot of the west ridge of Breitind (approx. 1300m). There are large cairns here. Walk across the snowfield to

Looking south towards Skarfjell   Ian H. Robertson

gain the rocks on the ridge. An easy scramble over large blocks will take you to the summit snowfield where the angle eases. From here it is an easy walk to the summit (1797m) and its glorious views.

Although Breitind's northeast face is not as famous as the Troll Wall, it is still a dramatic drop to the Romsdal valley bottom 1700m below. Breitind's East Pillar is a 2000m grade V rock climb and is one of the "Three Pillars of Romsdal" (the other two are Søndre Trolltind and Trollryggen). In short, you will need a good head for heights to look over the edge!

The return to Stigrøra is by the route of ascent.

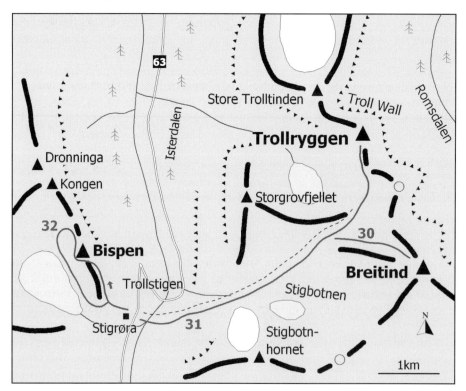

31. To the Top of the Troll Wall

John Baddeley

Trolltindan from the south   *John Baddeley*

Grading: Generally easy walking with a few rough sections and some steep snow patches. Some easy scrambling on the ridge, with harder options. *Time: 5 hours* *Overall distance and ascent:* *10km, 1050m*	*Access to starting point: From Stigrøra, on Fv63 at the top of Trollstigen.* *Maps: Statens Kartverk 1:80 000 Turkart "Romsdalen", or 1:50 000 sheets 1319-I & 1319-IV.*
Best enjoyed: Mid season, on a day with some shifting clouds to add to the drama.	

Route summary:
The easiest route to the top of the highest vertical rock wall in Europe. From the large car park at the top of the Trollstigen road take a faint path east towards the open corrie of Stigbotnen. Ascend north east from the lake in this corrie onto the east ridge of Storgrovfjellet, near to its lowest point and continue up the hillside to the north east onto a col on the south ridge of Trollryggen. Follow this north to the summit, taking in several rock steps or avoiding them by traverses on their southern flanks. Return by the same route.

Bispen (L) and Kongen (R) from Stigbotnen   *John Baddeley*

Trollveggen, the Troll Wall, has almost mythical status in world mountaineering. It is often regarded as the tallest vertical rock wall in Europe at about one mile high (1.6km), and its brooding presence dominates Romsdalen. Along its crest stands a succession of weirdly shaped and individually named pinnacles, the petrified Trolls that give the Wall its name. While the ascent of the main face is reserved for dedicated rock climbers, nothing more than an adventurous walk and a head for heights will get you to its highest point. Note that due to the complex nature of this area many of the peaks are un-named on the 1:50 000 maps. This chapter gives names and spot heights where known, derived from a variety of sources.

Most visitors to the area will be based in Romsdalen. From here, drive or take the bus south up the wildly hairpin road of Trollstigen, much photographed for tourist brochures. The large car park and souvenir shop/café at the top of the pass is likely to be busy, but this is soon left behind as you take a faint path eastwards, contouring the hillside above the large waterfall of Stigfossen. A clue to finding the start of the path is to look for the sign proclaiming that it is illegal to carry parachutes in the area – a reference to the sport of BASE jumping. Until its use was banned in 1986, the Troll Wall was a famous jumping site and appeared in the 1984 Guinness Book of Records as the scene for the first BASE jumping height record. Norway has more BASE jumpers per capita than any other country in the world, but a number of fatal accidents in this area led to the ban being imposed.

Looking along the Trolls from Trollryggen   John Baddeley

A path, faint in places, more defined in others, makes its way from the car park up into the open corrie of Stigbotnen. Cross the river flowing from the tarn in the corrie and head north-eastwards up steepening slopes of rock and large snow patches until you reach the broad East Ridge of Storgrovfjellet, near to its lowest point where it connects with the main Trolltindan-Breitind ridge. Continue eastwards to the col between Trollryggen and Søndre Trolltinden (1536m). For the final part of your approach to this ridge you may well start to feel gripped by the sense that there is nothing ahead, a wholly appropriate reaction. Indeed, for the last few metres you may feel inclined to crouch down for before you lies a drop that is likely to exceed any you have experienced before. Although not yet the Troll Wall proper, this subsidiary wall, whose North Face was first ascended by British climbers Rusty Baillie and John Amatt in 1967, gives a taste of the height and verticality of its larger neighbour. The experience of leaning over a drop of this magnitude is not easily forgotten, and is a taste of what is to follow.

From this col, turn north for the short but time-consuming trip to the summit of Trollryggen. This ridge rises in a series of rock steps of varying difficulty that may be attempted direct for those so inclined, or avoided by traverses on their southwest faces. Some of these traverses may involve tackling quite steep snow patches that, if frozen, would require ice axe and crampons. The two largest obstacles, Klumpen and Stabben are easiest if traversed around, as described above, and then ascended from the west.

149

Trollryggen from Breitind's west ridge   Ian H. Robertson

The summit of Trollryggen (1742m) is marked by a small cairn but there really is no doubt when you reach it. All around the ground drops away steeply and ahead lies the great void of the Troll Wall, topped by a bizarre array of pinnacles in all shapes and sizes. The walkers' route stops on this peak, but it is worth continuing westwards for a short distance to get better views of the pinnacles, the upper portion of the Wall and the immense drop. The col ahead between Trollryggen and the first pinnacle (Trollspiret) is where Rimmond Route, the most well-known route on the Wall, emerges. It was first ascended over five days in 1965 by a British team of John Amatt, Tony Howard and Bill Tweedale from the Rimmond Mountaineering Club.

Once you have torn yourself away from the spectacle of the Troll Wall, views of the other peaks of Romsdalen are interesting from here. Romsdalhornet looks surprisingly different because its profile from Åndalsnes is so well known; the effect is rather like seeing the Matterhorn from the Dent Blanche. Behind it are the spires and glaciers of the complex massif of Store Venjetind (1852m).

From the summit the descent is by the same route back to the road at the top of Trollstigen. An alternative for experienced and adventurous climbers is the grade 4/5 traverse of the pinnacles to Store Trolltinden before a choice of descents, as described in climbing guidebooks. Those wishing to extend the walking route described above into a full day trip can do so by starting with an ascent of Stigbotnhornet (1592m) and then traversing the ridge between it and Breitind (1797m) with some easy scrambling.

The map for route 31 is on page 146.

32. Bispen

Tony Howard

Bispen behind, Kongen in the background.   Tony Howard and Di Taylor

Grading: The route as described (up the south ridge and down the north ridge) involves grade 3 climbing (UK Mod – Diff) and requires a rope. Ascending and descending via the north ridge is an easy scramble. Time: 4–5 hours Overall distance and ascent: 4 km, 800m	Access to starting point: From Stigrøra, as for Chapter 31. Maps: Statens Kartverk 1:50 000 sheet 1319-IV.
Best enjoyed: In July and August when most of the snow has gone.	

Route summary:
From the large car park at the top of the Trollstigen road head northwest to gain the south ridge of Bispen. Ascend this ridge to the summit. From the summit, go down the north ridge and then trend west to reach the lake of Bispevatn. Follow the east side of the lake to the outflow and follow this back to the road.

For the alternative ascent via the north ridge, follow the stream to the Bispevatn and walk along the east side of the lake. Then head up to the col between Kongen and Bispen (some snow) to follow Bispen's north ridge. A path zigzags up between small rock walls.

Bispen viewed from Kongen.   *Øyvind Heen*

Bispen is the most southerly of a famous trio of mountains, Bispen, Kongen and Dronninga – the Bishop, King and Queen. The summit was first reached in 1882 by Carl Hall, Matias Soggemoen and Erik Norahagen who climbed one of the other Romsdal routes in this book, the Romsdalshorn, the previous year. They did not, however, climb Bispen by the route of our choice, the South Ridge. Instead they followed the nearby but easier southwest face, which provides an easier though less interesting approach to the summit as well as an optional way down. The climb of our choice was first made by the most famous of Romsdal's mountain pioneers, Arne Randers Heen, together with another local climber, Thørbjorn Krohn in November 1932. We had the pleasure of knowing both these gentlemen who made us welcome during our own years of Romsdal exploration in the 1960s.

The approach to their route starts from what is now the Trollstig Fjellstua café. Not far away across the road is the sensational viewpoint at the top of Stigfossen Waterfall – well worth a look despite the crowds! To escape the multitudes and gain immediate tranquillity, head northwest up the hillside from the Fjellstua, passing through a small cliff by an open gully (marker stone above). Continue up the hillside, making for the south ridge (possibly crossing some remnant winter snow patches dependent on the time of year).

The ridge is reached from cairned ledges on a shoulder to its right. The great tower of the East Ridge is beyond to the north and provides a classic route with pitches of Norwegian grade 3 and 4 when climbed directly. Our route is much more straightforward though care should be taken with route finding. Having gained the ridge, continue by scrambling up the left side of the lower section by shallow chimneys and broken rocks (some grade 2 and loose rock). Eventually a platform and short steep wall is reached which is passed by a grade 2 scramble to the right (exposed) or directly at grade 3. It is worth carrying a short rope to protect this section. From here, continue more easily and obviously to reach a knife-edge ridge and balance precariously across to reach the final summit scramble.

As just about always in Romsdal, there are great summit views: north to the steep south wall of Kongen and the upper skyline of its plunging 1500 metre east face and east to the impressive array of the Troll pinnacles standing sentinel above the hidden Troll Wall. Between two of the Trolls is the gap of Brur Skar with its frightening view down the face. Brur Skar is reached by another route in this book also starting from Stigfossen, the whole of that route being visible from Bispen. The Trollstig hairpins are directly below, small cars and coaches disgorging their occupants to experience the spray from the falls. Also down there close by the falls is the old packhorse and cattle drover's way down into Isterdal. This ancient trail was first recognised as a 'highway' in 1766 and resurrected in the 1990s. It descends through spray on the true left side of the falls down chain-protected cliffs, It is said that one farmer lost forty seven cattle here, having tied them together for the descent of the cliffs!

Looking south from the summit, ridge after ridge of snow capped peaks lead the eye on to the massifs of the Jotunheim and Jostedal on the distant horizon. Equally icy and much closer are the glacial slopes of Finnan (1786m) to the west, first climbed by its snowy south east ridge in 1898 by the ubiquitous trio of Hall, Soggemoen and Norahagen. Its east face drops down into the cold waters of Bispevatn along whose eastern shore (or, conditions permitting, frozen surface) our descent route passes.

As mentioned earlier, it is possible and quick to descend Carl Hall's southwest face route by scrambling down in that direction, mostly on scree then moving left at about half way into a gully (sometimes with snow) that leads down to the approach hillside. A more interesting and enjoyable way is to complete a traverse of the mountain and descend by the North Ridge towards Kongen. Cairns indicate the way down, which eventually moves onto the west side of the ridge. There are some steeper sections before the path descends to the lakeside. (In case of bad weather, there is a bivouac site in boulders on the col between Bispen and Kongen.)

Follow the lake round beneath Bispen and descend by the side of its exit stream or cross the shoulder to reverse your approach route.

The map for route 32 is on page 146.

Bispen from above Stigfossen   *John Baddeley*

33. Romsdalshorn

Tony Howard

Romsdalhorn from Vengedal, Troll Wall in background   *Tony Howard and Di Taylor*

Grading: Romsdalhorn is a grade 2+ (UK Hard Mod) rock climb. The descent involves abseiling (or a grade 3 downclimb). Two ropes of at least 40m are needed for the abseil. *Time: 5–7 hours* *Overall distance and ascent:* *3 km, 800m*	*Access to starting point: From Åndalsnes, follow road 64 eastwards along the southern shore of the fjord then, where the fjord ends after 6kms, take a minor road southeast rising up and round the hillside for 3kms to reach the toll road and honesty box at the entrance to Vengedal. From there it's a further 8kms to the road head.* *Maps: Statens Kartverk 1:50 000 sheet 1319-I.*
Best enjoyed: In July and August when most of the snow has gone.	

Route summary:
Walk up path from Vengedal (screes) to Romdalshorn's east face. Climbing and scrambling (see text) leads to the col between Lille Romsdalhorn and the main Romsdalhorn summit. Climb from here to the summit.
Return by the same route, with several abseils.

Having reached the end of the road, the high 'alpine' ridge of Vengetind is above and behind you to the left. Ahead is a dark, north-facing cliff glowering over the small lake of Hornvatn. On your right, above an expanse of scree and possibly snow is the dominating, almost forbidding, truncated tower of Romsdalshorn, one of Norway's best known and most popular summits.

From Hornvatn (760m) scramble slightly leftwards up the screes towards the east face of Romsdalshorn until a path is found marked by occasional cairns and red markers, leading left (south) between small crags towards a step in the skyline ridge. After some scrambling, the track zigzags back right to below a steep cliff. 'Den Gule Flekk', the Yellow Patch, a prominent overhanging wall of yellow rock, is high above to the right. Here you have a choice of routes: either climb a left-trending pitch of 3, or scramble up rightwards then back left across a slab at grade 2. There is an abseil point in position above this wall.

Continue the scramble up the east face, to reach a good ledge below and left of the Yellow Patch, before heading out left and up the east ridge with some scrambling (2) to reach the right edge of the ominous gully of Hall's Renne, which separates Romsdalshorn from it's smaller southern top, Lille Romsdalshorn.

The gully is named in honour of Danish mountaineer Carl Hall who, along with two climbers from Romsdal, Matias Soggemoen and Erik Norahagen reached the summit by this route in 1881. Arriving there, they found the cairn built in 1828 by Kristen Hoel and Hans Bjærmeland, two local farmers who claimed to have climbed the mountain after a "merry drinking party". This was a remarkably early date for such a climb and their rightful claim had consequently been viewed with some scepticism!

Following in their footsteps, scramble up the right side of the gully (there may be some snow) to its head, where a steep pitch of grade 2+ goes up the left side to the col and another abseil point. These rather curious looking metal hooks are actually the barrels of WW2 rifles hammered into place by one of Norway's most famous mountaineers, the legendary Arne Randers Heen, a tailor from Åndalsnes. From the 1930s to the 1950s Arne added numerous first ascents in Romsdal, both summer and winter, including the first winter ascent of this route with Karl and Osvald Oshaug in 1930. He is reputed to have climbed Romsdalshorn 233 times!

Arne continued to climb and take an active interest in his beloved Romsdal mountains until his death in 1991. A museum dedicated to his pioneering climbs will be found just over the bridge from Åndalsnes, heading west to Veblungsnes, then immediately left to reach the first house on the right.

156

Abseiling back down Romsdalhorn   *Tony Howard and Di Taylor*

Once at the col between Romsdalshorn's two summits, you become abruptly aware of your situation, perched 1500 metres above the green-blue depths of Romsdal, beyond which the cliffs of the Trolltind massif tower almost 2000 metres above the void. Above the col, and to its north, Romsdalshorn beckons you up and out of the cold shadows of the chasm onto what should be, if you are lucky, the warm sunlit crisp-dry rocks of its steep south ridge. Minor variations are possible, but the easiest way (grade 2) follows juggy cracks and corners first left then right and finally directly up past two abseil points to the summit 80 metres above.

Its many-cairned flat top has a shelter built from the summit stones by Arne Randers whilst amongst the summer alpine flora are other rocks carefully placed by Arne to collect rain water. It's a delightful place to enjoy the view: to the northeast are the twin peaks of Vengetind (1852m) with Kvandalstind to its south, described somewhat enthusiastically by Slingsby, as "the steepest mountain in Europe". South again, are Olaskardstind and Kalskratind with its high hanging glacier. Far below, the meandering blue snake of the Rauma River twists its way northwards between green meadows to Åndalsnes "the alpine town by the fjord". Immediately opposite to the west are the Trolltind peaks "home of the Trolls" and location of the immense Trollryggen Pillar, first climbed by Arne Randers and Ralph Hoibakk in 1958. With 2000 metres of climbing and some pitches of grade 6, it was a masterpiece of route finding and for many years was Norway's longest and hardest route. To its right is the grim verticality of the Troll Wall, first climbed in 1965 by two routes, Norwegian and British (the author of this chapter was on the British ascent). There were several massive rock falls on the wall in September 1998 (and others since) making many of the climbs either extremely dangerous or impossible.

Having enjoyed the summit vistas, there is a fast descent of five abseils down the North Face but this is steep and committing. It needs two fifty metre ropes, knowledge of the route and confidence on grade 4 rock should anything go wrong. The North Face can also be busy. The recommended descent route for those who ascend via Hall's Renne is to return via the same route, which also requires abseils, most people making one or two (of 20m then 40m) down the south ridge to the col at the top of Hall's Renne – though we once saw Arne Randers Heen taking six clients down this ridge. He had each of them on a short rope, three in each hand! He assured us he was fine so we abseiled swiftly down to the col and then 20m into the gully hoping that none of Arne's clients would come tumbling down on top of us!

From the col, make another abseil into Hall's Renne, and continue 90m or so until a path trends left. Zigzag down rock on the east face until another one of Arne's gun-barrel abseil posts can be found. A final 45m abseil is needed here. The rest of the descent is, weather and visibility permitting, straightforward although, having had the experience, I can tell you that finding your way down in a midsummer blizzard can be both slippery and time consuming! Once you reach the screes, if winter's snows are still lying deep and firm, enjoy the long glissade back down to the shores of Hornvatn.

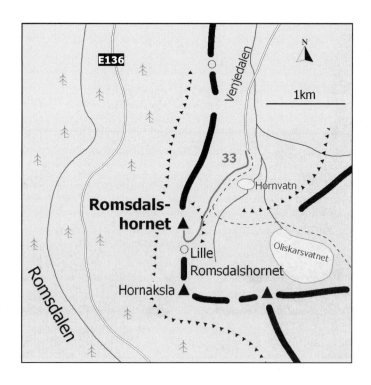

Romsdalshorn from the Southwest Pillar of Holstind   *Tony Howard and Di Taylor*

34. Walking through Innerdalen and Trollheimen

Anthony Dyer

Salen (1430m) and Rognebba (1497m) seen from the east   Anthony Dyer

Grading: Rough walking across marked paths. One glacier crossing on Snota. Time: 4 days (+ approach evening) Daily distance, ascent and time: Day 1: 21km, 800m, 8 hours Day 2: 22km, 1150m, 9 hours Day 3: 21km, 1250m, 9 hours Day 4: 21km, 1350m, 9 hours	Access to starting point: From Sunndalsøra head north on highway 70 for 10km to Virumdalen and head east to the end of the road at Dalen. Maps: Statens Kartverk 1:50 000 Turkart "Trollheimen"
Best enjoyed: This walk can be done in any benign weather in the summer season from mid July onwards.	

Route summary:
A linear walk from Innerdalen to Jøldalshytta. From the road end at Dalen, head east along a track to Innerdalshytta. On the first day, continue east along marked paths either via Innerdalen or via Renndalen to Bårdsgarden hut in Storlidalen. On the second day, head north to Trollheimshytta via the high path over Mellomfjellet. On day three, head west to climb the summit of Snota (1669m) before returning to Trollheimshytta. On the final day head east to Jøldalshytta over the summit of Trollhøtta (1616m) and continue along the track northeast to the end of a minor public road west of Highway 700.

Renndalen and Viromdalen seen from Slanglifjellet (1488m).   Anthony Dyer

Trollheimen is a mountain wilderness in the north part of southern Norway. It is roughly bounded by highway 70 to the south, highways 70 & 670 to the west, highway 65 to the north and highway E6 to the east. The mountain range is a popular weekend destination for people living in the Trondheim commuter belt being no more than a one hour drive away.

The mountains in this area vary greatly in character. The western mountains are quite shapely, with many of the peaks standing up in proud isolation and some being linked with long pleasant ridges. The eastern range is very much reminiscent of the Scottish Cairngorms, with large mountain plateaux and cliffs plunging many hundreds of metres down to some remote lakes. On the whole, these summits will appeal greatly to the general hillwalker who has no interest in scrambling.

In the southwestern part of Trollheimen lies the beautiful valley of Innerdalen. Innerdalen is very much a microcosm of Trollheimen, where the mountains take on a very alpine character. Trollheimen's highest mountain, Trolla (1850m), resides in Innerdalen. This is a paradise for scramblers, climbers and alpinists. Many rate Innerdalen as the most beautiful valley in Norway and it is in this valley that the walk starts.

Storsalen (1720m), the eastern gateway into Innerdalen   *Anthony Dyer*

This linear walk, takes a cross-country route from southwest to northeast Trollheimen and takes in the shapely peak of Snota (1669m) and the popular summit of Trollhøtta (1616m). The walk, however, can easily be extended to climb many other peaks and some summits are noted in this chapter that you may like to investigate further.

The walk begins from the end of the road at Dalen in Virumdalen. A four kilometre walk with 150m ascent on a vehicle track takes you to Innerdalshytta. It's recommended that you do this walk in the evening, ready for a fuller walk in the morning. At Innerdalshytta, a magnificent mountain presents itself. Innerdalstårnet (1452m) is the most celebrated mountain in Innerdalen. It's easy to see why, the mountain rises a full 1000m above the valley floor presenting itself as a slender pinnacle. The reality is that Innerdalstårnet is merely a subsidiary peak of the larger summit of Tåga (1840m).

From Innerdalshytta, two routes are described as they both have their own qualities. The quickest route is to walk up Innerdalen. This path is scenically very pleasing, but underfoot you'll find progress slow and very wet as you negotiate bog pools, slippery slabs and marshes while having to hold back the tree branches much of the time. Only when the valley turns east and you start ascending out of the forest does progress underfoot become easier and dryer.

Innerdalstårnet seen from the lake shore at Innerdalshytta

Anthony Dyer

The second route from Innerdalshytta walks through Renndalen and past the north shore of Langvatnet before joining the previous route at Innerdalen's watershed. This route starts by backtracking west 200m from Innerdalshytta and follows the path on the eastern side of the river Renndøla. Soon after this path starts, it enters a river gorge high above the Renndøla. The path is exposed but easy for 5 minutes. Only a short slab causes pause for thought.

The valley gradually opens out, and the path becomes easier, but in places it has collapsed into the slope below, and requires some care.

As the path climbs towards the tree line, the valley opens out before finally giving way to fine pastures in the upper part of Renndalen. Up ahead, a steep cliff can be seen behind which sits Langvatnet. The path ascends the slope to the south of this cliff and upon reaching Langvatnet, fine views can be had extending west back down into Renndalen.

The path skirts the north side of Langvatnet, before reaching Renndalen's watershed. The path then continues over rocky terrain to meet up with the path from Innerdalen. The scenery is now more gentle with wide open valleys and rounded summits. The path continues east descending to Tovatna; then it descends into the populated valley of Storlidalen with its pleasant grazing hillsides. The path finishes at Storlia where a gravel road is followed east down to the hut at Bårdsgarden.

Those wanting to climb a peak during this first day will find the summit of Storsomrungnebba (1798m) worth investigating. This summit appears to be one of the easier summits in Innerdalen and can be ascended via Tverådalen and a corrie between Storsomrungnebba and Storsalen (1720m).

An alternative summit to bag during this first day is Slanglifjellet (1488m). It is worth a detour from Langvatnet for the fine views offered of the rest of Trollheimen. It would add three hours to the day's journey. This summit is the eastern extremity of a long ridge extending westwards to the fine summit of Snøfjellet (1579m). Seen from below, there appears to be a steep scramble involved between Skjerdingfjellet (1500m) and Grinaren (1520m) but

Looking west from down Renndalen to Snøffellet and Skjerdingffellet   *Anthony Dyer*

otherwise the ridge appears to be a fine walk. This ridge can also be traversed from Innerdalshytta, taking the path on the west side of the river Renndøla upto the ridge. It will however, mandate an extra days walking.

The second day of walking on our main route (from Bårdsgarden) takes a series of paths over high ground north towards Trollheimshytta. This route takes in some fine high level scenery in eastern Trollheimen passing close to high mountains such as Gjevilvasskamben (1627m) and Blåhøa (1671m). The scenery is very reminiscent of the Cairngorms with high lakes surrounded by rounded mountains and cliffs.

From Bårdsgarden, backtrack west along the road to the path that takes you north. You begin by ascending up to the saddle between Okla (1564m) and Storbekkhøa (1504m). At the saddle, you reach a crossroad. Take the western path signposted for Trollheimshytta and follow it over the shoulder of a hillside. Fine views can be had east towards Gjevillvatnet where it sits below the mighty spurs of Gjevilvasskamben.

The path descends into Hyttdalen where another path crossing is met. Two paths go to Trollheimshytta, one low route following the river Folda and the high route over Mellomfjellet. Follow the high route up a grassy hillside to a higher, more barren hanging valley. If you wish, you can make an easy three hour detour to take in the summit of Gjevilvasskamben.

164

Snota seen from Bossvasshøgda to the east   Anthony Dyer

You soon gain the high point of today's route as you reach the watershed of a spectacular high valley in which the lake of Storfagerlitjønna nestles. Progress is very easy along this route, being largely dry underfoot without too many boulders to slow you down. The route stays high and undulates gently before reaching the spur of Mellomfjellet (1325m). This is a broad bulky spur, more like a plateau in character. The path goes up and down, eventually reaching the high point before dropping down to Trollheimshytta. The path follows the western side of the river Slettåa before crossing the river to reach the hut. The bridge has been relocated upstream due to flood damage at the original crossing point. You'll have to backtrack about 150m to the new bridge location.

The third day of walking is a circular walk climbing Trollheimen's finest mountain outside of Innerdalen. Snota is a complex, bulky mountain harbouring numerous corries and has spectacular cliffs surrounding two sides of the summit plateau. The summit itself sits right on the corner of these two cliffs. It is a popular mountain, and the current summit log, already half full, only goes back two years.

The route to the summit has a long approach over what is generally boggy and wet terrain. The way up the mountain itself is complex and involves an easy glacier crossing but is marked both on the map and with a liberal amount of red paint on the mountain itself.

From Trollheimshytta, a good path can be followed beyond the hut bridge to the river Folda where a suspension bridge crosses. Beyond, the path ascends up boggy ground to cross Bossvasshøgda (815m) and into the boggy basin of Bossvatnet. At a path junction, the ascent of Snota finally begins. Initially the path climbs west into a shallow corrie before turning south to ascend to a shoulder on a complex rocky spur. This route crosses extensive slabs up to the shoulder. Once you reach the shoulder, the path turns west to cross a knobbly, complex spur of Snota.

Trollhøtta seen from the west   Anthony Dyer

Eventually you reach a glacier. Cross this lower glacier at its top end just below a rock ridge, to where the lower glacier meets the upper main glacier. Cross the upper glacier close to its edge to meet Snota's broad summit ridge. Ascend easily to the summit where the large summit cairn greets you just before you reach the spectacular cliff corner. The return to Trollheimshytta is by the same route.

On the final day, your journey goes up and over the summit of Trollhøtta. This is another popular summit, more so than Snota as it's more accessible for weekend visitors living in Trondheim. The mountain as seen from the west is quite a lump. However, when seen from the east, it hosts a spectacular corrie harbouring a lake 600m below the summit. The mountain has a marked route for the entire ridge which is quite narrow between the north and east tops.

The approach path is generally good through the forest with just the occasional bog trot. The path continues up the steep lower hillside relenting only once you're above the tree line. Continue the steady pull to the summit, gradually getting steeper as you get higher up.

From the summit continue to the north summit along the ridge before turning east to cross the airy ridge going across to the east top. The mountain broadens out beyond the eastern top as you descend down to an extensive 1200m high plateau. Beyond Langfjellet (1264m), the path finally descends 400m to the valley floor where it continues for another two kilometres to Jøldalshytta. From this hut, a track can be picked up heading northeast for five kilometres to the end of the public road. This a minor road leading up from highway 700. Those without wheels will need to walk a further ten kilometres to the main highway between Melbu and Berkåk.

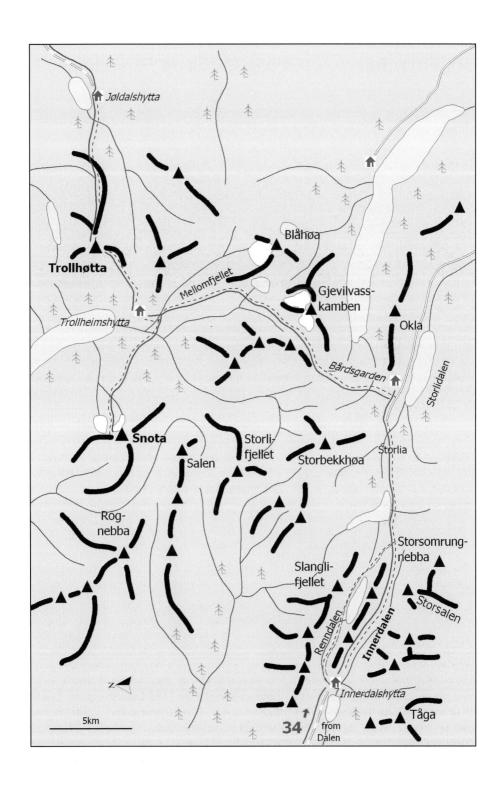

Jøldalshytta

Blåhøa

Trollhøtta

Mellomfjellet

Gjevilvass-
kamben

Trollheimshytta

Bårdsgarden

Okla

Storlidalen

Snota

Storli-
fjellet

Salen

Storbekkhøa

Storlia

Rog-
nebba

Storsomrung-
nebba

Slangli-
fjellet

Storsalen

Renndalen

Innerdalen

z

Innerdalshytta

5km

34

from
Dalen

Tåga

167

35. From Top to Top Along the Bodø Peninsula

Anthony Dyer

Breidviktinden (left) and Fagertinden (right) seen from Kvalhornet   Anthony Dyer

Grading: Mostly easy walking over slabby mountain tops. Time: 4 days. Daily distance, ascent and time: Day 1: 10km, 1000m, 4 hours Day 2: 13km, 1250m, 8 hours Day 3: 18km, 1600m, 12 hours Day 4: 12km, 450m, 5 hours	Access to starting point: From Fauske, head west along highway 80 to a carpark at the northernmost point of Valnesfjorden. Map: Statens Kartverk 1:25 000/1:75 000 Turkart "Bodø–Bodømarka"
Best enjoyed: Early-Mid July in dry weather to avoid slippery slabs.	

Route summary:
A linear walk from Valnesfjorden to Bodø. The route starts by ascending Kvalhornet before camping in a corrie just east of Stordalsfjellet. The second day continues by traversing west over Stordalsfjellet, Kistrandtindan, Innertinden and Mjønestinden before continuing west to camp high above Heggmovatnet. On the third day, the route descends to a gravel road, which is followed to the southwestern base of Heggmotinden. This summit is ascended before returning to the road. The road continues west to Vatnet where a path is taken north to the base of Steigtinden. From Steigtinden, take a broad ridge to a saddle to camp by Skauskardvatnet. The final day follows the moorland ridge southwest towards the town of Bodø.

Looking north from Kvalhornet to a myriad of summits   Anthony Dyer

Bodø is one of the larger towns in Arctic Norway. It sits right on the very tip of a mountainous and rather complex peninsula that extends out westwards from the main E6 highway. The peninsula is bounded to the south by Saltfjorden and Skjerstadfjorden, to the northwest by the Atlantic ocean and to the north by the Sørfolda fjord. The southern side of the peninsula has a relatively straightforward coastline, while the northern end is heavily indented with no fewer than seven fjords, which make some parts of the peninsula rather remote.

The mountains on this peninsula stand proud and majestic. While none of the summits exceed 1200m in height, many throw down vertical walls of rock some 600m high. What is more amazing about this mountain location is the complete absence of any marked paths despite being relatively close to two sizeable towns.

This walk describes a route that takes in numerous high tops on the southern end of this peninsula, as part of a westward journey following the highest ridgeline down to the town of Bodø. The walk starts on the northern tip of Valnesfjorden where a track, degenerating into a faint path, leads into the forest. The forest is open enough so that if you do lose the path, finding your way up out of the forest shouldn't be too arduous. The path disappears above the trees as you emerge into the valley in which the river Bothåga descends.

The river is followed up to the 600m contour where good camping opportunities exist in the corrie below Stordalsfjellet (986m). From this camping spot, the summit of Kvalhornet (962m) makes an easy three hour round trip.

The west face of Innertinden   Anthony Dyer

The vegetation on the southwestern slopes of Kvalhornet progressively thins out to boulder fields and slabs as you ascend. The route is easy but the slopes do have numerous undulations that make navigation tricky in mist.

The northern view from Kvalhornet suddenly bursts open as you reach the summit ridge. The view to behold can only be described as amazing! Serrated peaks and giant rock walls rising out of blue fjords, lakes and green forests is a sight that you rarely see in the more sterile Jotunheim mountains in Southern Norway. The route is reversed to get back to the camping spot.

On the second day of walking, four summits are climbed and this makes for a tough day. The first summit of the day is Stordalsfjellet. From the camping spot, ascend the ridge on the north side of the corrie. This ridge is broad and slabby in nature and is nowhere difficult. After reaching the first top (940m), continue west to the saddle before the main top. The saddle marks the point of descent to the next summit: Kistrandtindan (979m). However, you continue west along the ridge to the principle summit of Stordalsfjellet. Here the ridge begins to taper and narrow. At one point a rock step provides an interesting obstacle barring progress. The south side of the step provides an a short easy traverse with some exposure while the north side provides a weakness up slabs with less exposure but requiring some faith that your boots don't slip! Beyond the rockstep the ridge is narrow but continues more easily to the summit.

Return to the saddle on the ridge and descend down to the col before Kistrandtindan. From Stordalsfjellet, the ascent of Kistrandtindan looks rather steep.

Innertinden (left) and Mjønestindan (right) seen from Kistrandtindan   Anthony Dyer

The gradient however looks stepper than it is, the ascent in mid July was an easy mix of snow slopes and slabs with some minor steps getting onto the next slab. Kistrandtinden has a broad summit ridge which you follow west to the main summit.

From the summit of Kistrandtindan, descend steeply to the col with Innertinden (982m). Innertinden also looks steep but it turns out to be another easy ascent on slabs. From Innertinden's summit, a 300m high cliff face bars further westward progress. Return to the previous saddle and descend south to the tarn at 758m. From the tarn, do not follow the stream down, instead follow the less steep slabby slopes due south, east of the stream. At the 600m contour, the slope relents a little and here you can turn west towards the tarn located southwest of Innertinden at 627m.

The final summit, Mjønestindan (1058m), demands a 450m slog up its long southeastern slopes. The ascent is quite bouldery, but the rock stays firm underfoot and a line of posts leads the way up to the east ridge where you'll find an assortment of iron posts and cables littered across the boulder fields – remains of a old installation. Upon reaching the summit, the view west towards Bodø is unhindered while the southern views across Saltfjorden towards Børvasstindan are spectacular.

The descent towards camp proceeds along Mjønestindan's west ridge, high above its 150m high vertical south face. The ridge turns north west and descends easily towards a watercourse that drains Mjønestindan. Good camping opportunities can be had at this stream before its steep descent down Heggmovatnet. The evening views across this lake towards Breidviktindan (1154m) are amazing.

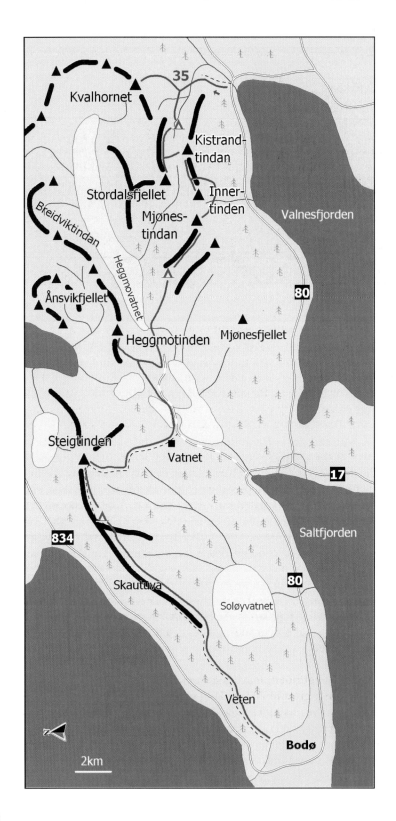

Kvalhornet

35

Kistrand-
tindan

Stordalsfjellet

Inner-
tinden

Breidviktindan

Mjønes-
tindan

Heggmovatnet

Valnesfjorden

Ånsvikfjellet

Mjønesfjellet

80

Heggmotinden

Steigtinden

Vatnet

17

Saltfjorden

834

Skautuva

80

Soløyvatnet

Veten

Bodø

2km

Looking along the basin of Heggmovatnet   Anthony Dyer

On the third day of walking, two summits are climbed. Heggmotinden (798m) and Steigtinden (793m) may be small summits, but the drop between them is nearly all the way down to sea level, and this makes for a long tough day. From the camping spot high above Heggmovatnet, make a diagonal descent west along easy slabs to the dam at the western end of Heggmovatnet. A forest track is picked up here that takes you down to the public gravel road. The road is followed southwest for 800m where the road turns northeast.

At the bend of the road, a narrow path heading northeast, pierces the forest and leads the way through thinner forest and up to long easy slabs on the western slopes of Heggmotinden. The way up is straightforward but is rather a relentless slog. With 100m of ascent left to the summit, the northerly view begins to reveal itself and on the summit itself, the view across to Storvikfjellet (814m), Ånsvikfjellet (1005m) and Småtindan (972m) is nothing short of spectacular. The way down follows the same route but splits at 260m to follow a more westerly route meeting the road further west.

A road walk continues west for three kilometres to the nunnery at the small hamlet of Vatnet. Here an old rough track heads north to the base of Steigtinden. The track degrades quickly to a path despite being marked on the map as a track.

At the base of Steigtinden, leave the track and ascend a path steeply through the woods to open ground above. This finally reaches expansive slabs leading to the base of the summit ridge. The summit ridge is steep, and isn't ascended directly as cliffs bar the way. The ridge is however ascended from its side using a well-worn earth path that zigzags easily up the very steep grassy slopes to its summit. Steigtindan is a popular mountain, probably due to it being the closest mountain to Bodø.

Ånsvikfjellet seen from Heggmotinden   Anthony Dyer

Looking east from Heggmotinden to Småtindan and Breidviktindan   Anthony Dyer

Return to the base of the ridge and continue west along broad gentle slabs to the saddle at Snokdalen. Here the lake of Skauskardvatnet provides a camping opportunity a short distance away from the saddle.

On the final day, the broad undulating ridge is followed southwest down to Bodø. From the camping spot, return up to the saddle and follow a good path up 100m to the plateau leading to Skautuva (626m). The path thins out on the plateau before the final rise to the summit. The continuing ridge rises right up from the Atlantic coast. The tarns of Sandfjordvatnan are passed on the north side and a thin path is regained that leads down to the 400m contour of the ridge.

The tree line gets ever closer and the vegetation gets ever thicker by the time you reach Omgamfjellet (421m). The path leads along the ridge and dips into a tree covered saddle before emerging back onto the open ridge. At the end of the ridge is a summit called Veten (366m). Military tracks and buildings occupy the summit area. With Bodø spread out before you, you can watch the hustle and bustle of normal life from high above. The final section continues southwest down a path reaching a forest track leading to a car park beside Svartvatnet and the road leads to the Vollen district of Bodø.

36. Stetind: Norway's National Mountain

Anthony Dyer

Stetind   *Frode Jenssen – www.stetind.nu*

Grading: Hard exposed scrambling with one short rock-climbing pitch. *Time: 10–18 hours* *Overall distance and ascent:* *9km, 1500m*	*Access to starting point: From Narvik, take highway E6 south to Efjord and turn off onto highway 827. Follow highway 827 to the carpark at the bottom of Stetind.* *Maps: Statens Kartwerk 1:50 000 sheet 1331-III*
Best enjoyed: Late June onwards, preferably when the weather is dry to have the best chance of completing the rock climb.	

Route summary:
A return walk from highway 827 to Stetind. From highway 827, follow the well worn path southeast into Storelvdalen and up to Svattvatnet. Continue east to the saddle between Stetind and Prestind. From the saddle, head northwest to Stetind's foretop and onwards on the narrow, exposed summit ridge to Stetind itself. Return by the same route.

The south pillar (right edge of shadow) of Stetind seen from Svattvatnet   Anthony Dyer

In the year 2002, Stetinden (more popularly known as Stetind) was officially designated as Norway's national mountain. Anyone who has seen the famous view of Stetind from Tysfjord will instantly understand the reasons why. The mountain rises up right from the fjord in a majestic symmetry resembling a shark's fin. Smooth walls of granite support the summit on the east and west faces and the easiest way to this peak is on a slender ridge separating these two faces.

The crux of the route: The famous "Hand Traverse"   Anthony Dyer

In the opinion of many, Stetind is by far the most beautiful mountain in Norway. My opinion is that it probably ranks as one of the world's top 100 beautiful mountains.

The first serious attempt on Stetind was made in 1870, but it wasn't conquered until 40 years later in 1910. Any climber who lays eyes on this summit will feel compelled to climb it. The summit can be climbed in a day from the road. Despite being a round trip of only nine kilometres and 1500m ascent, the final summit ridge should not be underestimated. Parties inexperienced with moving together on rope should allow 3–4 hours *each way* on the summit ridge alone. Queuing for other parties often occurs below the crux and I found myself waiting an hour for another party of six to complete the short crux.

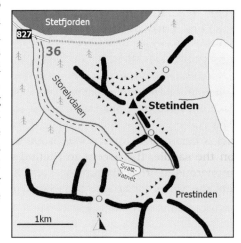

Exposed Scrambling on the south ridge
Anthony Dyer

The north face of Prestind seen from Stetind
Anthony Dyer

The route starts from the highway 827 in a carpark at the southern end of Stefjorden. The path is well worn with occasional boggy sections as it ascends southeast through the birch forest into Storelvdalen. Beyond the forest, the path continues beneath the west face of Stetind and clambers up boulders between the west face and the steep slab beneath Svattvatnet.

Upon reaching Svattvatnet you are presented with two routes: A steep climbers' path makes a diagonal ascent up to the south ridge beneath Stetind's foretop. An alternative easier-but-longer route is to continue to the saddle between Stetind and Prestinden (also popularly known as Prestind). Prestind is another magnificent mountain, harbouring a sheer 500m tall north wall. Despite appearances, it isn't wise for climbers to climb the north face of Prestind. I observed terrific rock falls crashing down this north face. The route to the saddle is quite slow and torturous crossing large boulder fields before arriving at some broad slabby ledges beneath the saddle. Once on the saddle, the ascent to Stetind's foretop is easy for the main part but numerous short walls provide some short scrambling opportunities. Higher up, the ascent to the foretop is non-eventful.

The south ridge of Stetind: exposed and nauseating   Anthony Dyer

Once on Stetind's foretop, the full scale of what you are about to face becomes all too apparent. Two friends accompanying me to the summit described themselves as "feeling nauseous" when confronted with the view of the south ridge immediately in front of them. We had our doubts, but we continued with caution and safety in mind.

The journey from the cairn on the foretop begins easily enough by traversing below the ridge to the left (west) on a broad ledge. Continue on this ledge as it gradually narrows. If you continue on the ledge back to where it meets the ridge, you are confronted with a tricky 2m downclimb. Instead, 15m before this point, make a diagonal descent down exposed-but-easy ledges, round a shoulder and then scramble 3m up to the relatively broad ridge beneath the previously described down climb.

The ridge is easy for another 50m before dramatically narrowing to a sensational but short knife edge on top of two 50° granite slabs. This ridge offers some gear protection just off the main crest, but is otherwise seamless.

Beyond, a small scramble gets you down to a broader part of the ridge which continues for another 150m to a point where a deep slanting gash halts further progress on foot. Here a bolt provides protection for a slightly awkward 5m downclimb. Beyond, broad ledges on the left (west) side of the ridge gradually narrow as they ascend beneath the Mysosten block towards a

Walking along towards the Mysosten Block   *Nicola Barnfather*

very steep 80° slab. A belay ledge is found underneath an overhang at the start of the crux pitch above this slab. Rucksacks are frequently left here by parties who can't do the climb with them on.

The pitch is about 20m and makes a rising traverse. It starts on a ledge that soon narrows to a crack used as a handrail. An overhang above prevents you walking along here. Bury your fingers into the crack and smear your feet on the featureless slab below (rock boots advised). You then hand traverse for about 3m before you can get a foot back onto the ledge. The move requires finger and arm strength and a good dollop of determination. You definitely need a head for heights above the 700m drop below you. If you let go here, you pendulum onto the 80° slab that is quite sheer without any foot or handholds. The overall grade is about Severe / Hard Severe on the UK scale.

Beyond the climb, the ridge continues initially as an exposed scramble with one 4m climb, but gradually widens to become a steep walk with some easy scrambling. You suddenly arrive on the summit plateau and it's quite a contrast (and a relief) to the ridge that has just been done. The summit log can be found in the direction of the northwest ridge. It's located in a metal box bolted to a boulder. However, the logbook is full. Make a point of bringing a new logbook up with you!

Stetind and Prestind seen on approach into Harstad-Narvik airport   *Anthony Dyer*

The relief of reaching the summit is soon replaced by the excitement of facing the whole summit ridge all over again! The return journey is by the same route. However, at the top of the crux, walk out along the summit crest for 20m to an abseil point on the Mysosten Block. Abseil 20m back down to the belay ledge at the start of the crux. Once you get to the bottom of the mountain, give yourself a big pat on the back. I didn't return to my tent until 1 a.m.!

37. From Swedish Border to Norwegian Coast: the Mountains of Ofotsfjorden

Anthony Dyer

Leigastinden seen from the east near Kubergvatnet   Anthony Dyer

Grading: Valley & moorland walking requiring good route finding skills. One steeper section on steep grass. Time: 4 days Daily distance, ascent and time: Day 1: 18km, 600m, 8 hours Day 2: 16km, 650m, 10 hours Day 3: 15km, 500m, 6 hours Day 4: 21km, 900m, 11 hours	Access to starting point: At the station and ski resort of Riksgränsen on the E10 east of the Swedish border. Maps: Statens Kartwerk 1:50 000 sheets 1432-II, 1432-III, 1332-II. (Swedish Map) Lantmäteriets Fjällkarta 1:100 000 "BD6 Abisko-Kebnekaise Narvik"
Best enjoyed: Mid July – Autumn to avoid the worst of the snow	

Route summary:
A linear walk from Riksgränsen to Bogen, on the Norwegian coast. On the first day, head north from Riksgränsen to a path junction 10km north. Follow the path west to a confluence at the 600m contour. On the second day head west on the path to Bukkedalen and then continue west to camp west of Læigasvatnet. On the third day heat west down to the E6 at the hamlet of Øse. Continue west into Labergsdalen and then south into Beadvalahku and camp at lake Beadvajávri. On the final day walk southwest to road 829 at Skoddeberghytta, continue west over Tverrfjellet and then down into Bogen.

Beassetčohkka seen in June from the south.   *Anthony Dyer*

The journey described here takes the backpacker right from the Swedish border, across empty moorland and neglected paths, underneath magnificent mountains, camping at delightful wild spots and finishes at the small village of Bogen located on the coast of Ofotsfjorden. The mountains here are on the other side of Ofotsfjorden to Narvik and whilst being lower (1100–1400m), they are just as spectacular as the higher mountains just south of Narvik. The walk, whilst only climbing one small summit, provides far more extensive views than the Narvik chapter (see chapter 38).

I did this journey in late June. Snow cover was extensive down to an altitude of 600m. My original plan was to walk a mountain route all the way to Harstad–Narvik airport, but I found that one section of the route was too dangerous to traverse due to a high risk of avalanches. The journey to Bogen is along the same route as that to the airport, but is one day shorter.

Officially, a marked route exists all the way to Bogen from Riksgränsen, as described in DNT literature, but the route is only illustrated for part of the way on Statens Kartwerk 1:50 000 M711 series maps. The paths frequently only exist by the presence of few cairns here and there as well as red paint on trees that is often peeling off. Despite this, the route for the main part covers easy terrain, and forests are thin enough to walk through if you do find yourself off route.

Midnight sun shining on Bukkefjellet and Beassetčohkka   Anthony Dyer

*Exhausting walking south
of Bukkedalen*   *Anthony Dyer*

At the ski resort of Riksgränsen, a small convenience store will provide basic food as well as small essentials that you may want. A path starts next to some modern apartments heading north on the west side of Lake Vássejávri. The path is well worn here with board-walks across boggy ground. After a bridge, don't miss the path junction: continue north where the path goes through a pass west of Rohččevárri (726m). The path is now much fainter as it winds its way north through undulating terrain and birch forest. Sometimes the path is a struggle with tree roots, branches and moss-covered boulders doing their best to slow you down. The path skirts the western edge of Lake Bajip Njuorajávri and finally ascends above the tree line to make easier progress across heather.

At lake "447m", depart from the path and take a short cut to meet the other path at lake "479m". The paths only exists here by the presence of a few cairns every now and again, there was no erosion pointing the way. Keeping a good eye on your map is essential.

Looking northwest towards Labergsdalen   *Anthony Dyer*

Soon after lake "479m", the Norwegian border is met and you are greeted with a yellow metal sign saying "Riksgränsen mot Norge". Beyond the sign, the path makes a slow rising traverse up to the 600m contour. It's easy to drift off course here, as the path only exists on the map with few cairns present.

The 600m contour is easy to find, it's located on a saddle separating a small knoll from the bigger mountain of Beassetčohkka (1420m). Beyond, a stream can be followed to where it reaches a confluence with another stream, which then flows south to form the river Karenejva Gádjajohka. At this confluence, idyllic camping can be found on cropped heather.

On the second day, continue west following the path. The path initially ascends the slopes above the gorge in which the stream flows. The path then levels off and branches south of the stream and lake "775m" to reach a saddle at 820m (highest point). During my walk in June, this part of the route was completely snow covered above 650m, however there were numerous cairns poking through the snow to point the way. The path beyond the saddle continues over more open ground with grand southern and western vistas while the mountain of Beassetčohkka dominates the northern view.

The path drops to Kubergvatnet and beyond, the path follows the north side of the stream down to a confluence with the stream draining Næverfjellvatnet. Here, the map shows the path as crossing the stream and continuing down the west side of the stream. However, frequent cairns show that there is

186

Idyllic camping beneath Dudalstinden (1260m) and Nonstinden (1238m)   Anthony Dyer

a path on the east side of the stream, contrary to what is shown on the map. I stuck with the latter and ended up in Bukkedalen at a major river without a bridge. This was obviously of some concern, however the river at this point was wide and shallow enough to cross (depth to the top of my shins), with wet feet being the only penalty.

On the north side of the major river a faint path can be picked up in the forest. The path leads to a bridge crossing the river draining Grasvatnet. Throughout most of this day's walk, the westward view has been dominated by Leigastinden (1332m). Now you stand at the foot of the mountain ready to walk round the southern base of it. The path initially heads north along the west side of the river draining Grasvatnet, but a path junction is reached where you turn west to follow a path up the slope to the large lake of Læigasvatnet.

This lake is big and is completely dominated by Leigastinden. At an altitude of 576m, the lake was completely frozen over in late June. The path follows the north side of Læigasvatnet and remains easy to follow until near the end, where a short steep section provides access to easier slopes beyond. Numerous streams here provide good camping opportunities.

The third day returns to civilisation very briefly before continuing into the wilderness beyond. The path descends towards the small hamlet of Øse on the E6. The path is well cairned, but it deviates from the direction shown on the map. Nevertheless, the forest which the path descends into is quite thin,

Revtind (1219m) seem from lake Beadvajávri   Anthony Dyer

so it doesn't matter whether the path is followed or not. The ground east of Storvatnet is quite wet underfoot. A small dam on the northern side of Storvatnet is reached which you cross. Beyond, some small paths serving numerous cabins are followed out onto the road.

On the other side of the E6, a dirt road is followed past a small ski centre to its end where a neglected track continues. At times this track is faint, and not marked on the map, but red paint on the trees assure you that this is the correct route. Ahead, the spectacular summit of Nonstinden (1238m) dominates the view. The track frequently disappears into open boggy ground, but reappears the other side as it descends into Labergsdalen.

Note the river falling down the deep gorge on the left side of the valley. The path goes just to the left of this river above its gorge. Follow the paint marks to the bottom of the slope but note that two marked routes go up this slope, one is some distance away from the stream, while the proper route is just above the gorge. Look out for a big T painted on a boulder to assure you of the correct way.

The ascent up these slopes is easy enough to begin with, but the menacing sight of cliffs ahead causes doubt in some minds. Ascend more steeply up slippery grass and roots to the base of these cliffs, without much in the way of red paint to show the way. Then traverse right, where a cairn shows the way into the river gorge. Once past the river gorge, the valley of Beadvalahku opens out into a more pleasant walk. Lake Beadvajávri at the south end of

Trangdalsfjellet (1065m) and Novatind (1211m) in winter time   *Anthony Dyer*

this valley provides idyllic camping with spectacular views out across Ofotsfjorden.

The final day takes you through extensive birch forest and the third group of mountains before descending into Bogen. Head south down into Maridalen following a path and paint marks on the eastern side of the stream. At a confluence, cross the stream and follow paint marks as best as you can. If you lose the path as I did, you'll need to aim for the 460m high treeless hill just east of Hornet (471m). Progress through the forest is quite easy with frequent open boggy ground and local paths. When you reach the 460m high summit, the path again becomes obvious with frequent cairns showing the way down the saddle and up again to the summit of Hornet. Despite the height of the summit, the views from here are uninterrupted. Here you can clearly see Narvik as well as the previous and next group of mountains that you'll traverse. From Hornet, descend west following the marked route down towards road 829 at Skoddeberghytta.

On the other side of the road, a paved track can be followed to the entrance of a military installation. At the entrance, a path skirts left around the perimeter fence. Rather than follow the path up to Runddalen (path unmarked on map), I decided to ascend the summit of Tverrfjellet (782m). The ascent up the head of Runddalen is quite steep, but Tverrfjellet is easier and offers better views. Despite being off track, the ascent through the forest is easy and quickly gets up to the moorland above. A trig point at 710m hosts a summit log. Continue up the ridge to the true summit before

Camping at the eastern end of Blåvatnet, Litletinden in the background   Anthony Dyer

descending to the saddle with Butinden (714m) and then head north down to Buvatnet.

At Buvatnet, you are reunited with the main path. At the southern end of Buvatnet, a path junction exists where a path descends down towards Strandvatnet to a track which is followed round the north side of Strandvatnet towards Bogen.

If time and conditions allow, it is well worth continuing this route west from Buvatnet. Cross the dam on the south side of Niingsvatnet and follow a well cairned route up the slopes of Niingen (1073m). Cross a shoulder below Niingen and descend north down to Blåvatnet. Following the shores of Niingsvantet is not possible since cliffs bar the way. The views around here are simply stunning. The whole mountain range held its snow long into June 2004. Despite being at an altitude of 564m at Blåvatnet, there was only one exposed patch of grass to camp on at its eastern end.

The continuation path follows the south shore of Blåvatnet but this was dangerous to follow because of avalanche risk. It would be well worth your time to explore this mountain range further, taking in the summits of Litletinden (1134m) and Rismålstinden (1012m) before continuing west or south to get down to a suitable road.

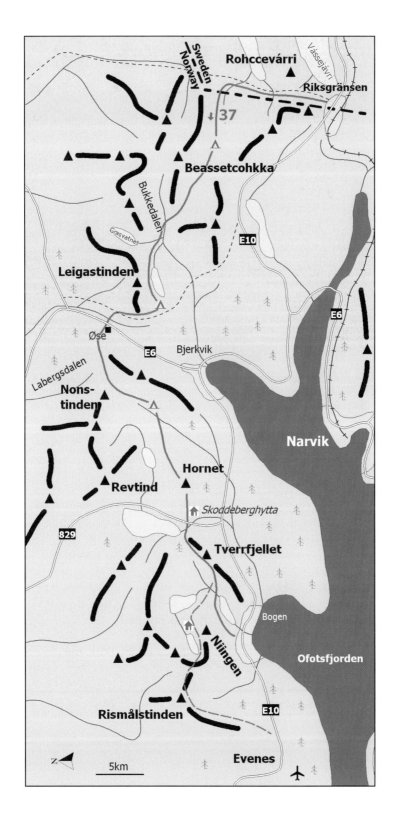

Rohccevárri

Riksgränsen

Sweden
Norway

Väsejávri

↓37

Beassetcohkka

E10

Bukkedalen

Grasvatnet

Leigastinden

Øse

E6

Bjerkvik

E6

Narvik

Labergsdalen

Nons-
tinden

Hornet

Revtind

Skoddeberghytta

829

Tverrfjellet

Bogen

Ofotsfjorden

Niingen

Rismålstinden

E10

z

5km

Evenes

38. Exploring the Valleys of Narvik

Anthony Dyer

Nihkevárri seen from the southeast   Anthony Dyer

Grading: Valley walking along faint paths which frequently disappear and some gravel tracks. Time: 3 days Daily distance, ascent and time: Day 1: 26.5km, 900m, 12 hours Day 2: 20km, 400m, 7 hours Day 3: 20km, 200m, 6 hours	Access to starting point: From Narvik, take highway E6 south to Fagernes where a minor road is followed southeast to Beisfjord. Maps: (Swedish Map) Lantmäteriets Fjällkarta 1:100 000 "BD6 Abisko-Kebnekaise Narvik"
Best enjoyed: Late June – Autumn to avoid the worst of the snow.	

Route summary:
A linear walk from Beisfjord to Katterat. From Beisfjord, follow a gravel track south into Skamdalen. Cross a bridge north of lake "180m". Continue on a thin path south into Skandalsbakken then east along Nihkevággi then south to camp in Skearrogieddi. On the second day continue east on a gravel track to reservoir "639m" and continue on a path east to Cunojavrrehytta and then continue north to camp on the slopes above lake Sealggajávri. On the final day, continue on a thin path north through Oallavággi down to a river ford in Hunddalen. Continue north on a gravel track down to Katterat.

The view from Skamdalen towards Rienatčohkka   *Anthony Dyer*

Narvik is one of the major towns in the north of Norway. The town sits north of the 68° line of latitude and despite receiving a warm current from the North Atlantic Drift, snow lingers long into June high in the mountains.

The mountains around Narvik typically rise 1400m – 1900m above sea level. At 1892m, Storsteinsfjellet is the highest summit in the Narvik area. Being so close to the coast, the scale of these mountains is significantly bigger than the mountains in Scotland. These mountains are more alpine in character, with many glaciers and large crags falling 600–700m from the summit crests. Further inland, there is a lot more open moorland rising up between 700–900m. The inland mountains are more rounded, similar to the Cairngorms in appearance with many corries and broad plateaux.

The proximity to Sweden is of note, across the border a world famous walking route known as "Kungsleden" stretches for 400km from nearby Abisko to Hemavan in the south. Just across the border is Sweden's highest mountain, Kebnekaise (2111m). Arctic Norway by contrast has mountains of equal stature in terms of beauty, but walking on the marked routes is much quieter here. Paths frequently only exist by the presence of a splash of red paint every hundred meters or so. Huts in Arctic Norway tend to be unstaffed and locked, so DNT membership is essential to guarantee access if there's no-one else around.

Looking down Skamdalsbakkan   Anthony Dyer

I came up to Narvik in mid June 2004 to attempt a walk deep into the wilderness and then into Sweden. That walk, as I found out, couldn't be done as it mandated the use of skis or snowshoes for over 90% of the journey. Snow was lingering in the valleys and sheltered slopes above 800m. One year on, in June 2005, the snow cover in the Narvik mountains was significantly more extensive.

The walk described skirts around the base of Storsteinsfjellet (1893m) and its satellite peaks. Over three days the walk sticks to the valleys surrounding this mountain group. The walk starts in the village of Beisfjord and starts by heading south into the spectacular valley of Skamdalen. A gravel track is followed on the east side of the river where a bridge is crossed, the river drains Stubblidalen. The track then enters Skamdalen as it gently ascends to the lake at the end of this valley.

Before lake "180m", a bridge is found crossing the river. A thin sketchy path is picked up and this goes along the western shore of the lake before ascending the slopes into Skamdalsbakken. Below these slopes, a bridge is seen crossing the river, though I didn't use it and followed a path on the river's west side. I then crossed the river without difficulty further south at the 600m contour.

Despite the presence of high voltage power lines in this valley, Skamdalsbakken is wild and remote. Avalanches could be heard high on the slopes of Mattačorru (1457m) but I was confident they wouldn't reach the bottom of this wide U shaped valley. The path then turns east into the valley of Nihkevággi with the slopes of Nihkevárri (about 1740m) rising above.

Looking southwest to the mountains across the Čunovuopmi mountains.   Anthony Dyer

The path turns south around the shores of Lossivatnet and the DNT hut of Lossistua is available for those with a key. The massive bulk of Nuorjjovárri (1727m) comes into view here. Camping around Lossivatnet in high summer is recommended to avoid the mosquitoes that will plague the valley down in Skearrogieddi. However this valley, with its trees, provides warm sheltered comfort when Lossivatnet is snow bound in June.

The second day of walking follows a broad valley east to Cunojavrrehyttta, just three kilometres west of the Swedish border. A bridge is crossed in the valley of Skearrogieddi and a gravel track is picked up on the southern slopes of the valley. This track is followed to the reservoir at lake "639m". Here a small hydroelectric installation is present and is part of a much larger reservoir system which includes Lossivatnet.

The summit of Storsteinsfjellet is hidden behind its lower convex flanks. Glimpses of its glacier (Sealggajiekna) add to Storsteinfjellet's elusiveness. Beyond the gravel tracks, an unbridged glacial river is crossed. In June, crossing this river involved getting no more than wet feet. Beyond the river, a good path is followed over old glacial moraines now covered in vegetation. As such, the path undulates a fair bit over each ridge and hollow.

Cunajavrrehytta is a remote hut, 21km from Katterat in the north and 22km from Bogholmen in the west. Despite this, 80km separate you from the next road further south and 60km from the next road to the east in Sweden. In the grand scheme of things, 21km from the nearest settlement isn't all that remote!

195

Ristačohkka seen from Cunojavrrehytta   Anthony Dyer

The path now turns north towards Katterat. Soon the path crosses a deep river using a bridge. The view north gradually opens out to reveal the shapely summit of Ristačohkka (1688m) and later the lake of Sealggajávri. Comfortable camping can be found by the path next to a stream 30m above this lake.

On the final day, the path continues north into a valley called Oallavággi. In mid June, this valley was covered in deep snow and progress was very slow. The path has a few cairns to show the way and it stays on the east side of the lakes that sit in this valley. Further along, a tiny DNT bivouac hut, called Oallavagge, is found. Bed spaces are not listed in DNT literature but it probably provides bunk space for 4 people.

The path gradually descends into Hunddalen and is initially quite distant from the river and its gorge. As you get closer to the river, you come across a small dam which channels the river away from its natural course into pipes. The river down at Hunddalen is therefore easy to cross being no deeper than the top of your ankle.

Once on the other side of the river, a gravel track can be picked up and this is followed easily down Sørdalen to Katterat, where there is a railway station. For those wanting to kill time while waiting for the train, a path can be followed close to the track in the direction of Sweden. This path is well maintained with lots of information posts about the history of the Kiruna – Narvik railway line.

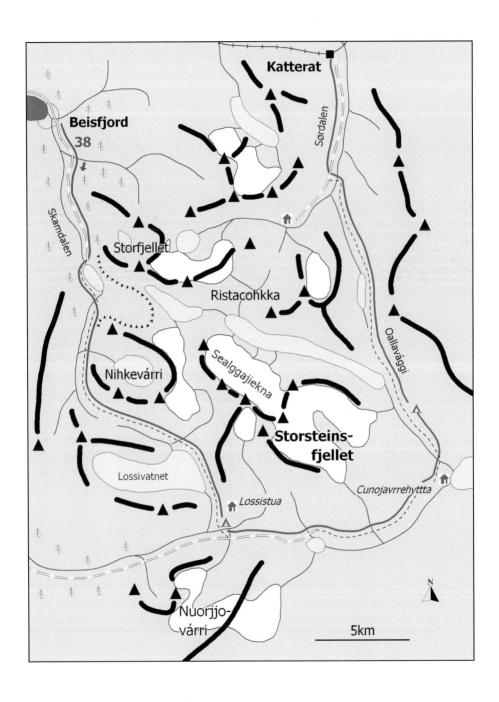

39. Introduction to the Lofoten Islands

Ian H. Robertson

The classic view from Reine, Moskenesøya   Denis Wilson

In Europe, there is nowhere else like Lofoten. Whether you arrive by air, by sea or by road the experience is the same, a complete assault on the senses. Jagged mountain after mountain rises straight from the sea, with seemingly impenetrable rock faces and knife-edge ridges. All of this is next to fantastic fjord and sea landscapes, with white sandy beaches and a turquoise sea. And of course the summer midnight sun. The reality of Lofoten will surpass all the photographs you might have seen, it is no wonder that this archipelago has been called "The Magic Islands".

If you only visit Norway once, you should come here – mountain lovers of all kinds will not be disappointed. Therefore it is only fitting that *Walks and Scrambles in Norway* features eight outings in Lofoten, four of them in the most magnificent island of them all, Moskenesøya.

Up until now, Lofoten has been considered the preserve of rock climbers. There are many quality climbs, especially on Austvågøya, but there is also much to excite the hillwalker, scrambler and mountaineer.

The island of Litlmolla seen from Rundfjellet   Krystina Lotoczko

The island chain lies north of the Arctic Circle, so the best time to visit is July to August. Whilst it protrudes into the Atlantic, and can be subject to the same maritime weather that plagues Skye and the Scottish Hebrides, it can also have long periods of settled "Scandinavian High" weather.

It is a long drive from the ferry terminal at Bergen to Lofoten, but you travel through some magnificent mountain scenery en route. A more practical alternative for a shorter (i.e. normal length) holiday would be to either fly or take the train to Bodø and then catch the ferry to Moskenes. For Austvågøya, take the coastal fast-boat, ferry or plane to Svolvær. If you want more mobility, you can fly to Harstad–Narvik airport (Evenes) and hire a car. This will give you a stunning day's drive down the island chain to Å but will seriously damage your wallet!

Whichever means you use to get there, (assuming the weather plays its part of the bargain) you will have one of the best mountaineering or walking holidays of your life.

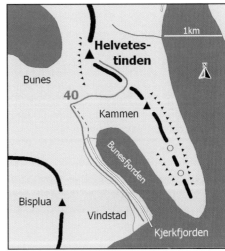

40. Helvetestinden

Ian H. Robertson

Helvetestinden's summit ridge with Moltbærtinden in the distance   Krystina Lotoczko

Grading: A straightforward walk with an airy ridge at the end. *Time: 4 hours* *Overall distance and ascent:* *11 km, 600m*	*Access to starting point: From ferry pier at the harbour in Reine.* *Maps: Lofoten Garn & Gaver Turistkart 1:50 000 "Vest-Lofoten" or Statens Kartverk 1:50 000 sheet 1830-I.*
Best enjoyed: The route is practicable under any weather, but is best left for a day of clear visibility when the stunning views will be best enjoyed.	
Ferry note: Best done on a Monday or Friday when more time is available between ferries! Alternatively, go in with a tent.	

Route summary:
Take the foot passenger ferry from Reine to Vindstad. Walk from the pier at Vindstad along the track to the col at the head of the fjord. Go up the easy slopes to the col south of Helvetestinden. Turn left and follow the ridge to the summit. Return by the route of ascent.

The view from the ferry up Kjerkfjorden   Denis Wilson

This is one of the shortest walks in this book. It is also one of the best, offering airy ridge walking amidst fantastic Lofoten rock peaks.

The start of this walk is at the ferry pier in the village of Reine. At the time of writing, ferries leave Reine at 10:00 and the return from Vindstad is at 15:15, so you have a limited time for this walk. Alternatives are to do the walk on a Monday or Friday (when there is an earlier ferry at 7:30) or to take a tent. It should go without saying that you must find out the return ferry time as there are no facilities at Vindstad.

The ferry journey up Kjerkfjorden is magical. All too soon, the ferry arrives at Vindstad and it is time to disembark and start walking.

Go along the track from Vindstad that follows the shore of Bunesfjorden. Avoid a false trail towards the cemetery, but continue to the houses at the head of the fjord. Follow the marked path as it winds its way up to a low col. It is worth the short detour to the far side of the col for a look at the beautiful sandy beach of Bunes, flanked on two sides by steep rocky mountains. The rock slabs that plunge down from the summit of Helvetestinden are particularly impressive, but are totally out-of-bounds for non rock-climbers – you will need to take a more circuitous route.

Helvetestinden's airy summit ridge, looking towards Kammen.   *Denis Wilson*

From the col, take a traversing line to the right and aim for the right of a large boulder field. A faint path will eventually be picked up that will take you to the col between Helvetestinden and its neighbour, Kammen. If you miss the path, don't worry – it is easy to pick a line out that ascends between the slabs and the boulder field.

After a stiff ascent, you will at last reach the summit ridge. This offers glorious views towards Moltbærtinden and is a good photo-opportunity. Don't wait too long, as the best bit is yet to come. Follow the path towards Helvetestinden's summit along the narrow airy ridge and one of the best mountain views anywhere will be yours. The summit is small and airy, perched precipitously overlooking the sea: its views of the sweeping granite ridges of the Lofoten Wall are unsurpassed.

The return is by the route of ascent. Those who have camped or have plenty of time before the ferry may wish to explore the other end of the ridge out towards Kammen. Alternatively, a detour to the beach at Bunes is a very worthwhile diversion.

The map for route 40 is on page 199.

41. Munkan

Ian H. Robertson

Munkan from Djupfjorden   Ian H. Robertson

Grading: A straightforward walk with an optional easy scramble at the end. Time: 7 hours Overall distance and ascent: 11 km, 900m	Access to starting point: From highway E10 in Sørvågen. Maps: Lofoten Garn & Gaver Turistkart 1:50 000 "Vest-Lofoten" or Statens Kartverk 1:50 000 sheet 1830-I.
Best enjoyed: The route is practicable under any weather, but is best left for a day of clear visibility when the stunning views will be best enjoyed.	

Route summary:
From the E10 at Sørvågen, follow a side road at GR166319 until a path is reached signposted "Munkebu". Follow this to the top of Djupfjordheia (GR166355). Follow a developing path to the col between Djupfjordheia and Munkan. Now follow a path until the cairn of Munkan is reached. A higher top can be reached by a short easy scramble. The return is along the same path, but branch off and descend to the hut at Munkebu. Return over Djupfjordheia. An alternative descent is from the col between Djupfjordheia and Munkebu along the path beside Djupfjorden.

Seiltind and the Kjerkfjord from near Munkebu hut   *Ian. H. Robertson*

It is difficult to believe that an island so rugged and mountainous as Moskenesøya has some easy ascents, but it is true. Those with an eye for a route, the ability to map-read and a bit of knowledge can experience mountain settings normally reserved for extreme Alpinists or rock climbers.

One of the best ascents is Munkan. Its main summit is only for rock climbers, but there is a walking top and a scrambling top that are within the capabilities of most hillwalkers.

Start at the village of Sørvågen on the E10. There is a small crossroads near the crest of a hill, and a side road leading north offers limited parking. From the end of this side road follow the path signposted "Munkebu". This is a well-marked path which leads into the interior of the island, and gives access to several hills as well as the DNT hut.

After passing the enchanted lochan of Stuvdalsnet, the fun starts with a wire rope assisted ascent of some easy angled slabs. The wire rope is a luxury in dry conditions, but is useful when the slabs are wet, especially on the descent. At the top of the slabs, it is time to get the camera out, as now the first mountaintops come into view.

From here, there is a steady uphill pull to the minor summit of Djupfjordheia. You will now get your first view of the spectacular triple summits of Munkan. The main summit and the two northern tops look spectacular from here.

204

The path to Munkebu hut   *Krystina Lotoczko*

Carry on towards Munkebu on the main path, but as the path begins to descend left towards the hut, stay high and aim for the col between Djupfjordheia and Munkan. There is a vague path which becomes more distinct as you near Munkan. Eventually this develops into a well defined path which winds its way up the mountainside to a small corrie. Carry on across the base of the corrie and pick up a better path which climbs steeply to the top. If you are lucky enough to have good weather, you will have breathtaking views over the rest of Moskenesøya.

The main summit to your right is for rock climbers only, but there is an middle top which is recommended. The approach is by an airy ridge and very easy scramble. This ends abruptly overlooking Munkan's jagged summit peak, with a dramatic drop below. After you have drunk your fill of the view, return by the route of ascent.

Three alternative routes of descent are possible from Munkan. Instead of returning the same way, at the edge of the corrie, carry on downhill on a well defined path which takes you to Munkebu hut. This offers slightly different views from the ascent and is worth the extra climb back up to Djupfjordheia.

An alternative, which can be included to make a good circular walk, is to descend from near the Djupfjordheia col (the path is signposted) to the head of the Djupfjord. From here, a very rough path traverses the south side of the fjord to the E10 at the fjord mouth.

A final alternative on the way back to Sørvagen, is to include the summit of Merraflestinden. This is easily ascended from the col between it and Djupfjordheia. It is probably best to return to this col and pick up the main Munkebu path, rather than try and descend direct to Sørvagen – the slopes off Kjølen are steep and vegetated.

Munkebu   *Denis Wilson*

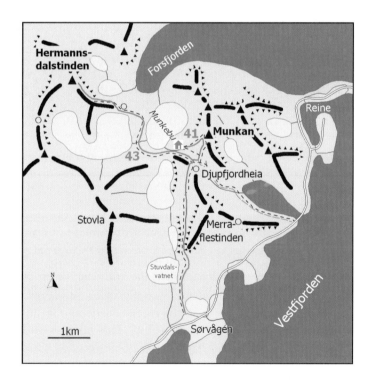

42. Markan and Brandtuva

Ian H. Robertson

Markan's north ridge   *Krystina Lotoczko*

Grading: A walk over rough terrain into magnificent country. Any scrambling can be avoided. *Time: 9 hours.* *Overall distance and ascent:* *12 km, 800m*	*Access to starting point: Leave highway E10 at Finnbyen (on Flakstadøy) and take the side road to Fredvang. Across the bridge, take the rough side road to Selfjord (partly unmetalled).* *Maps: Lofoten Garn & Gaver Turistkart 1:50 000 "Vest-Lofoten" or Statens Kartverk 1:50 000 sheet 1830-III.*
Best enjoyed: The route as far as Markan is practicable in any weather, but is best left for a day of clear visibility when the stunning views will be best enjoyed. Navigation to and from Brandtuva would be very difficult under misty conditions.	

Route summary:
At the parking space at the end of the Selfjord road, follow a Landrover track which then becomes a (rough) DNT path. Follow the cairned path to the col at the head of Fageradalen. Turn right (west) and follow the ridge to Markan. Follow the ridge north to Brandtuva, avoiding the bad steps on the ridge. Descend to the col south of Brandtuva and follow a rising traverse to the DNT path at the col at the head of Fagerådalen. Return to Selfjord on this path.

Krokhammertindan from Markan's east ridge   Krystina Lotoczko

The northern part of Moskenesøya contains rock scenery which would not look out of place in the high Alps or Patagonia. A walk into the rough interior is a test of stamina, but will give views and memories that will last a lifetime.

The roads on this part of Moskenesøya are not connected directly to the rest of the island, so access is from the neighbouring island of Flakstadøya via a bridge. As you drive down the unmetalled road to Selfjord, the mountains come into view and whet your appetite for the day ahead. There is an obvious car park at the end of the road – cars should not be taken past this point (the Landrover track is private).

The next three kilometres take a surprisingly long time – the going underfoot is rough (and boggy) and is a test of resolve. Eventually the lochan of Fageråvatnet comes into view and is a good spot for a break. Continue through the rough ground over boulders beside the lochan and then up to the col at the head of Fagerådalen. When at last you reach the col, the view makes all the effort worthwhile. Seiltind is magnificent, but it is the rock towers of Krokhammartindan that catch the eye.

You will not find it difficult to motivate yourself to climb the next 200m to the summit of Markan, which is a superb viewpoint. An easy-to-follow path marks the way.

The going so far has been easy, but that soon changes. On Markan's north ridge, the way is barred by a slab of rock, lying perpendicular to the ridge. Rock climbers and competent scramblers can move across this easily (grade II), but a slip would almost certainly be fatal – the end of the slab projects

208

Brandtuva's summit   Ian H. Robertson

over thin air and would result in a huge fall. This "bad step" can easily be bypassed for those who wish – this is certainly advisable if the lichen covered rock is at all wet. Go back down Markan's east ridge, keeping to the crest. About 20m below the height of the summit, there is a break in the summit rocks, and an easy bypass path can be found that leads back onto the north ridge.

The going now is easy and gives a delightful ridge walk with expansive views on either side. Before too long you come to another rocky hiatus in the ridge. It may be possible to down-climb this directly, but the author has not done this. Again a bypass route can be found – on the right (east) side. Once the crest is regained, more ridge walking followed by a final easy scramble leads to the col below Brandtuva.

From here, it is a straightforward walk to the summit over moss and boulders. The views are magnificent. Competent scramblers may be tempted to try for the next peak along, however this involves a down-climb over a narrow ridge that seems to be composed more of moss than rock, so this guidebook cannot recommend more than going to the end of Brandtuva's summit to have a look.

Reluctantly you must leave Brandtuva's magnificent views and set off back down the mountain. Return to the col between Brandtuva and Markan, then follow a rising traverse to the col at the head of Fagerådalen. Your way back to Selfjord is the DNT path.

Navigational note: do not try and descend direct to Fageråvatnet without using the DNT path – the slopes below Markan and Brandtuva are lined with crags that are unseen from above.

The sea is a magnificent backdrop to many Lofoten walks   Denis Wilson

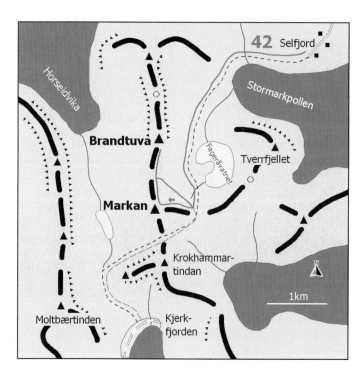

Note: for those without a car, the foot passenger ferry (see route 40) can also used to access Markan and Brandtuva. Disembark at Kjerkfjorden and walk to Horseid. This is another fantastic sandy Lofoten beach.

Just north of Brandtwa is as far as walkers can go...   Ian H. Robertson

43. Hermannsdalstinden

Ian H. Robertson & Krystina Lotoczko

Looking from Hermannsdalstinden towards Reine and Munkan   Krystina Lotoczko

Grading: A long and tiring walk with intermediate exposed scrambling. A half-length rope should be carried in case the fixed ropes are not usable. Time: 10–11 hours Overall distance and ascent: 22 km, 1700m	Access to starting point: From highway E10 in Sørvågen. Maps: Lofoten Garn & Gaver Turistkart 1:50 000 "Vest-Lofoten" or Statens Kartverk 1:50 000 sheet 1830-I.
Best enjoyed: Route finding both on the summit and on the long approach would be very difficult and serious in mist. Recommended only on a clear day.	

Route summary:
From the E10 at Sørvågen, follow a side road at GR166319 until a path is reached signposted "Munkebu". Follow this to the top of Djupfjordheia (GR166355). At the sign marked "Djupfjorden" follow a faint cairned path left to the col at GR159360. Follow the cairned DNT path to point 448m. Look for a faint path leading west (difficult to find) and follow this round point 536m to below the southeast ridge of Hermanndalstinden. Follow this ridge (fixed ropes at difficulties) to the summit. Return by the route of ascent.

Hermannsdalstinden (on right) from the approach path   *Krystina Lotoczko*

The island of Moskenesøya is as rugged and mountainous as they come, but surprisingly its highest summit is easier than most on the island. You won't need extreme rock climbing skills to ascend it, but you will need a good head for heights and be comfortable with exposed scrambling. You will also need good route-finding skills, both on the approach and on the summit. It is not a mountain to be attempted under conditions of low mist.

Take the Munkebu hut path (as described in route 41, Munkan) until the top of Djupfjordheia. When you get to the sign that indicates the Djupforden path to your right, this is your cue to look for another path to the LEFT (heading northwest). This skirts the crags below Munkebu hut and takes you safely to the col at GR159360. If (like this author) you mistakenly head for Munkebu hut and then try to descend to the col from there, you will end up down-climbing near-vertical rotten rock. This is not recommended!

The correct path is the one to the passenger ferry at the head of Forsfjorden and is marked with frequent cairns. This passenger ferry or a stay at Munkebu hut are ways to make Hermannsdalstinden a more manageable day, but the ferry is not scheduled and would need to be requested at Reine.

From the col at GR159360 you will have the first of several ups and downs during the course of the approach walk. This makes the total ascent 1700m, even though the summit only attains a height of 1029m. This should not be under-estimated – there is a lot of re-ascent on the return walk. The first

At the foot of the southeast ridge   Krystina Lotoczko

climb takes you over some snow below the crags flanking Moldtinden. Those with time to spare can hunt out mini-bergschrunds and snow bridges. There is then another dip past a beautiful icy lake and a climb to top 448m. This is a superb viewpoint and is a good place for a well-earned rest.

At this point you leave the main DNT ferry path, and you will need to scout around to find a safe route of descent to the col between top 448m and the next top, point 536m. From the col, the path is tricky to locate. It then takes a rather muddy and often eroded traversing line around point 536m. At last you emerge below the southeast ridge of Hermannsdalstinden. Now the "real" mountaineering starts.

The character of the route changes here too – for the first time there are the long, steep sweeps of glaciated slabs characteristic of Moskenesøya's mountains. There are two dramatically placed lochans beneath 300m sheer rock walls. One of these drops down from Hermannsdalstinden's southeast ridge.

To climb the ridge, go up some grassy slopes and look out for the correct route of ascent – it starts off following the crest of the ridge before moving round to the left. The angle increases and you have to ascend some steep grass. You will then come to a rocky groove – fortunately a fixed rope is here to aid your ascent. (See note in Appendix G on fixed gear). You then top out onto the crest of the ridge – this is in quite an exposed position with a dramatic drop below. Again, there is a fixed rope here.

On the narrow ridge between the summits   *Krystina Lotoczko*

Continue easily up the ridge which soon ends and deposits you on a grassy plateau. This eventually leads to the boulder field on the broad southeast ridge. A well cairned path carefully avoids much of the boulder slope and leads through the summit rocks. There remains some easy scrambling over huge blocks before you reach the very exposed summit ridge. The summit itself is recognised by its small cairn. It is tricky to get onto and has standing room for one only! It is not a place for those who suffer from vertigo.

West of the summit can be seen the further tops of Hermannsdalstinden. Those who have not yet had their fill of mountaineering, can scramble along to the next (subsidiary) summit. There is a narrow rocky arête that connects these tops which provides more exhilarating scrambling. The view back to Hermannsdalstinden's summit from this ridge is particularly impressive. You will need to climb back up to the summit ridge to pick up the descent route.

The descent retraces your well cairned route of ascent back to the southeast ridge and then picks up the path back to Munkebu.

The map for route 43 is on page 206.

Hermannsdalstinden's summit has standing room for one only...

Krystina Lotoczko

44. Past Austvågøya's Hidden Lakes

Ian H. Robertson

The icy waters of Botnvatnet with Botntinden beyond   *Ian H. Robertson*

Grading: A hike over terrain which is frequently rough. There is some optional easy scrambling. *Time: 6–7 hours* *Overall distance and ascent:* *Circular walk: 15km, 800m* *Through trip: 13km, 600m*	*Access to starting point: Leave the E10 in Svolvær at the Shell garage (signposted Knutsmarka). Go along Caroline Harveys vei, then Meyerbakken, then Strømbrubakken. Over the bridge, follow the signs for Knutmarka Feriesenter. Park at the Hjelpekorps.* *Maps: Statens Kartverk 1:100 000 Turkart "Lofoten". Cappelens Kart 52 "Lofoten med Vesterålen" for street map of Svolvær.*

Best enjoyed: The route is practicable in any weather, but navigation around Botnvatnet in mist is only for the experienced.

Route summary:
From the Hjelpekorps hut, follow Vannsverkbakken to a ski trail. Follow the ski trail over a wooden footbridge. Turn north and follow the path alongside Øvre Svolværvatnet to Sæetra. 200m past Sæetra, follow a path over the shoulder of Botntinden. Continue on the path past Botnvatnet and descend to the north

end of Isvatnet. For a through trip, follow the path north over Damheia to Haugen and Sandsletta. For a circular walk, ascend from Isvatnet to the low col north of Isvasstinden. Scramble over this ridge, and pick up a flanking path round point 539m back towards Botnvatnet. Return to Svolvær by the route of ascent.

This route follows one of the few marked paths across the centre of the rough island of Austvågøya. It is by no means easy going, but the views of the wild interior and its magnificent lakes are more than ample compensation for the effort expended. For those who want to do this as a circular walk (or for those doing a north-south traverse) there is an optional easy scramble over the rocky little peak of Isvasstinden.

Navigation on this route is at times tricky, and even finding the start of the path in Svolvær is not easy! The Cappelens road map to Lofoten (Kart 52) has a very useful street map of Svolvær on the reverse. Leave the E10 at the Shell garage and follow the signs for Knutsmarka and then the Feriesenter.

If you have a car, park it near the Hjelpekorps building – there is very limited parking beyond here. Follow the street of Vannsverkbakken until a gravel track leads left. This is a ski trail, illuminated by street lights in the winter. This takes you to a suspension footbridge over the narrowest part of the lake of Svolværvatnet. The ski trail turns south and heads back for town, but you need to leave it and head on the path that now follows the west bank of the lake. The first part of this is boggy and progress is slow, however after one kilometre or so the going becomes drier and easier. Before long you will reach the head of the lake, and there is a water pipe which feeds a small hydro-electric power station. 200m beyond the hut of Sætra, the main path ducks under the elevated water pipe and heads off north-northwest to climb the shoulder of Botntinden. This path is cairned but is still easily missed.

If you miss this turning and instead follow the rough path alongside the waterpipe, you will end up at the small lochan of Svartvatnet. If you have the time to spare, this is an impressive lochan and worth the detour. There is a path which continues alongside Svartvatnet which looks like a tempting way to get to Botnvatnet, but this path crosses some steep slabs which fall straight into deep water. A slip here (especially with a heavy rucksack) would have serious consequences. There are wire ropes, but they are corroded and this guidebook author could not recommend trusting them. In other words, you are recommended to turn back and look for the correct path!

So, back on the correct path at Sætra, it goes under the water pipe and heads up a series of steep slopes with small slabs. This section deserves care if the ground is wet. Before long, the path heads right and contours into the corrie well above the end of Svartvatnet (Rundfjellet's southwest ridge looks very impressive from here). The path is well cairned, but crosses a boulder field

Retreating from the slabs beside Svartvatnet   Ian H. Robertson

and the route can be difficult to pick out, especially in mist. However, the boulders are soon passed and there is a short climb to the haunting lochan of Botnvatnet. In mid August, Botnvatnet can still be frozen and is a reminder that you are truly north of the Arctic Circle. It is an atmospheric place to linger and have lunch. Fit walkers could easily include the summit of Torskmannen in the round.

From Botnvatnet, it would be an easy downhill walk back to Svolvær, but that would be missing out on two absolute gems in this part of Austvågøya. These are the beautiful lochan of Isvatnet and its neighbouring top of Isvasstinden.

Follow the cairned path northeast from Botnvatnet. It leads over an outlying gentle ridge and descends gradually to the north end of Isvatnet. Those doing a through walk will follow the path north (see description below). If you are doing a circular walk back to Svolvær, head off the path and aim east for a low col to the north of Isvasstinden. The peak's broad north ridge is an easy scramble on beautifully rough "white" granite, nowhere exposed, and is a real delight for the scrambler. Even if you normally baulk at the idea of putting hand to rock, this is an enjoyable ridge and it finishes all too soon at the summit.

The blocky scramble over Isvasstinden is easy and good fun   Denis Wilson

Rundfjellet looks very tempting from here, however the southwest ridge is interrupted by a couple of rocky pinnacles/buttresses. There is a break in Rundfjellet's crags on its west buttress, however this involves an ascent on dangerously steep grass in an exposed situation. In short, this approach to Rundfjellet cannot be recommended and a better way is the long northwest ridge over Utjordtinden (see chapter 45).

Leave Rundfjellet for another day, and start to head back to Svolvær. The south side of Isvasstinden is an easy angled grass slope – head southwest from the summit to the col between Isvasstinden and point 539m. Just west of the col, there is a path which winds its way round the side of point 539m. This crosses an icy couloir, but it should be possible to get across this obstacle by losing a little height and crossing it at its narrowest point. Before long, you will meet your main outward path and the return to Svolvær.

If you are doing a through walk, the path heads north from Isvasnet, and gains the ridge just north of point 472m. An easy walk along the ridge and down through the trees will take you to the farm buildings at Haugen, from where it is an easy two kilometre walk to the campsite at Sandsletta.

~

The North to South Through Walk

This walk can also be done as a through walk from North to South, or as a circular walk to Botnvatnet. The following notes may be of use to walkers approaching from this direction.

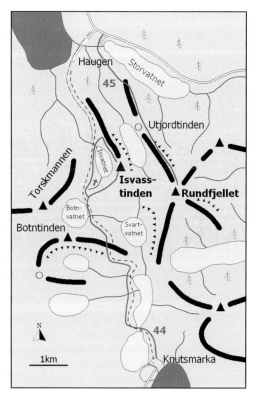

The start of the path is at the farm at Haugen (GR 793783), however you cannot drive here. Cars cannot be taken beyond the bridge at Løvland (GR 796789) or else leave them on the public road (limited parking).

At Haugen, follow a tractor track south down a hill. At the bottom of the hill, this track turns left. At this bend, the path to Svolvær heads straight on and heads up the hillside, near the right hand edge of a firebreak. The start of the path is difficult to find, but once you are on it and gain height, the path is easy to follow all the way to point 472m.

From here, follow the crest of the ridge to Isvasstinden. The rest of the route is described above.

The beautiful Isvatnet   Denis Wilson

45. Rundfjellet

Krystina Lotoczko & Denis Wilson

Rundfjellet's summit cairn, looking towards Litlmola   Krystina Lotoczko

Grading: A rough hike to a superb viewpoint, with some easy scrambling. *Time: 8–9 hours* *Overall distance and ascent:* *11 km, 900m*	*Access to starting point: Leave the E10 in Vestpollen (GR 872791). Take the minor road to Sandsletta. Start at Ytreidet (GR 800792). There is only limited parking here.* *Maps: Statens Kartverk 1:50 000 sheet 1131-I*
Best enjoyed: There are no paths over much of the route. Navigation would be difficult in mist. Best kept for a clear day to enjoy one of the best viewpoints in Lofoten.	

Route summary:
From Ytreidet, head for the northwest ridge of Isakheia. Follow the crest to Utjordtinden, picking the easiest way over the easy angled rock slabs. From here drop to the col and then head up the northwest ridge of Rundfjellet. Return by the same route.

The start of the walk. *Krystina Lotoczko*

Rundfjellet is a magnificent mountain. It has four main ridges radiating out from its summit and the corries between these ridges are exceedingly craggy. Its Norse name means "Round Hill" and does this hill a great disservice – it is not round and it is not easy!

On the map, Rundfjellet looks as if it may be easily ascended from several different directions. In practice this is not so: the path from the east (alongside Vatterfjordpollen) ends at the head of the sea inlet. Any further progress is barred by near-impenetrable birch scrub.

The attempt from the west, via Isvasstinden, has been mentioned in Chapter 44. This way up goes through a grassy break in the crags that form the western buttress of Rundfjellet. This is very steep and insecure (one of the party used hands, feet and stomach for grip!) and it is not recommended as a route in this guidebook. However, the way the party went down, over Rundfjellet's northwest ridge, turned out to be quite easy. This is the route described below. It should be pointed out that the authors have not climbed the mountain by the northwest ridge, only descended it, but the description below should still be useful. All this effort is worthwhile, as Rundfjellet is the highest mountain in this part of Austvågøya and is a tremendous viewpoint.

Start at Ytreidet, cross the fence and skirt round the hayfield. Cross the small river that comes out of Storvatnet and head for the small top of Isakheia. This is easily identified by the electricity cables heading towards it.

Rundfjellet's northwest ridge, seen from Isvasstinden   *Krystina Lotoczko*

The ridge is clear of birch trees and you now need to follow it to Utjordtinden. There are some rocky slabs, but occasional faint cairns mark the way. From the top of Utjordtinden, drop down to a shallow col, then climb the northwest ridge of Rundfjellet. The ridge has several pinnacles, but these can all be avoided. Further up, there is a large section of boulder slope and slab, but an easy angled rake affords a way through. At last the top will be yours, with one of the best viewpoints in Lofoten.

Return by the route of ascent.

The map for route 45 is on page 221.

On Rundfjellet's northwest ridge   *Krystina Lotoczko*

46. Onto the Geitgallien Ridge

Ian H. Robertson

Geitgallien   *Krystina Lotoczko*

Grading: An Alpine snow romp as far as the summit glacier. The summit glacier and tower are for experienced climbers and Alpinists only. *Time: 8–9 hours.* *Overall ascent: 900m* *Distance: 11 km.*	*Access to starting point: Leave highway E10 at Eide and take the road to Liland. Start at the shop in Skinvollen 200m south of the E10.* *Maps: Statens Kartverk 1:50 000 sheet 1831-I.*

Best enjoyed: The route has complex route finding and is only recommended for clear weather. A sunny day will give an enjoyable glissade for the descent. Ice axe and crampons are required. For an attempt on the summit tower, a rope is also needed.

Route summary:

Take the ski trail behind the shop in Skinvollen and follow it into Lilandsdalen. At the top of the trail follow a faint path through the scrub until a junction of two streams is reached. Follow a faint path (see text) into the middle part of the corrie. Take a ramp through the upper rock band into the snowy upper corrie. Follow the snow ramp to the summit glacier. Either go left to gain the ridge or for the summit, cross the glacier and then ascend the summit tower. Return by the route of ascent.

The approach up Lilandsdalen   *Ian H. Robertson*

The eastern part of the island of Austvågøya (called Nordre Austvågøya) is almost a separate island, connected to the main part by a narrow isthmus at Higrav. Nordre Austvågøya has some of the most rugged mountains in Lofoten. Access is difficult and so most of these summits require a multi-day expedition and a boat drop-off: usually from the Raftsund or Trollfjorden. A glimpse into the hidden world of these peaks can be had from east of the Raftsund (see route 47) but for those who want a closer look there is a part of the ridge that can be ascended in a single day – Geitgallien.

The summit tower and glacier require some Alpine skills and climbing experience but the rest of the route is little more than an enjoyable romp over snow. Even if you don't intend to bag the summit, this is still an excellent day out and is one of the best in Lofoten. Note that errors in route finding would be serious, so this is an outing only for a clear day. You must also be experienced in the use of ice axe and crampons, as a slip could be fatal.

Your start is via a ski trail. These have street-lights for use in the dark days of mid-winter, so the first part of the route is easy to follow. The ski-trail starts behind the shop in the little village of Skinvollen, just south of the E10. Don't park in the shop car park – space for parking cars is available a few metres along the road. The start of the trail is at a gate – look for the street lamps.

Into the upper snowy corrie　　　　　　　　　　　　　　*Krystina Lotoczko*

Follow the ski-trail upwards into Lilandsdalen. Although called a dale, it is more like a corrie than a true valley. When the ski-trail starts to descend on its return trip, look for a faint path leading through the scrub; starting a few metres right of a green post box. Fortunately the scrub soon eases off and takes you into a grassy meadow, in the lower part of the corrie.

The day's first obstacle is now before you – a steep slope and two waterfalls. The 1:50 000 map does not show the stream system in Lilandsdalen correctly. There are two main streams converging in the lower meadow by two waterfalls. Take the route *between* the two streams – the path seems to go left, but is a false trail and leads onto dangerously steep vegetated terrain. Follow the path between the waterfalls with care, especially where it crosses above some steep slabs.

Soon the angle eases and affords a good view of the middle part of the corrie. Store Higravtinden rises above you on the left, but this is a peak for climbers only. Follow the left-hand (north) bank of the stream until you are above a second set of slabs. This is the middle part of Lilandsdalen. To get to Geitgallien, you need to gain the snowy upper corrie.

The next obstacle is a band of cliffs that separates the snowy upper corrie from the middle corrie. However, there is an easy-angled terrace over to the right (south) which offers a way through. Cross over the stream and head for the bottom of the terrace. Ascend the terrace on an easy angled slope. At the top of the terrace, an easy-angled snow couloir leads to the upper corrie.

The "plughole"   *Ian H. Robertson*

If you are equipped with ice axe and crampons put them on now and start on your way to the top. Alternatively, an easy scramble to the left of this snow couloir lets you gain more height on rock.

Regardless of method, you will soon come to the upper corrie where you have no choice but to take to the snow. Carefully note the route leading back down to the terrace – this is the route you will need to follow to get safely back off the mountain.

From here, it is an enjoyable walk on snow up several snow slopes of varying steepness to the edge of the small summit glacier.

At last you come to Geitgallien's small summit glacier. The way to the top is now obvious – but it is also very intimidating! This is a mountain with a real sting in its tail. The small summit glacier swirls round like a basin and discharges into a "plughole" – this is a gully that tumbles off over the edge of the mountain. Any climber slipping on this glacier would slide straight down this plughole and would have a long drop awaiting them.

You now have three options open to you:
1. Take the opportunity for a photo-stop then retrace your steps down the mountain. This is still a very worthwhile expedition.
2. Head on up to the summit.
3. Head on up to the summit ridge without crossing the glacier.

Trolltindan   *Krystina Lotoczko*

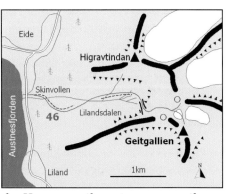

When the author did this route, he had mistakenly left his crampons in Scotland. Cutting steps up Lilandsdalen was easy, but cutting steps above the "plughole" was more serious. His party therefore opted for (3) and headed up directly onto the ridge. This is over some very loose rock and deserves care. The continuation from here along the ridge to the summit is exceptionally loose and unstable – it cannot be recommended. However, the views over the Trolltindan are immense and the ascent to the ridge is still worthwhile.

To gain the summit tower directly, cross the glacier and head for a rocky rake. Climb this to the ridge, then ascend the summit tower.

Note: the author's party has not ascended the summit tower. It was originally graded a "moderate climb" by the first to ascend it by this route in 1910. It is certainly very steep and very, very exposed so a rope would be required. As with all climbs that have not had numerous re-ascents, take this grade with caution. The summit is therefore for experienced Alpinists or climbers only.

Whichever option you choose, the way down is by the route of ascent. However, if you are lucky enough to have climbed it on a hot summer's day, the descent should be good fun – the upper slopes catch the afternoon sun and can give a good glissade on soft snow back down the mountain. However, be careful – if you are not confident about ice-axe braking or if the snow is still hard, keep your crampons on and walk down.

Care needs to be taken in locating the position of the couloir and the terrace to get you through the upper cliff band. After you get down the terrace look for the start of the path. This is on the right hand bank of the stream (looking out). It is much further to the right than you may think.

Geitgallien's summit tower   Ian H. Robertson

47. East of the Raftsund

Ian H. Robertson

The Raftsund from the slopes of Snøtinden, with Rulten beyond   Ian H. Robertson

Grading: Easy hillwalking amidst spectacular views. Time: 6-7 hours. Overall distance and ascent: 12 km, 700m	Access to starting point: Leave highway E10 at the bridge over the Raftsund. Take the minor road to Digermulen. Start at a picnic site about 300m south of the ferry pier. Maps: Statens Kartverk 1:100 000 Turkart "Lofoten"
Best enjoyed: The route is practicable in any weather, but is best left for a day of clear visibility when the stunning views will be best enjoyed.	

Route summary:
From the picnic site in Digermulen, follow a path signed "Digermulen kol". Continue over the minor top of Keiservarden to a small lochan. Follow the path beyond the lochan to a high moor. Turn right and ascend Snøtinden. Continue to a col and then ascend Nipen. Return to the col and then descend a corrie with care. At the foot of the corrie, turn left and pick up a marked path which returns you to the lochan and then Digermulen.

The Vest Fjord and the mainland from Snøtinden   Ian H. Robertson

The Raftsund is the famous channel that separates the islands of Hinnøya from Austvågøya. As explained in chapter 46 on Geitgallien, the mountains of Nordre Austvågøya are hard to access. However, whilst they may be difficult to reach and even more difficult to climb, they are spectacular and give a magnificent backdrop to a walk on the hills of south-western Hinnøya.

This part of Hinnøya has, until recently, also been difficult to access; however the extension of the E10 highway and a new bridge over the Raftsund has meant that Digermulen is within reach of a car-based day trip from Svolvær. Alternatively, Digermulen could be reached by ferry from Svolvær but this would require an overnight stay (tent required).

The hills east of the Raftsund are more gentle than their counterparts west of the sound on Austvågøya; but they are still rocky in places. They would not look out of place in the Scottish Western Highlands or parts of the English Lake District. The walk given here just touches on the edge of this area and there is much potential for hillwalking of an exploratory nature. There is also a network of marked paths above Digermulen that are not shown on any map, so for once access to above the tree-line is straight-forward.

From the ferry pier, go about 300 metres south along the road until you see a path to the left signposted "Digermulen Kol". There is parking opposite this and a picnic table. Follow this well marked path which zigzags its way through the trees until you top out on a rocky knoll called Keiservarden ("the

Snøtinden's summit looking towards Austvågøya   *Denis Wilson*

Kaiser's cairn"). Here are two plaques commemorating visits by Wilhelm II of Germany in the years before the First World War. It is easily seen why Kaiser Bill visited this spot, as the views over the Raftsund towards the seemingly impregnable mountain of Rulten are simply magnificent. It is a good spot for an early lunch.

Head roughly northeast from Keiservarden and then drop down to a small lochan surrounded by birch trees. It is a lovely spot to linger but the next top awaits. Follow the well marked path to a high moor. Another (unmarked) path leads up the hillside on your right – to Snøtinden. The path does not lead to the summit itself, but contours round the top part, so you will have to leave it and head for the top. Again the views make all the effort worthwhile, but this time it is the Norwegian mainland and the waters of the Vestfjord that catch the eye.

After this second photo-opportunity, head slightly right to outflank Snøtinden's summit cliffs then descend a steep and partly loose grass and scree slope to reach a high col that separates you from the next peak, Nipen. Again a vague path leads round the mountain slopes but not to the summit itself so you will need to leave the path. This is a splendid piece of high level walking with good surfaces underfoot.

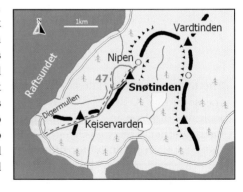

From the top of Nipen, we headed back towards Digermulen. Adventurous walkers could try and extend the walk north – there is plenty of scope in this area. An alternative to re-ascending Snøtinden is to descend from the corrie between the two hills and pick up a path that leads back to Digermulen.

233

48. Breidtinden

John Baddeley

Breidtinden as seen from the north   John Baddeley

Grading: Short walk-in to an easy scrambling ascent of an airy ridge. Time: 5–7 hours Overall distance and ascent: 7km, 1000m	Access to starting point: From Svarthola, on the road between Mefjordbotn and Mefjordvær. Maps: Statens Kartverk 1:50 000 Turkart "Senja", 1:50 000 sheet 1433-IV
Best enjoyed: Whenever the route is dry and clear of snow.	

Route summary:
From Svarthola, follow a marked path up through the birch forest to Svartholvatnet. Go north of Breidtindvatnet to gain the col below the South Ridge and scramble up the ridge to the summit. Return by the same route.

The peaks above Mefjorden from the south   *John Baddeley*

Senja is the second largest island in Norway and one of its most attractive. The east coast is mainly gently rolling countryside and farmland, fringed by areas of white sand beaches with a backdrop of the rugged mainland peaks. To the west, the coast is indented with deep fjords separated by steep mountains, reminiscent of the Lofoten a short distance to the south but generally lower and easier to access. Plant life is interesting, there is a small National Park, and animals include abundant sea eagles. It is also one of the best whale-watching locations in Norway, with both sperm and killer whales seen frequently. This combination of characters within a short distance means that Senja is often called "Norway in Miniature". It is an ideal holiday venue for those wishing to mix some spectacular but relatively easy hillwalking with more traditional holiday pursuits. For those spending any time on Senja, the map "Turkart Senja", which covers the whole of the island, is a worthwhile purchase. Published locally and available from shops on the island, the map is based on Statens Kartverk 1:50 000 mapping and has many local paths marked.

Breidtinden (often called Breitind) is the highest mountain on Senja and is a real gem. Standing on the west coast at the head of Mefjorden, its three summits appear impregnable from most angles. The route described here ascends the higher, South Peak by its South Ridge. The Central Peak (985m), sitting atop a huge rock wall, is also reported to be accessible to scramblers, but the ascent of the lower West Peak involves technical climbing.

The summit of Breidtinden   *John Baddeley*

The route up Breidtinden begins on the minor road between Mefjordbotn and Mefjordvær. Coming from the east, go through two tunnels and an open-sided rockfall/avalanche shelter to a small parking area on the west side of the small, rocky bay of Svarthola. Several metres further west a path, marked by red paint, finds a route up through steep birch woods to the small collection of fishing huts at the north end of Svartholvatnet. Head slightly north of east onto a broad ridge and follow this to the higher lake of Breidtindvatnet. Cross the small stream at the outflow of this lake and make a rising traverse across the rough hillside up to the col at the head of the valley. Throughout this section the South Ridge is seen well in profile and looks rather steep and intimidating.

From the col you have two options. Maximum scrambling is achieved by getting onto the ridge as soon as possible and following the crest upwards. Alternatively there are vague, scrappy paths that make their way up the slopes to the right of the ridge. Although there isn't much reason to do so, these can be taken to avoid the lower sections of ridge but do not leave it too long before attempting to rejoin the ridge. In particular, do not be fooled by the sight of a pointed peak ahead to the right, which appears like it might be the summit. This is a subsidiary top and, while its ascent gives good views across the main face of the mountain, it does not provide a scrambling route to the summit.

The South Ridge gives high quality, easy scrambling all the way to the summit. In one or two places there is some exposure but not at the more difficult parts. The route stays on or close to the crest of the ridge and is not hard to follow as, unusually for northern Norway, it is well-enough used for signs of wear to be present. The summit of Breidtinden (no definitive height available but about 1030 ± 15m) appears suddenly when only a few metres from it, and is perched on a block that overhangs the North East Face of the mountain. Being the highest mountain on the island, views are extensive in all directions, but the immediate view across the main face of the mountain and down Mefjorden is the one that holds the eye. The eastern side of this fjord is made up of a great rollercoaster ridge of mountains that while rarely more than 800m high, have great vertical faces of granite dropping from their summits to sea-level. The return to the road is by retracing the ascent route.

Just to the north of Breidtinden is the spectacular Øyfjorden. It is long and narrow, confined by two slender peninsulas of jagged mountains. Part way along it is the fishing village of Husøy, which entirely occupies its eponymous island and is well worth a visit. The easiest way to appreciate Øyfjorden is by making a short ascent of the hillside above the southern entrance of the tunnel to Fjordgård. This can easily be extended to take in Barden (659m), which gives probably the best views of Breidtinden. The more energetic can make a straightforward ascent of Keipen (938m) from the same starting point.

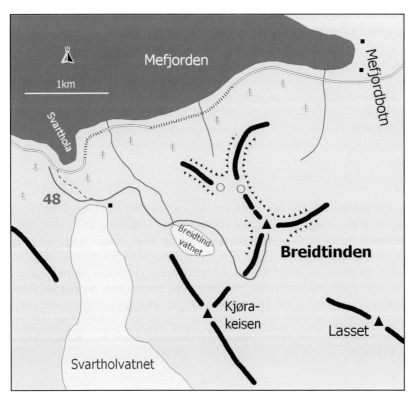

49. Hamperokken

John Baddeley

Hamperokken from the north   John Baddeley

Grading: A stiff ascent followed by a long section of easy scrambling, turning into intermediate scrambling near the summit. Descent over rough, unstable boulder fields. Time: 6–8 hours Overall distance and ascent: 10km, 1350m	Access to starting point: Parking area at GR 326206 on Rv91 between Fagernes and Breivikeidet. Maps: Statens Kartverk 1:50 000 Turkart "Tromsø fastland – Stuoranjárga"
Best enjoyed: Whenever the route is dry.	

Route summary:
From the road, go south east up the steep hillside to Middagsaksla, then along a ridge with some sections of easy and intermediate scrambling to the summit of Hamperokken. Descend towards the outflow of Lilleskarvannet and stay on the east side of the stream back to the road.

Looking up the North West Ridge   *Mike Forrester*

Standing just a short distance south of Tromsø, above the road to Lyngen, Hamperokken makes an ideal introductory ascent for visitors new to the area. It has most of the elements found on the higher mountains such as long, steep ascents, insect-ridden forests, rock scrambling, unstable boulder fields and a superb summit, contained in a relatively short day out.

The most practical way up Hamperokken begins from the south side of the Rv91. Park in a short section of track that forms a loop off the road and has a notice board at the western end with local fishing information. At the eastern end (not western as on the map) a rough grassy track heads south into the forest. This continues for several hundred metres before becoming a narrow, twisting path, marked with plastic tape on trees. Finding this path is a great aid, as the forest hereabouts is a dense mixture of birch and conifers. These

Airy scrambling near the summit of Hamperokken   *John Baddeley*

trees soon end abruptly in a flat area of bog, and it is well worth making sure that you will be able to relocate this end of the path on your return.

The route continues southeast, aiming for the steep hillside of Middagsaksla. Cross an area of mire vegetation and enter the open birch forest on the lower slopes of the hill. The walking though this is easier than is often the case, although insects may well be a problem. Carry on up through the trees and out onto the open and increasingly steep hillside. This ascent is hard work but the underfoot conditions are relatively easy and height is gained rapidly. At around 1100m the hillside narrows into the start of the ridge proper, and coming over a small rise you get the first good view of the summit pyramid. It stands at the end of a long, leftwards-curving ridge and at first sight looks rather formidable. Below the ridge to the east is a small glacier, unmarked on the map.

The ridge traverse is an excellent route to the summit and is mainly walking with some easy scrambling in places. Initially, any difficulties are turned on the left, but further along the right hand side is easier. The route goes over many small undulations but overall gains height slowly until close to the summit pyramid. Here is the hardest section of the ridge, where you must cross a large tower with an exposed and narrow descent on the far side. The crossing of this tower establishes you on the start of the summit section, which involves some passages of quite steep intermediate scrambling. In less than good conditions, some may like the reassurance of a rope on this last part of the route. Make a traverse right below very steep rocks until a broad, open gully is reached. This may be wet with drainage and will have some snow early in the season. Scramble up this gully with care as there is much loose rock in the lower section. The easiest line trends to the right to reach a spectacular position on the South Ridge of the mountain, overlooking Tepphaugdalen. Go up this very exposed but easy ridge for 40m to a short broken wall, which is then climbed to emerge suddenly at the small, pointed summit of Hamperokken (1404m). The worst of the exposure on the South Ridge can be avoided by the slightly harder option of continuing straight up the gully rather than exiting onto the ridge.

The cairn contains a log book, and a handy panorama of the peaks of Kvaløya to the north west, beyond Tromsdaltinden. The summit is very airy, with steep drops all around. The views west are enticing but just too distant to really hold the attention. The peaks to the south are much closer but cannot compete with the panorama of Lyngen to the east. The great glacier-topped mass of Jiehkkivárri is an arresting sight, with large blue/white icefalls dropping into dark corries, while to its north are the serrated, alpine peaks of the northern Lyngen peninsular.

Descend from the summit by the same route to regain the North West Ridge. From here the route goes down steep boulder slopes to the outflow of Lilleskarvannet, either directly or by first continuing back along the ridge for about ½km. This descent is quite loose and unstable and thus heavy going, but the hardy will be rewarded by a refreshing swim in the icy blue Lilleskarvannet at the bottom. Beyond the lake there is an open corrie filled with huge boulder fields. Avoid these by traversing out to the east side of this corrie, where the going is somewhat easier. Soon after this the outward route is rejoined for the journey back though the trees to the road.

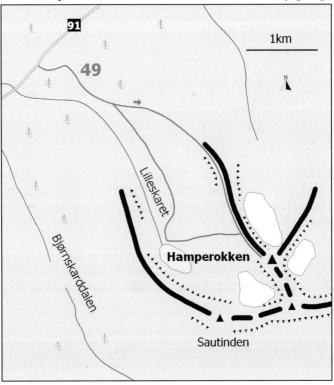

50. Piggtinden

John Baddeley & Espen Nordahl

Piggtinden from the west   *John Baddeley*

Grading: Excellent scrambling in superb situations, becoming harder with height, to summit tower. Ascent of this is grade V- (UK HS) for one pitch. *Time: 8–11 hours* *Overall distance & ascent:* *13.5km, 1450m*	*Access to starting point: Parking place just west of where the road crosses the Lakselva, east of Fjellås.* *Maps: Statens Kartverk 1:50 000 Turkart "Lyngenhalvøya"*
Best enjoyed: Whenever the route is clear of snow, most likely in July/early August. The rock is extremely slippery when wet.	

Route summary:
From the road, follow a track then path (marked on map) on the north side of Storelva to the 500m contour. Traverse north east to the base of Piggtinden's West Ridge, and follow this to the summit. Return by the same route.

Superb scrambling on the West Ridge of Piggtinden   *John Baddeley*

Situated near the base of the Lyngen peninsula, the commonly-used access roads bypass the striking pyramid of Piggtinden, meaning that many visitors miss one of its most spectacular mountains. The route described here makes a direct ascent of the 800m-high West Ridge, obvious from the road and visible throughout the approach walk. Although reaching the summit proper requires climbing harder than most of the other routes in this book, the ascent as far as the final tower gives over 700m of top-quality scrambling and is highly recommended.

From the parking place, take the track immediately east of the road bridge over the Lakselva. Unlike many of the routes marked on the Turkart, this one actually exists on the ground and makes for easy progress through the birch woods. The intermediate gradient is also a welcome change to many of the ascents in this area. After about two kilometres the track becomes a less distinct path but it is marked by red poles and is easy to follow as far as the confluence of streams that run from north and south of Piggtinden. After crossing the northern stream, the easiest line follows a moraine ridge towards the pass of Piggtindskardet. Follow this until, at about 500m, it is possible to make a gently rising traverse to the northeast across heathland, to the base of the West Ridge at 700m.

Despite its imposing appearance from the road, the ridge is surprisingly straightforward and up to 1000m there is nothing harder than occasional easy scrambling between sections of rough walking.   Above this the

Looking down the West Ridge of Piggtinden   *John Baddeley*

scrambling becomes more continuous as the ridge steepens and becomes slabbier in nature up to 1250m. At this point there is a small tower on the ridge, followed by a narrow neck of rock before another steep but short section.   Once on top of this, the summit tower comes into full view. The drops on each side, which have been slowly increasing, now begin to make themselves felt more fully, and the whole route takes on the more serious edge of a hard scramble.

A 4m descent (*in situ* peg at top) leads to a short rise, beyond which two pinnacles must be negotiated by descending traverses on their south sides. On this section the quality of the coarse gabbro becomes highly questionable in places, and care is required. Thereafter the ridge is almost entirely comprised of much sounder rough slabs. Follow these to the left-hand edge of the rock wall ahead, into a small notch where a loose open gully comes up from the right. This is the base of the summit tower. Up to now there has been nothing to deter the competent scrambler, but to continue further requires climbing proper. Climb up, then make a small traverse right before continuing up again in an open groove system (Grade V-, UK HS). The first part may be wet early in the season, but the rock is reasonably sound. As the route levels out you see some old abseil points. Take note of these for the descent. From here is it a short walk to the West Peak of Piggtinden (1505m).

An alternative route is available from the pinnacles. Continue along the main ridge for a short distance until you see a small cairn on the South West Ridge. Traverse the loose, open gully (possibly filled with icy snow) and use

244

The summit of Piggtinden, with climbers on the South West Ridge   Mike Forrester

an obvious horizontal break in the wall of slabs to gain the South West Ridge just below the cairn. Scramble up the ridge for about 50m to the final steepening. Rope up (*in situ* peg) and climb up and right on some very insecure rock for 20m to a large ledge that crosses the whole wall. From this ledge head up to the summit (Grade IV, UK S). Although this route is technically easier than the more direct line, the very poor rock quality on the former must be taken into account.

The outlook from the summit is tremendous and gives you views of famous Lyngen peaks such as Lakselvtindane and Jiehkkevárri. For those not content with the view from this summit there is the option of continuing to the East Peak, also 1505m. This involves a short abseil (Grade V, UK VS to re-ascend) and an easy walk. The descent from the West Peak can be made by either of the ascent routes. Many will choose to abseil at least the first section, in which case the direct route back to the notch is the best option, using the anchor points noted above. This requires two 50m ropes, and care is needed due to the amount of loose rock. Thereafter follow the ascent route back to the road.

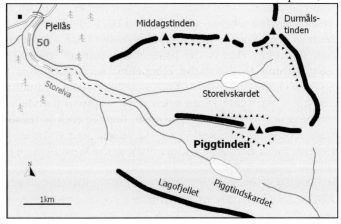

51. Jiehkkivárri

John Baddeley

Jiehkkivárri (L) from Holmbukttind in late summer   Espen Nordahl

Grading: A demanding mountaineering route that includes some moderately steep snow, a complex glacier crossing, and hard rock scrambling that may be snowy. Escape routes problematic. Time: 12-16 hours Overall distance and ascent: 23km, 2300m	Access to starting point: Holmbukta, on the road between Lakselvbukt and Jøvik. Maps: Statens Kartverk 1:50 000 Turkart "Lyngenhalvøya"

Best enjoyed: In July/early August, when snow cover is likely to have reduced enough for easy walking and there is 24-hour daylight. Clear, settled weather is strongly recommended for a first ascent.

Route summary:
From Holmbukta, follow a grassy track/path up Goverdalen. Ford the river and go up Sløkedalen, staying on the north side of the stream to the base of the South Ridge. Ascend this to the South Top and go north, then east over the icecap to the summit of Jiehkkivárri. Head west, south of Point 1738m and go down northeast through a crevassed area. Ascend the East Ridge of Holmbukttind (1666m, unnamed on map), descend its North Ridge to Point 1396m and then go south west into an open corrie. Stay north of the Tverrelva back to the road.

Lakselvtindane seen from Goverdalen   *Mike Forrester*

Slingsby called Jiehkkivárri the "Mont Blanc of the North" and it is not hard to see why. It is a huge mountain, of massive bulk and higher than any other for over 150km. The summit area is comprised of several square kilometres of icecap, girdled by precipitous cliffs and icefalls with few lines of weakness. This, combined with the length of day required and the often unpredictable local weather conditions make for a challenging mountain whose ascent is highly prized. The route described here is a full, committing day of mountaineering adventure that traverses Jiehkkivárri using the infrequently-ascended South Ridge.

The route starts at Holmbukta, a collection of widely spaced houses and small farms on the road up the western side of the lower Lyngen peninsula. There are several places to park along the few hundred metres of road on either side of the bridge over the Goverelva. A track leaves the road about 200m south of this bridge and heads southeast, up Goverdalen. Follow this track, which changes into a path marked by red paint splashes after a few kilometres, up the birch-filled valley to the open, flat area of Vassbakk. Here, flat-topped, vegetated moraines provide good camping spots with views up to the steep glaciers on the eastern side of the Lakselvtindane range. Rather bizarrely, there is also a post-box mounted on a stick that holds a logbook.

The first challenge of the day now presents itself; the crossing of the river, which could be difficult after wet weather or with lots of snow melt. In these conditions the best place may be where the moraines almost dam the river into a wide, shallow and lagoon-like lake of slowly flowing water. Wading across here will be cold and the clear water is deceptively deep, but may be much safer than the faster-flowing sections of river up and down stream.

Once on the other side, cross the almost flat area of mire and scattered trees to the stream that flows down Sløkerdalen. Keep this stream to your right for the next 600m of ascent. At first the going is easy and you can stick close to the stream, but higher up its sides steepen and it is better to quit the banks for some moraine ridges. These flatten out at around 600m, where there is a vegetated hollow. Head up and left to a prominent lateral moraine. This avoids the large areas of slab nearer to the stream and gives easy access to the upper corrie, several hundred metres north of its small lake. The lake is likely to be well frozen as a glacier from Bálggesvárri falls directly into it. From here you get your first views of the South Ridge of Jiehkkivárri, high on the left. The route to the base of it continues straight ahead, up a broad ridge of stones and slabs that separates the two northernmost corries of upper Sløkerdalen, until you are just south of Point 1308m. This location can also be reached from the east by a long, gentle ascent of Lyngsdalen and the Bálggesváhjiehkki glacier (also called Sydbreen) from Furuflaten. To gain the

South Ridge an initial rock tower must be negotiated on its western flank, either by a level traverse with some tricky moves, or by descending loose boulders to reach a rotten gully that is ascended to regain the ridge beyond the tower. From here there are good views down the large glacier of Bálggesváhjiehkki, whose sweep away eastwards is accentuated by the presence of bands of medial moraines.

The ascent of the South Ridge is mainly a high-quality, hard scramble, comparable in character although undoubtedly easier than a late-spring ascent of one of the classic ridge routes on the North Face of Ben Nevis. The route sticks on or very close to the crest throughout, with most of the difficulties in the lower half. Considerable expos-ure occurs in places but these

The South Ridge   *John Baddeley*

Emerging into midnight sun from the South Ridge　　　　　　　　*John Baddeley*

generally correspond with the easier sections. The rock is gabbro, in the main very rough and sound although loose in a few places. It is worth noting that as the route is at an elevation of between 1300 and 1500m it may have some snow cover at any time of year. The extent of this may not be very obvious from the approach and it may be frozen and icy. However, as you will already be carrying rope, ice axe and crampons, this should not present too much of a problem. In this case an indicative grade would be alpine PD+, UK winter II/III.

From the top of the ridge, ascend an easy slope to the South Top of Jiehkkivárri (1672m). The final part of this ascent establishes you on the icecap, and full glacier travel equipment is essential from here. The views are spectacular and give the first indications that the South Ridge was only the beginning of this excursion. The eastern edge of the South Top is a corniced, 100m-high almost vertical snow/ice cliff topping an 800m fall to the glacier below. Ahead to the northeast is the rounded summit dome, and below to the right and left are sizeable icefalls where the icecap finds its way into the corries below. Behind you, the jagged peaks and tumbling glaciers of Lakselvtindane are well displayed.

Go due north, down a moderately steep snow slope, to the col between the South Top and the rest of the mountain. Then head slightly east of north, towards the western end of a boulder field that lies west of the summit. This

Approaching the South Top of Jiehkkivárri   *John Baddeley*

route crosses a slight bowl in the icecap, which restricts the views. This, however, is an advantage as it heightens the impact of reaching the summit ridge, when all the peaks of the Northern Peninsula burst into view. The scene of steep mountains rising out of bright snowfields and dark fjords is striking, especially if this part of the trip is timed to coincide with the midnight sun. Just before reaching the boulders, be on the lookout for small crevasses that run lengthwise along the summit ridge in this area. Turn east across the boulder field, then complete the trip across ½km of icecap to the unmarked summit of Jiehkkivárri (1834m). As you would expect, the views on a clear day are simply stunning in all directions, out over the Lyngen peninsular to many distant peaks. To the east are the great rolling hills of Finnmark, topped to the north east by the glittering mass of Øksfjordjøkelen far in the distance. This icecap gives rise to the only glacier in mainland Europe to fall directly into the sea. Far south are the peaks above Narvik, while to the west lies a complex jigsaw of islands and fjords.

Leave the summit by your ascent route as far as the western end of the boulder field. Continue south west for about one kilometre, then head due west, either walking over or contouring south of Point 1738m, and continue until you reach the rocks that mark its western end. This passage takes you through a relatively narrow gap between these rocks, and cliffs to their south west. Care is thus needed with navigation, especially as there are some large crevasses to avoid. Once west of Point 1738m you are on top of a steep slope of glacier that drops away to the north, which must be descended. Directly

Crossing the Jiehkkivárri icecap   Mike Forrester

below lies an ice cliff not yet visible, so head northeast, into a heavily crevassed area and take the best line through it. The slope soon eases and it is possible to curve back towards the west to a flatter area below the ice cliff, being careful not to get too close to it. Ahead of you now lies the final top of the day. Go up the increasingly steep snow and rocks that form the East Ridge of Holmbukttind (1666m, unnamed on map). This summit provides a fine panorama of most of the route from the now distant South Top and over the summit, and also of the steep icefall leading down to the glacier of Blåisen, sometimes used as a winter route to the tops.

The descent begins down the North Ridge. This is reasonably narrow at the top and may have a cornice, so care is needed if you are tempted eastwards to look at the large glaciers tumbling down Jiehkkivárri's northern flanks. As the ridge widens and the angle eases, bear more to the west to reach Point 1396m. The route from here follows the line of the path marked on the Turkart, which is not present on the ground. A small, upper snow bowl ends in a line of broken crags breached by a narrow, often snow-filled gully. Two arrows scratched into the surface of a huge boulder indicate the top of this gully. Once through the gully you emerge onto another small glacier. Sticking to the north and west edges of this glacier, to avoid avalanche or rockfall danger from the steep cliffs of Holmbukttind, provides an easy descent, perhaps as far as the 900m contour. Below this the route degenerates into loose rock and boulder fields. Make the best way you can down these, keeping north of both the stream (not on map) issuing from the corrie and, further down, the Tverrelva. Once below the treeline, vague paths begin to appear, mainly down slight ridges of moraine. Go down these to join the riverbank and follow this until a track emerges through the forest, then take this back to the road just north of the starting point.

The normal ascent route for Jiehkkivárri starts from Holmbukta, following the descent route described above. If in doubt about the weather this route is much safer. The icecap, and in particular the heavily crevassed area, is difficult to navigate in poor visibility and the presence of a track should not be relied upon. While the use of GPS waypoints may help with general navigation should the weather close in, it is of little use in negotiating crevasses (see Safety Notes). Thus the ability to retrace your own steps in the event of a retreat is an invaluable option, especially given the lack of easy routes on or off the icecap.

It is worth noting the considerable ski potential of the Jiehkkivárri area. Ski ascents are made between March and September but the prime season is from March to May, when snow cover is at its peak and days are long. The normal ascent route from Holmbukta is often used but there are many other options, depending on snow cover and avalanche conditions. The classic route is the south-north traverse of the whole massif. This starts up the normal ascent route to Holmbukttind, crosses Jiehkkivárri and its north eastern top of Kveita before tackling Fugldalsbreen and Fornesbreen, exiting to Forneset. Allow at least 12 hours.

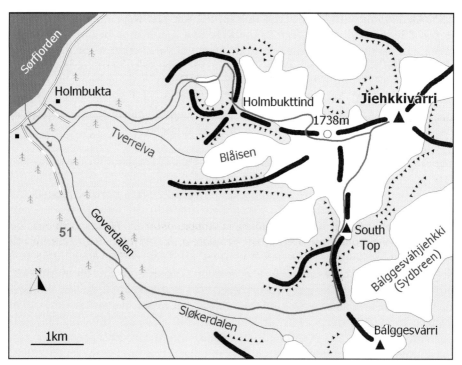

52. Store Lenangstinden

Espen Nordahl

Looking east from the summit of Store Lenangstinden   Espen Nordahl

Grading: A long day out that includes easy glacier crossings, steep snow climbing and easy rock scrambling. Time: 10–12 hours Overall distance and ascent: 17km, 1650m	Access to starting point: From Koppangen, at the north end of the road from Lyngseidet, on the east side of the Lyngen peninsula. Maps: Statens Kartverk 1:50 000 Turkart "Lyngenhalvøya"
Best enjoyed: In late June to early August when snow covers the bergschrunds and there is 24-hour daylight.	

Route summary:
From the road, go up Koppangsdalen to Koppangsbreen. Head northwest up Koppangsbreen and continue across Strupbreen to reach a steep snow climb up to the East Ridge. From here it is an easy scramble to the summit. Descend the same way, or a by a longer but easier alternative further along the East Ridge.

Store Lenangstinden (centre) from Strupbreen   *Jan Fredrik Frantzen*

Store Lenangstinden is the highest peak on the northern part of the Lyngen peninsula, but in spite of that it is seldom visited. The peak is situated in the heart of one of the most alpine regions of Lyngen, surrounded by glaciers, icefalls and many other attractive peaks. It was first climbed in 1898 from the west by the formidable team of G. Hastings, W.P. Haskett-Smith, W.C. Slingsby and E. Hogrenning, by what is now known as Hastings' Couloir. The route described in this chapter climbs the peak by its easiest route, from the east by a long ascent across magnificent glaciers.

The route to the summit starts from the little settlement Koppangen on the east side of Lyngenhalvøya, where the road ends. It is very popular among foreign fishing tourists and if you want to spend a night here, there are some really nice cottages to rent, Koppangen Brygger. If you arrive by car, please ask the locals where to park. Walk north west along the shoreline for 150m and then take a path along the east side of the river. At the beginning it may be difficult to locate, but it soon becomes easier to follow. After you have left the treeline you are on the way into Koppangsdalen and some typical Lyngen terrain; loose scree and boulders. You now have to zigzag up a boulder field. A path may be recognizable in parts of the ascent, which levels out near the top where there is a cairn. Traverse back north towards the river and follow a faint path up loose rocky terrain. As you gain height you will see a notch to the left of the river, which is your destination. Once there you will see Koppangsvatnet. From here the walk is flatter and easier. Head for the snout of Koppangsbreen. This glacier has retreated tens of metres in the last 10-15 years and the front has become steeper, but climbing onto it presents no difficulties at the time of writing (ice axe and crampons necessary).

At around 600m the glacier flattens out. There are some crevasses but there should be no problems crossing or avoiding these. Keep right of a large medial moraine at first, but cross over this high up. Leave Koppangsbreen at 780m and start the easy climb up the wide icefall, which is to the right of some prominent rocks, to reach the large glacier of Strupbreen. From here you can finally see your destination; Store Lenangstinden. Your route goes north west across Strupbreen, directly towards Store Lenangstinden. Crossing Strupbreen is a more or less straightforward undertaking. Early in the season it should all be snow covered. Later in the year, when melting has started, there may be some small lakes in a basin in the middle of the glacier at around 1000m that must be avoided.

Continue across the glacier to the broad snow gully directly south of the summit (obvious directly below the summit in the second picture of this chapter), ascend it and cross the bergschrund at its top. Climb straight up steep snow for 200m, then turn right and start climbing a narrowing snow gully. The steepest sections of this are at a gradient of 50°, and may well require crampons. The gully ends on the East Ridge at 1520m. Go up the ridge by easy scrambling to the summit of Store Lenangstinden (1625m, but 1596m on the M711 map). When dry and snow-free, a rope is not normally required on this section of ridge.

A cairn marks the summit and the view is spectacular. To the north you look down on parts of the big mountain wall that makes up the north side of Strupskardet. Støvelfjellet and Veidalstindan make a particularly majestic view, while to the west you look straight into the famous Jægervasstindane massif. The descent can be made by reversing the ascent route. Alternatively, you can take an easier option of continuing down the East Ridge, past the snow gully you ascended, to a saddle at around 1450m. From here you can downclimb a snow slope to the south, taking care when crossing the bergschrund, and being aware of falling rocks from above. Thereafter retrace your outwards route back down the glacier to Koppangen.

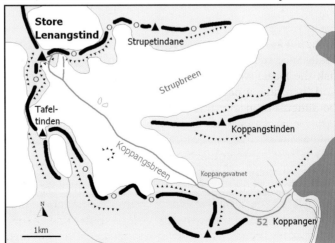

53. The Northern Tip of Lyngen

Espen Nordahl

On Gammvikbláisen, looking towards Lille Peppartinden   *Espen Nordahl*

Grading: A short camping trip that involves some easy walking into a base camp, easy scrambling on Lille Peppartinden, and some easy glacier walking and easy scrambling on Store Peppartinden. Time: 2 days. Daily distance, ascent and time: Day 1: 7km, 700m, 4–6 hours Day 2: 14km, 900m, 7–9 hours	Access to starting point: From Russelv, at the end of the road on the west side of the Lyngen peninsula. Maps: Statens Kartverk 1:50 000 Turkart "Lyngenhalvøya"
Best enjoyed: Before the last week in July and in clear weather, to savour the midnight sun.	

Route summary:
Day 1: Walk southeast from Russelv, up Russelvdalen and cross the watershed to reach a campsite just south of Lomvatnan. Ascend Lille Peppartinden and return to your tent. Day 2: Head south to gain the snout of the Gammvikbláisen glacier, go up the east side of this to a col on the South West Ridge of (Store) Peppartinden and scramble up this to the summit. Descend by the same route to your tent, and then back out to Russelv.

Store Peppartinden (L) and Gammvikbláisen from Lille Peppartinden   *Espen Nordahl*

The northern part of the Lyngen peninsula is an ideal place to feel the closeness of sea and mountain so typical of northern Norway. If you bring camping and glacier equipment you can spend a relatively easy but adventurous weekend out, and if you are lucky you may be rewarded by seeing the midnight sun in majestic surroundings. The route described in this chapter involves easy walking on gentle terrain, some easy scrambling and an easy glacier crossing.

Drive along the west side of Lyngen nearly to the northernmost point. At Russelv, leave the main road and drive several hundred metres up a small road on the west side of Russelva to a gate. From here you start walking first on the road and then out into the terrain. You may be able to find a faint path but generally it's better to find a good line up the south side of the main river in Russelvdalen. The ground ascends gently with some undulations. Cross all three branches of the Tverrelva and head towards Dalbruna (414m). Then descend south east until you are some 300-400 metres south of Lomvatnan, where you will find a lovely spot for your tent. If you are lucky you will wake up the next morning with a herd of reindeer as visitors.

If the weather is good an evening trip up Lille Peppartinden (640m) is highly recommended, to enjoy the midnight sun. The 300m ascent is just an easy walk from the camping spot, with some loose rocks in places. On the summit you will be amazed to find a really solid and impressive cairn, which may contain a logbook. As is often the case with small mountains set amongst larger ones, the view from the summit is amazing.

Midnight sun from Lille Peppartinden   *Espen Nordahl*

To the east and north you can enjoy the fantastic serrated outlines of the islands of Kågen, Skjervøy, Uløya and Arnøya. To the south you see Gammvikblåisen and the rocky peak of Peppartinden. Best of all though is the sight of the midnight sun rolling along just above the sea in the north.

The next day is mainly an ascent of Peppartinden. The route from the campsite heads due south. Pass a small lake at the 440m contour, north east of the summit of Kalddalstinden, and continue ascending on the west side of a small river. To reach the glacier of Gammvikblåisen, first turn east and scramble up to a point just north of the glacier, then descend a short distance to reach the northern part of the glacier front. Gammvikblåisen is gently sloping and, in the lower parts, generally free from crevasses. Cross the glacier heading south towards the saddle on the South West Ridge of Peppartinden. The glacier has been in retreat recently, so late in the season when the snow has melted you may have to scramble up some dirty loose rocks for about 50m to the saddle at 970m. From here it is an interesting but easy scramble up big rock steps, with a great drop down to the glacier on the left, to the summit of (Store) Peppartinden (1252m).

This is the route used by G. Hastings and E. Hogrenning on the first ascent in 1899. To the east you can admire similar views as from Lille Peppartind. To the west you look over to Storgalten, which is a popular peak with visiting ski-mountaineers. Farther away to the south are the seldom-visited peaks of Tverrbakktind, Synbakktind and Rappgamtind. Follow the same route back to your tent, and from there walk out to the road by the approach route.

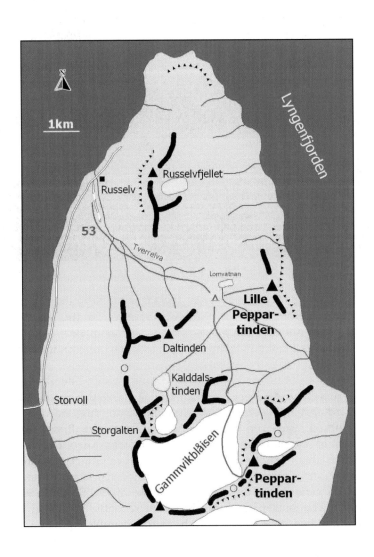

Appendix A. Transport

Flying: A cheap, fast way of getting you and your luggage to Stetind   Anthony Dyer

Flying

By far the easiest way to get to and around Norway is by plane. Several flights a day to Oslo leave from London, Manchester, Glasgow and Aberdeen. Additionally, direct flights to Stavanger, Bergen and Trondheim can be made from London each week. Direct flights also reach Stavanger and Bergen from Aberdeen and Newcastle. In recent years, the cost of flying to Norway has fallen dramatically. Big carriers like SAS-Braathens and British Airways offer return flights starting at £100 while budget carriers like Ryanair and Norwegian Air Shuttle offer cheaper bargains.

Internal domestic flights are the fastest way to get around Norway, and it's actually more popular to fly long distances than it is to drive. Flights between the major towns and cities are frequent and cheap. A 90-minute flight to Arctic Norway from Oslo would otherwise take two days of driving, and this means that you could be hillwalking in the far north within seven hours of taking off from London. Prices for an internal flight have seen dramatic reductions in recent years. It isn't too difficult to find an internal return airfare to Arctic Norway for £90. Even as recently as 2000, such a flight would have cost a prohibitive amount. Now, a whole new playground is within the financial reach of a lot more people.

Airline Information

SAS-Braathens	www.scandinavian.net	Daily flights from London Heathrow and Gatwick, and Manchester to Oslo Gardermoen. Daily flights from Aberdeen to Stavanger. Extensive internal flights to the larger airports.
Norwegian Air Shuttle	www.norwegian.no	Flights from London Stansted to Oslo Gardermoen, Stavanger, Bergen and Trondheim. Extensive internal flights to the larger airports.
Wideroe	www.wideroe.no	Daily flights from Aberdeen and Newcastle to Stavanger and Bergen. Extensive internal flights to many smaller airports in Norway.
British Airways	www.ba.com	Daily flights from London Heathrow and Manchester to Oslo Gardermoen.
Ryanair	www.ryanair.com	Daily flights from London Stansted and Glasgow Prestwick to Oslo Torp and Haugesund.
City Star Airlines	www.citystarairlines.com	Daily flights from Aberdeen to Oslo Gardermoen and Stavanger.
Coast Air Aviation	www.coastair.no	Internal flights in southern Norway.

Rail

The railway network is fairly limited in geographical extent. The main lines of interest to the hill-goer head from Oslo out west across the Hardangervidda to Bergen, and north across Dovrefjell to Trondheim and Bodø, with a branch down Romsdalen. Access to Narvik is possible but this is a very long journey *via* the east coast of Sweden. If heading for somewhere not too far from these lines then rail offers the fastest way of getting to numerous mountain destinations in southern Norway. Most of the inter-city rail network is single track and rather twisty, making trains in Norway slower and less frequent than on the faster lines of the British rail network. It is, however, much faster than coach travel. Train travel from Oslo to Bergen or Trondheim typically has a journey time of about seven hours with departures about every two to four hours.

An inter-city train at Oppdal station   *Anthony Dyer*

Trains are generally clean, the staff are polite, the carriages are wider with more comfortable seats and you can get "*minipris*" tickets where you book in advance to get a single between any two stations for 199kr, subject to availability. An interesting feature is that first class often doesn't cost much more than a standard-class ticket and is quite luxurious with movable armchairs sat overlooking full height windows, and complimentary drinks and newspapers. Irrespective of tickets, you'll need a compulsory seat reservation, even on fully flexible tickets. Another handy feature is the sleeper carriages, which mean that you can have a day out in Romsdalen, get on a train that night and wake up in Oslo. The extra cost is much less than a UK sleeper.

Timetables, Prices and Booking:
www.nsb.no

Buses and Coaches

Where the railways stop, the buses continue. An extensive network of inter-city coaches link the large and small towns together with some rather comfortable coaches offering bags of legroom and seats that recline to a position where sleeping is quite comfortable.

Many routes in the commuter belts of major cities offer half-hourly express services to places in the foothills of mountain regions. Many smaller domestic

Coastal steamer and bridge, both essential coastal transport links   *Anthony Dyer*

airports have prompt bus connections for specific arrivals and departures, and these provide very handy links for the local towns.

As a general rule, buses are rather infrequent outside of city catchment areas. Many destinations only see two to three coaches a day, even on express routes. For the distance covered, fares tend to be quite expensive in comparison to railway and airline tickets. A typical four-hour bus journey is likely to cost around 300kr. A recent introduction is the concept of maximum fares on many routes. Although these are set quite high, if you are travelling a long distance they can offer real savings.

Bus Information

Nor-way Bussekspress	www.nor-way.no	Express Bus Services throughout Norway.
Rutebok.no	www.rutebok.no	Timetables for all bus services in Norway.

Ferries

For people travelling in a group, taking the ferry across from England is the cheapest way of getting to and around southern Norway. Ferry services to

Norway from the UK sail from Newcastle to Kristiansand with DFDS Seaways. Sailings take 18 hours. Sailings from Newcastle to Bergen, Haugesund and Stavanger can be made with ferry operator Fjordline. Sailing times take 18-26 hours. Another ferry service runs during the summer from Aberdeen to Bergen via Shetland.

Around the heavily indented coastal areas of Norway, the fastest way of getting around is often by ferry/hydrofoil. In regions such as Nordland for instance, road transportation is very circuitous. As an example, it can take six hours to take the bus from Svolvær in the Lofoten Islands to Narvik. The hydrofoil service, however, takes three hours and costs a lot less money. Where ferry services provide an essential road transportation link, the service provided is often very frequent and for foot passengers is quite cheap.

A very useful service, particularly in the north of Norway is the "Hurtigruten". A daily service operates from Bergen to Kirkenes calling in at every major port along the way. The entire journey takes six days, but each leg of the journey can be very handy for those needing just a short hop.

Ferry Information

DFDS Seaways	www.dfdsseaways.co.uk	Services from Newcastle to Kristiansand.
Fjordline	www.fjordline.co.uk	Services from Newcastle to Stavanger, Haugesund and Bergen.
OVDS	www.ovds.no	Services in Nordland.
Fjord1	fjord1.no	Services in Møre, Romsdal, Sogn and Fjordane.
HSD	www.hsd.no	Services in Rogaland.
Hurtigruten	www.hurtigruten.no	Daily ferries from Bergen to Kirkenes.

Car Travel

Taking your own car across is often the best option for those who have plenty of travel time in their holidays. The road network varies greatly in quality, but generally speaking it is intrinsically slower than the British road network on account of the challenging terrain. Motorways remain confined to the immediate catchment areas of major cities. Elsewhere, the trunk "E" roads are single carriageway roads that vary in quality in a similar manner to the A82 linking Glasgow with Fort William. The more local, numbered roads are similar in importance to the A roads in the UK and are generally hard surfaces but quite twisty and frequently bumpy. Many local side roads are composed of gravel.

Generally speaking it is advisable to have an up to date road atlas of Norway. Within the last 15 years, the Norwegian government has ploughed a lot of money into improving the road network. Many new roads, tunnels and bridges have appeared and have made portions of the old trunk routes obsolete. Together with road renumbering, it can be quite easy to get totally lost on Norwegian roads without a current atlas.

The national speed limit on normal roads is lower than the UK at 80-90km/h (50-56mph). Fines and penalties linked to your income await those that get caught breaking the speed limit by as little at 5km/h (~3mph). The maximum permissible blood-alcohol level is also much lower, making it unwise to consume more than a single drink if driving the next day. Short prison sentences are usual for offenders. Fuel prices are nowadays similar to the UK. In winter, winter tyres are mandatory throughout Norway, although many parts of southern Norway do not allow studded tyres. Many high trunk roads crossing from Oslo to the West Coast are closed between November and May, and some remain shut until July.

The cost of car hire in Norway is highly variable, with rates from major companies costing 350-800kr per day. Taxis are also expensive with fares costing up to 15kr/km + 90kr call-out fees. Despite the high prices, both options can offer similar value to the buses for those who travel as a group of four or more people. Minibus taxis, offer particularly good value for large parties.

Hitchhiking in Norway is certainly possible, even with a large pack. You will often get a lift sooner than waiting for a bus, especially in remote areas, and whilst hitchhiking has its risks, rural Norway must be one of the safest places to try. Don't be surprised if an enquiry about buses at a local shop results in someone offering you a lift straight away!

Taxi / Car Hire Information

Rent a Wreck	www.rent-a-wreck.no/eng	Budget car hire
Norges Taxiforbundet	www.taxiforbundet.no	Directory of taxi firms

Plus the multinational hire companies in most larger towns

Appendix B. Accommodation

Sandhaug hut, Hardangervidda   *Anthony Dyer*

Mountain Huts

Den Norske Turistforening (DNT, or local organisations affiliated to it) run an excellent network of huts throughout Norway, especially in the south. While called huts, they vary in standard from well-maintained bothies to simple hotels. They can be used either as bases or for grand cross-country backpacking expeditions. If you intend to stay in one for several nights, it is worthwhile becoming a DNT member before you go. The current cost is 455kr. Members get a discount on hut fees, from 260kr to 195kr in staffed huts and from 255kr to 155kr in unstaffed huts. The other benefit of membership is that it gets you a hut key. This will give you access to all the unstaffed and self-service DNT huts, and to the huts of many of the affiliated local organisations (although it is wise to check the latter before setting off).

Huts in popular area can be exceptionally busy at peak times; it is not unheard of to have 60 people sleeping on the floor in Spiterstulen! However, the huts have a policy of not turning anyone away, no matter how crowded they are. Either book ahead, or be prepared to camp instead if you want some peace and quiet. Incidentally, DNT members over 50 years of age are guaranteed a bed even if it means turfing a younger hiker out of one, so depending on your age this may be another benefit of joining.

Stetind basecamp   *Anthony Dyer*

Wild Camping

Within Norway, the law allows you not only to roam across uncultivated land, but also to camp anywhere more than 150m away from a dwelling. It is always wise to make inquires locally if you are in a well-inhabited area. This may often result in you being directed to a much better place to camp, and possibly in some fresh supplies. Certain exceptions apply to this law, for example in Jotunheimen, you can only camp more than 1km from a dwelling, to protect land near to tourist huts from too much pressure. You are allowed to camp in any one spot for a maximum of two nights. Camp fires are forbidden between 15th April and 15th September. At times, the ground becomes tinder dry and so there is a strong danger of fires spreading in an uncontrollable fashion.

Wild camping is often the only practicable solution to climbing many of the more remote summits. Mountain huts are typically located about a day's walk apart from each other, so adding some summits along the way will often add an extra day to your journey. Unlike upland areas of Britain, popular wild camping spots (such as Styhead Tarn in the English Lake District) are not a common sight. In all probability you'll have a perfect pitch next to a lake with grand mountain views, and not have any near neighbours.

While the law allows you to wild camp anywhere, nature dictates its own rules. Within the higher mountain areas, the corries are so high that they are completely devoid of vegetation. If you camp too low, you'll have thick forests to deal with. The best opportunities for camping lie generally between 100–400m above the local tree line, where you will have a mixture of grass, heather and moss to pitch on. In areas with high valleys, like Jotunheimen and Dovrefjell, it is wise to be prepared to spend some nights camped on rocky ground. A heavyweight polythene sheet or sleeping mat under the tent will help protect the groundsheet, although the latter can't be recommended if you use a self-inflating mattress.

Official Camping

At the end or in the middle of your trip, when in need of a shower and clean clothes, official campsites in Norway normally have very good facilities including showers, washing machines and tumble dryers. The campsites tend to be spaced well apart, similar to many areas of the Scottish Highlands.

An important thing to understand about camping in Norway is that the Norwegian interpretation of the word does not necessitate the use of a tent. Thus many campsites are really set up for caravans and camping *hytte* (see below), but two backpackers in a small tent will usually be squeezed in somewhere. As their main customers are families arriving by car, rather than hillwalkers on foot, campsite prices tend to be per tent rather than per person. Generally, you can expect to pay around 70–90kr per night for a tent + 10kr for use of a hot shower. In most areas you are also allowed to camp in the vicinity of DNT huts and use their facilities for 60kr.

Campsite Huts ("*Hytte*")

Many official campsites have huts on them that can be booked by the night. These *hytte* are useful as replenishment stops between camping exploits, as refuges in the event of inclement weather, or they make good self-catering accommodation in their own right if camping is not your scene. The standards vary from little more than a small shed with bunks, to large well-equipped huts with cookers, bathrooms and heating. The costs vary depending on the size and standard, but for a high-quality, well-equipped four-person hut you could expect to pay about 140-220kr per person per night. It is often possible to take a small *hytte* and have some people sleeping outside in tents at no extra charge, which makes for a very cheap night's accommodation if you are in a small group.

Rorbuer

In the north of Norway and especially in Lofoten, there are fisherman's cabins called *Rorbuer*. These offer well equipped self-catering accommodation. There are "old-style" ones available built on wooden piers over the sea, which are now mostly for the tourists (and priced accordingly), or else actual seasonal workers' accommodation. The main cod fishing season is from March-April, so during the summer months the fish workers' accommodation is rented out to tourists. The cost is about 220-300kr per person per night.

Youth Hostels

There are some good youth hostels in Norway and the quality of accommodation is high, as are the prices. Some of the state schools in rural areas are boarding schools and in the summer these are run as hostels.

Hotels and Serviced Accommodation

Norway's reputation as an expensive country is nowhere more evident than in the costs that you may be quoted for hotel accommodation. Prices are often considerably higher than in Britain and elsewhere in Europe. If you walk in off the hill you are highly unlikely to find a bargain. Also a word of warning; make sure that you know if the price quoted is per person or per room. That said, if you are able to book in advance some reasonable room rates can be found. For example, some of the hotels around Oslo Gardermoen airport have double rooms for around 700kr per room, and similar rates can be had in Central Oslo.

Accommodation and Tourist Information

www.visitnorway.com	A good portal for accommodation and tourist information
www.turistforeningen.no	DNT mountain huts
www.vandrerhjem.no	Youth hostels

Appendix C. Food and Fuel

Breakfast in bed   *Anthony Dyer*

Food

Eating out in Norway can rapidly drain your cash reserves but is often unavoidable at various stages of a trip. Few places in Norway serve filling food at a reasonable price. There are, however, some notable exceptions to this, such as the pizzerias found in many towns. Hotel meals tend to be extortionately priced, but the breakfasts can be remarkably good value. The traditional buffet breakfast, ranging from hot bacon and eggs through to cold meats, bread and drinks will often cost no more than 100kr. While this may seem expensive for breakfast, the "all you can eat" policy can be tested to the full by hungry backpackers fresh from the hills, and a generous lunchpack can also be assembled.

Eating in the mountain huts is also an expensive option, where non-members will pay 80kr for breakfast and 240kr for dinner. Moreover, because full-service huts have no self-catering kitchens, you have to cook outside on your own stove if you choose to forego the food from the hut. Most visitors to the Norwegian mountains will thus be self-catering for most of their trip.

From a small supermarket, a week's worth of backpacking food will cost maybe 20% more than in a premium supermarket in the UK. Large supermarkets are not found outside the largest cities; instead there are smaller supermarkets more akin to the Co-op. As such, the range of food on offer is proportionally less and the prices higher. You'll be able to get all your fresh produce, but you may be more challenged to find palatable dried food for a week of camping meals. Once in the hills, full-service huts will also sell basic supplies, including bread and cheese as well as sweets and chocolates. Self-service huts often have food and other basic supplies (but not fuel) for sale on an honesty basis, although note that the food will usually be tinned.

The opening hours of small shops can be quite restrictive. They usually close around lunchtime on a Saturday and are unlikely to open on Sunday, so a bit of forward planning is useful. When you're on public transport, finding a time or place for shopping is not always easy. Bringing most of your own food to Norway allows you to plan your food rations without having to "make do" with food that is too bulky to carry. Customs allows the import of up to 10kg of foodstuffs, including meat and cheese from another EEA country.

Outside the main cities, vegetarians are not well catered for in Norway, either eating out or self-catering. This is not too surprising in a land where hunting and fishing at the personal level are an integral part of the culture. Small supermarkets in the towns sell a reasonable selection of pasta, vegetables and fruit; but expect to struggle in a small shop in the country. Salads are very expensive in the north of Norway, root vegetables less so. Dairy products are, however, very common and available in an interesting variety.

Most visitors will find alcoholic drinks in bars prohibitively expensive. One beer can easily cost 60kr. However, in most areas supermarkets sell beer at prices similar to those in bars in the UK. Wines and spirits can only be bought at special shops (*vinmonopolet*) and are roughly two to three times UK prices. If you want a dram in Norway, it is best to take it with you.

Fuel

Camping fuel, including gas cartridges (both screw and pierceable fittings) and methylated spirits, is reasonably easy to get in Norway. In most mid-sized towns, there will be an outdoor store, usually of the "hunting and fishing" style, that sells these items. A large fuel canister will cost about 70-80kr. Many filling stations also sell gas and meths, which can be useful if you arrive in a town outside normal opening hours. You should note, however, that not all filling stations, including the otherwise handy one at Oslo Gardermoen airport, sell gas or meths, so you should plan trips on the assumption that they don't. One note of caution is that few campsites, unlike in the UK, sell fuel for the use of hillwalkers.

Appendix D. Maps

Turkart, M711 and Swedish mountain maps   Anthony Dyer

Maps for hill walking in Norway cover the whole country at the 1:50 000 scale and are published by Ugland IT Group (formerly Statens Kartverk). The 1:50 000 scale M711 map series is much akin to the British Ordnance Survey's Landranger series. Special maps called the *Turkart* series cover popular areas. These maps are derived from the M711 map series, but they cover larger areas and incorporate extra tourist information. On some of the older sheets the information is shrunk down to the 1:80 000 or 1:100 000 scale (without loss of detail) but 1:50 000 issues are gradually replacing these.

For maps covering the Swedish border, Norwegian *Turkart* maps show neighbouring Swedish areas whereas the M711 series maps do not. You can also buy Swedish 1:100 000 maps for the border areas and these are known as "*Lantmäteriets Fjällkarta*". These Swedish tourist maps include Norwegian data.

The maps are very accurate in the detail shown, but there are some key differences to note between them and the British 1:50 000 maps. First of all, the contour interval is 20 metres rather than 10 metres. While this helps cope with the generally much higher and steeper mountains in Norway, it can be challenging to estimate height gains and losses across undulating terrain. As an extreme example, a 39m height gain may only be marked by a single contour line. Furthermore, it is harder to estimate how narrow a ridge really is. Another note of caution is that cliffs and outcrops are not explicitly marked on the maps. While large cliffs are evident by tight contour lines, small cliffs require very careful inspection of the contour lines for any hint of their existence. Glaciers are marked on the maps but the location of crevassed areas are not, unlike on many maps of the European Alps. The authors have also seen several instances of small, crevassed glaciers present on the ground that don't appear on the map at all.

There are numerous suppliers of Norwegian maps in Britain. Most maps in the *Turkart* series are normally available from stock and are reasonably up-to-date. However, the authors have sometimes had M711 and *Turkart* maps delivered that have been old, out-of-date editions so it is wise to check the revision date of the map you are buying. We have found that The Map Shop is normally best for M711 series availability. They often have maps for quite obscure areas ready for next-day delivery.

Per square km, the *Turkart* map series represent good value for money and cost £11-12. The M711 series maps cover much less area for £9-10. However, for some popular areas Cordee sells the M711 series maps in bundles of six to nine maps for £22.95. Buying M711 maps like this makes them much better value for money.

Note that unlike Britain, where most newsagents and garages stock Ordnance Survey maps, very few places in Norway sell them. Bookshops are frequently sold out of maps of the local area, so you are strongly advised to purchase them before you go.

Stocklists

Cordee	www.cordee.co.uk
kartbutikken.no	www.kartbutikken.no
Maps Worldwide	www.mapsworldwide.com
Stanfords	www.stanfords.co.uk
The Map Shop	www.themapshop.co.uk

All of the 1:50 000 data can be viewed online, for free, with a very good zoomable map. This is especially useful in evaluating a particular area before buying the map.

Online Map

ngis2.statkart.no/norgesglasset/default.html

Appendix E. Weather

Atlantic Maritime weather in Norway is much the same as in Britain   Ian H. Robertson

The book assumes that the reader is familiar with typical Scottish weather conditions and the equipment required for a hill-walking trip in Scotland. The teaching of general weather principles for the purposes of mountaincraft is covered in other, more specialist books. This appendix aims to highlight differences in weather, climate and required equipment between Scotland and Norway.

Norway is a long country, stretching over 13° of latitude from Nordkapp (71°N, the most northerly point) to Lindesnes (58°N, the most southerly point). To put this into context, equivalent distances are from London to the southern tip of Italy in Europe, or from Boston, Massachusetts to Orlando, Florida in the USA. This inevitably gives rise to a wide range of weather conditions, although not as much as you might expect due to the moderating influence of the sea never being far away. Overall, however, the climate of Norway, like Scotland, is temperate maritime and is heavily influenced by the warm North Atlantic Drift current. Like Scotland, there is a pronounced east/west split in weather conditions. Western mountain ranges receive the brunt of the Atlantic weather fronts and showers while the eastern mountains and lower-lying areas enjoy a more continental climate, with less precipitation, warmer summers and colder winters.

Arctic Norway: a typical early evening temperature in March   Anthony Dyer

Most of the country is very close to the sea and this gives Norway a lot of precipitation. While there can be many days of rain, there are also long periods of settled weather, with high-pressure systems extending in from the Arctic or Russia. It is often the case that while Atlantic weather systems batter the southern half of Norway, the northern half is under a settled polar high-pressure system, and vice-versa. It is worth noting though that Norway is generally much less windy than Scotland. In terms of general summer trends along the country, the mountains of the north are cooler, drier and less windy than those in the south.

Summer

One of the key differences between Norway and Scotland is that Norway, being further north, is several degrees colder at sea level. During July and August, temperatures at sea level typically vary between 15°C to 25°C in southern Norway and 11°C to 25°C in northern Norway. In the mountains, temperatures vary between freezing point and 20°C. Snow on the highest tops during summer is not uncommon, but rarely will any new snow cover remain for more than two or three days. Old snow, however, lingers in large patches, often right through the summer.

Winter

Unlike their broadly similar summer climates, winter time in Norway is rather different to Scotland. Winter in the former extends over a greater number of months, from October to late April or early June high in the mountains. While coastal air temperatures can look just a little colder than Scotland (0–6°C), the inland temperatures get much colder. Often a drive of just 10km inland is enough to take the night time temperatures down by 10°C. You should be prepared for typical days out in temperatures of -15°C to -20°C. Whilst in still, sunny conditions this may feel quite pleasant, do not underestimate the effect of wind-chill at these temperatures. Night temperatures of -30°C are not uncommon inland during clear nights. In the mountains, snow depths often reach 3m and unlike Scotland, this may often be powder snow. This means that chokingly thick blizzards can be stirred up by even a moderate amount of wind and hold you hostage in a snow hole or hut for days on end. The snow starts to recede in earnest any time between mid-May and mid-June.

Midnight Sun

The Arctic Circle is the parallel of latitude that circles the globe at 66.6°N. It marks the southern boundary of midnight sun in the summer and polar night in the winter. This means that on the Arctic Circle there is one night at midsummer when the sun never sets. The further north, or the higher up a mountain, you are, the longer the midnight sun lasts. In Tromsø (70°N) it lasts from about May 21 to July 21. However, for latitudes further south, or indeed outside of the midnight sun period, twilight periods in summer last much longer than in Britain, often extending to several hours. The overall effect of midnight sun is that even in the mountains of southern Norway, routes are often possible at any time of day. Indeed, in Arctic Norway many will prefer to time their ascents to experience fully the amazing sight of a low sun rolling along the northern horizon for several hours. This freedom from the constraints of day-length also makes it much easier to cope with periods of bad weather.

Interesting weather facts

	Highest	Lowest
Mean Annual Temperatures	Rogaland 7.7°C	Finnmark Plateau -3.1°C
Mean Seasonal Temperatures	Oslo 22.7°C (summer)	Finnmark Plateau -15°C (winter)
Record Extreme Temperatures	Buskerud 35.6°C (summer)	Finnmark Plateau -51.4°C (winter)
Annual Precipitation	Sogn and Fjordane 5576mm	Saltdal 118mm

Data Source: met.no

Online weather forecasts

www.met.no	Norwegian Meteorological Office
www.met.no/snokart	Snowmap for Norway – updated weekly between October and June
www.ecmwf.int	European Centre For Medium Range Weather Forecasting
www.bbc.co.uk/weather/world/ north_europe/pressure.shtml	BBC weather – pressure and frontal information for Norway.
www.snoskred.no	Avalanche Information Service

Online forecasts are all very good sat at home on your computer, however on location in Norway you'll need further weather information. One tip is to get a friend with internet access to send you suitably detailed weather briefings by text message. Alternatively, daily newspapers are available in the most remote of shops and carry map-based forecasts, in one case up to five days ahead.

Below is a conversion table for wind strength, which is usually expressed as km/h or m/s in Norway, together with the Norwegian adjectival terms.

Norsk	English	m/s	km/h	miles/h	knots	Beaufort
Flau vind	Light air	1	3	2	2	1
Svak vind	Light breeze	3	9	5	4	2
Lett bris	Gentle breeze	5	16	10	8	3
Laber bris	Moderate breeze	7	24	15	13	4
Frisk bris	Fresh breeze	9	34	21	18	5
Liten kuling	Strong breeze	12	44	28	24	6
Stiv kuling	Near gale	16	56	35	30	7
Sterk kuling	Gale	19	68	42	37	8
Liten storm	Strong gale	23	81	51	44	9
Full storm	Storm	26	95	60	51	10
Sterk storm	Violent storm	30	110	68	59	11
Orkan	Hurricane	>33	>118	>75	>64	12

Appendix F. Equipment Recommendations (summer only)

In all mountain areas, you will often encounter snow (especially early in the summer season), even when you're not crossing glaciers. As such, depending on your chosen routes, it's advisable to bring your ice axe and crampons.

The key difference between what you carry in a Scottish summer pack and a Norwegian summer pack is some extra, warm clothing. Otherwise the equipment required is very similar and a checklist is provided below.

Those who have grown up walking in the European Alps may be accustomed to wearing capes in wet weather. These are not recommended for use in Norway, because the weather is often too windy and effective rainwear is essential. It is wise to remember the saying often attributed to Norwegians, "there is no such thing as bad weather, only bad clothing".

You should bring good sun protection. When walking at higher altitudes or on snow the intensity of UV radiation is much higher. Thus you should at the very least bring high factor suncream and consider wearing a sun hat. The glare from the snow and rocks can be very powerful and it is strongly recommended that you bring sunglasses with UV protection, to prevent snow blindness and other long-term ailments.

As with Scotland, a midge hood is good to have if needed, and DEET-based repellents provide some effectiveness.

Visiting climbers tempted by more difficult routes should note that in almost all of Norway, and certainly on mountain routes, there is a very strong traditional climbing ethic, for clean climbing and against the use of pegs or bolts. Anyone contemplating some of the roped routes in this book will need to able to place non-damaging protection, although pegs are acceptable on winter ascents and as abseil anchors if there is no alternative. Advice specific to an area, particularly to modern sport climbing venues, is best sought in local outdoor shops or by posting questions on relevant websites before your trip. The amount of climbing hardwear required for most of the roped routes in this book is a matter of personal choice – what is one climber's epic is another's solo. However, the authors have found that a selection of about 5 wired nuts, 2/3 medium-large hexes and some long slings are sufficient for most routes. The routes that involve more technical climbing (Romsdalshorn, Stetind and Piggtinden) will need a full leader rack.

Below are some lists of recommended essentials to bring:

Basic summer day trip
Boots, semi-stiffened if walking in snow
Gaiters
Good quality breathable waterproof jacket & trousers
Fleece jacket
Rucksack & dry liner
Hat & gloves
Wicking t-shirt, thermal top and bottoms
Quick drying trousers
Lightweight down jacket
First-aid kit
Map & compass
Waterproof map case
Food & water
Midge hood & insect repellent
Sun protection (hat, glasses, cream)
Ice axe when walking in snow. Consider crampons for some routes

A phone, GPS and camera are useful extra items, but not essential. Walking poles are good for stability on the extensive loose boulder-fields and during river crossings, especially when carrying a backpacking rucksack.

Additional items for backpacking
Tent (good-quality 3- or 4- season)
Kitchen set, ignition source & fuel
Mattress (foam or self-inflating)
Summer sleeping bag

Additional items for glacier travel
Helmet
Climbing harness (consider a chest harness also)
Rope (at least 30m × 9mm)
Prusik loops
Slings & screw-gate karabiners
Ice axe and crampons
Snow/ice anchors as appropriate

Additional items for scrambling
Helmet
Climbing harness
Rope, at least 30m × 9mm
Slings & screw-gate karabiners
Assortment of nuts and hexes
The technical rock climbs require a full leader rack, and twin 9mm ropes to ease abseils. Ropes for Norway should be at least 50m, and dry-treated are recommended.

Appendix G. Safety Notes

The notes in this chapter are to assist the reader in anticipating those characteristics encountered on a trip to the Norwegian mountains that differ from those found in the UK. We do not aim to summarise general mountaineering techniques and skills, which are described fully in specialist publications and taught on numerous courses.

Scrambling or Climbing

The authors wish to stress that unroped scrambling is potentially the most dangerous mountaineering activity, as a slip can easily have serious, possibly fatal consequences. That said, the pleasure of making rapid progress up an interesting route, unencumbered by the paraphernalia of pitched rock climbing, can be exhilarating. Despite many routes being on normally attractive scrambling rock such as gabbro, the rock is often less sound than visitors will be accustomed to. This is due to more vigorous frost weathering and a lack of traffic. The latter means that whereas many mountain scrambles in the UK involve following a well-worn track on polished rock, routes in Norway almost always involve much more route finding. Also, rocks often have a healthy cover of moss and lichen, making them very slippery in the wet. Be mindful of these factors, particularly if tempted to lunge for the comfort of a prominent spike at a tricky moment, or when setting off in unsettled weather. Progress steadily, pressing down rather than out on holds. Be conservative in your choice of route, especially on the first few outings in a new area, and don't hesitate to rope-up. The wearing of helmets is strongly recommended. Also, take note that in contrast to the common UK practice of scrambling up and walking down, you will often be required to descend the ascent route. This should be taken into account during the ascent, and the prudent will carry abseil equipment on the harder outings.

Glaciers

Many of the routes in this book involve glacier crossings, and it is this aspect of the Norwegian mountains that will be the source of much concern for visitors who may be experienced walkers but are unfamiliar with glacier travel. Whilst this is understandable and well-justified, glaciers add an extra element to any ascent and give a real mountaineering feel to what may otherwise be relatively mundane outings. They are, however, no place for the inexperienced. It is essential that you are properly equipped and have the appropriate skills before undertaking any glacier crossing. A good way to do this is to engage the services of a qualified Norwegian guide for several days at the start of a trip.

Even for those familiar with the technical aspects of glacier travel from, say, visits to the European Alps, there are additional hazards to be faced in some areas of Norway.

Crossing dry glaciers can be problematic
John Baddeley

Few Norwegian glaciers are more than several tens of kilometres from the sea. This makes weather conditions on them particularly fickle, and navigation on glaciers is notoriously difficult in poor visibility. The necessity to avoid crevasses means that it is hard to maintain a compass bearing and judge distance travelled as you would on normal ground. The use of GPS greatly aids general navigation, but cannot be relied upon for the safe passage of crevassed areas, even on a route safely traversed some days earlier. Where the descent is made by reversing the ascent route then the GPS trackback facility can be useful, allowing you to at least retrace your route should tracks become obliterated. The descent of any unknown glacier is potentially dangerous and difficult, especially so in poor weather with low-contrast lighting. Even detailed directions are insufficient as crevasse hazards change rapidly. Thus this type of route can be recommended only in clear weather.

Ice-caps of various sizes occur along almost the entire length of Norway. These great, open plateaux of snow and ice, ringed with cliffs and icefalls, offer unique and special mountain experiences, but they also present additional dangers. The weather over ice-caps is often worse than on nearby mountains of similar height. One further hazard is the increased exposure time to the weather. Due to the technical problems of travel, and the distances often involved, rapid descents are rarely possible should the weather change. There is a lack of natural shelter, and these large, frozen bodies have a noticeable cooling effect on the local environment. Being unconfined by the ridges that bound an alpine-type glacier, navigation is both more critical and more difficult. Of particular importance is the ability to locate the safe entry and exit points to the ice-cap. Typically there are few of these and they are situated on the steeper parts, around the edge of the ice-cap. Whilst finding a route up onto the ice may be relatively easy, locating a descent from above is usually much more difficult.

The authors have occasionally seen certain glaciers referred to as being "safe", with no need to rope-up. One look at photographs taken in a season with low snow cover exposes the fallacy of this view. While people with detailed local knowledge may be able to reduce the risks significantly, we recommend that users of this guide never travel unroped on a glacier. A possible exception to this is in the case of ski ascents with good snow cover, but even here a high degree of local knowledge is necessary before an informed decision can be made.

Fixed Equipment

Some of the routes in this book (e.g. Hermannsdalstinden, Råna) have fixed ropes in place. Like all fixed ropes in the mountains, these may not be in the same condition as they were when this guidebook was written. Nylon does deteriorate badly when exposed to UV light.

Anyone using equipment found in the mountains does so at their own risk. If in doubt, use your own rope. For example, although we ended up not using it, we took a 25m 9mm rope along for our ascent of Hermannsdalstinden.

The guidebook authors cannot be held responsible for the condition of any fixed gear nor for any mishaps or accidents from their use.

River Crossings

Mountain rivers and streams in Norway are generally much larger than those found in the UK. In most areas, high-level snow patches or glaciers supply water throughout the summer, meaning that levels stay high, or are even increased, after warm, dry weather. Furthermore, the generally sparse vegetation cover and thin soils mean that rain runs off soon after it falls, resulting in a rapid rise in water levels. Many crossing points, even on marked paths, are unbridged and where bridges are marked they may not be present. This is especially true of "summer bridges", intended to be there for the main summer season but removed so that they are not washed away by snowmelt in the spring. Detours to find places to cross safely may sometimes be measured in days rather than hours.

Visitors are recommended to familiarise themselves with safe river-crossing practices before visiting Norway. Remember that rivers are likely to be cold, swift-flowing and have a rough bed of boulders, and glacial rivers are opaque. Walking poles, or a handy piece of birch, can be a great asset to safe crossing.

Animals

There are few hazardous animals in the mountains of Norway. Of the large mammals, only musk ox (see chapter 23 on Dovrefjell) and moose are at all likely to attack humans, and then only when threatened. Much like the rest of Europe, the real problems come from the smaller animals. The only poisonous animal in Norway is the adder. Take the same precautions against these as you would in the UK.

The biggest animal-related problem comes from the healthy population of biting insects. Midges, mosquitoes and clegs (horseflies) are present in the mountains throughout Norway, and are particularly numerous in July and August. Although they are not vectors for human diseases, mosquitoes are the most troublesome of these pests as they can bite through a surprising amount of clothing. Penetrating thick woollen socks to get to blood-rich ankles is a particular favourite. Proprietary repellents are largely effective.

Lakes

The main hazard posed by lakes is caused when they are part of hydroelectric power schemes, which can result in large and rapid fluctuations in water level. Whilst unlikely to be a major problem in summer, in winter the effect is less obvious. Unseen under a layer of ice and snow, lake levels can drop by many metres. Unsupported and stressed, the ice weakens and may break suddenly with low additional loads. Extreme caution should therefore be used around such lakes, which are distinguished by distinctive shading on newer maps. On older maps, look for the lake surface height being given as a range rather than a single value.

Mountain Rescue

Mountain rescue services in Norway are organised through the police. If you require assistance in an emergency, dial 112. It is worth noting that, although it should in no way be relied upon, mobile phone coverage is surprisingly comprehensive in mountain areas.

Mountain rescue is normally free of charge, but there are cases of costs being passed on. You should consider purchasing an insurance policy that includes a substantial sum for mountain rescue, as helicopters are often used. Emergency medical treatment is free of charge for UK nationals. Other treatment must be paid for, although costs may be reduced if you carry a European Health Insurance Card (formerly E111).

Appendix H. Mountaineers' Norwegian Dictionary

English is spoken widely in Norway, often to a very high standard, meaning that English-speaking visitors generally experience few serious language problems. This does not mean that it is not worth learning some Norwegian. In many of the more remote areas, people either may not speak English or may be reluctant to do so. In these situations, opening a conversation with some bad Norwegian (*Norsk*) can be a great icebreaker. A further reason to learn some Norwegian is to access the many excellent guidebooks available.

With these factors in mind, we have compiled a short guide to Norwegian for the mountaineer. After some very brief grammatical notes there is a Norwegian to English dictionary that concentrates on words specific to the mountains, plus a few other essentials. Armed with these, plus a basic travellers' phrasebook/dictionary, you should be able to make good sense of many route descriptions.

The Norwegian Language

There are three official languages in Norway. Bokmål and Nynorsk are variants of what can generally be termed Norwegian (comparable with the relationship between Irish and Scottish Gaelic), and are inter-intelligible with Swedish and Danish. The third language is Sami, spoken in the far north and related to a group of languages found across Siberia. This guide is only concerned with the first two.

Bokmål is the variant used by about 90% of the population and the version usually encountered abroad as "Norwegian". Its use is concentrated in urban areas, principally Oslo and the South East. Nynorsk is found along the West Coast and, although far fewer people use it, it is the prevalent form in many mountain areas. Although not that hard to decipher when written, the traveller with only a few phrases to hand will probably be stumped by the spoken Nynorsk. An easy way to tell which area you are in is to see whether your milk carton says *melk* (Bokmål) or *mjølk* (Nynorsk). This guide uses Bokmål, due to its prevalence in the vast majority of publications.

Grammatical Notes

Norwegian has different genders for nouns and the effect of this is to alter the words used for "a" or "the". In addition, "the" is put onto the end of a word:

Neuter gender	*et hus* a house	*huset* the house	*husene* the houses
Common gender	*en bil* a car	*bilen* the car	*bilene* the cars

Taking this into the mountains, *Jotunheim* = home of the giants, *Jotunheimen* = the home of the giants. Occasionally, *-a* is added to the end of a word, *e.g.* *sola* = the sun. This is an example of the much-less-frequently used feminine gender and tends to be restricted to nouns that refer to objects found in the natural environment. A further variant is the use of *–ane* at the end of mountain ranges (*e.g. Trolltindane*). This is Nynorsk and reflects local practice, whilst the "official" version on maps might still be *–ene*. This generates much variation in the spellings of place names.

Telling the Time

Telling the time in Norwegian certainly takes some getting use to. Without going into the more obscure variants, note that if you hear a Norwegian time mentioned as *halv fem* (literally half-five) this is actually half-way to five; half-past four in English. It is an easy way to miss your bus, although timetables tend to use the 24-hour clock. Another time-related peculiarity is somewhat more useful. *Dag* = a day, but *døgn* = a 24-hour period (often used for hire periods, tube tickets etc.)

Dictionary notes:

The main point to note is that the endings of words are subject to much change, in addition to the definite article mentioned above. If the first part of the word matches, then you are probably on the right track but looking at, for example, an adverb. Compound words are common in Norwegian, which results both in some very long words and in many words that are not in smaller dictionaries (*e.g. breutstyr* = glacier equipment). These are easier to translate once you have got your eye in, and can attempt to spot the component words. The meanings can be somewhat harder to discern however. A well-know example is *røykfritt* (smoke-free) or *røyk fritt* (smoke freely). Also note that the letters peculiar to *Norsk*, æ, ø and å, are at the end of the alphabet. There is a good general-purpose Norwegian/English dictionary available at: http://www.tritrans.net/

Bakke	Hill, slope	Furu	Pine
Bekk	Stream	Før	Before
Berg	Mountain	Gamasjer	Gaiters
Bjørk	Birch	Geit	Goat
Botn	Corrie, hollow	Gleppe	Opening
Bratt	Steep	Grei	Easy
Bre	Glacier	Gå	To walk
Bregleppe	Bergschrund	Hakk	Notch (in ridge)
Bru	Bridge	Halvøya	Peninsula
Bu	(small) Hut	Hammer	Cliff, mountain
Bål	Campfire	Helle	Rock slab
Dal	Valley	Hestesko(tur)	Horseshoe (route)
Dyr	Animal	Hylle	Ledge, shelf
Egg	Ridge	Hytte	Hut
Elv	River	Høe	Hill
Enkel	Simple (easy)	Høst	Autumn
(ski)Feller	Skins (for skis)	Høyde (Høgde)	Hill
Fjell	Hill, mountain	Høyre	Right
Fly	Plateau	Is	Ice
Foss	Waterfall	Isbre	Glacier

Isøks	Ice-axe	Slutt	End
Kam	Crest	Smal	Narrow
Kant	Edge, rim	(ski)Smøring	Ski wax
Klatring	Climbing	Snø	Snow
Klyving	Scrambling	Snøfonn	Snowdrift
Kolle	Hill	Sommer	Summer
Komme	To come	Sovepose	Sleeping bag
Lett	Easy	(bre)Sprekk	Crevasse
Li	Hillside	Sted	Place
Lille	Little, small	Stegjern	Crampons
Liten	Little, small	Stein	Rock, stone
Luftig	Airy, exposed	Sti	Path
Løs	Loose	Stige (opp)	Ascend, climb
m.o.h	Metres above sea-level	Stor	Big, large
Man	One (third person)	Stup	Precipice, cliff
Mat	Food	Støvel	Boot
Meget	Very	Sva	Rock slab
Mellom	Between	Tak	(hand)Hold
Middels	Intermediate, Moderate	Tau	Rope
Morene(rygg)	Moraine (ridge)	Telt	Tent
Myr	Bog, marsh	Tind	Peak
Ned	Down	Tjønn	Tarn, mountain lake
Nedfiring	Abseil	Topp	Summit
Nes	Promontory, headland	Tung	Hard going (lit. heavy)
Norge	Norway	Ulv	Wolf
Nøkkel	Key	Ur	Scree/rocky ground
Opp	Up	Utstyr	Equipment
Os	Mouth of river	Vann	Water, lake
Pigg	Spike, pinnacle, peak	Vannhull	Water hole
Rapell	Abseil	Vanskelig	Difficult
Redning	Rescue	Varde	Cairn
Ruglete	Rough, uneven	Varm	Hot
Rygg	Ridge	Vatn	Lake
Sæter	Mountain farm	Vei	Road/route
Sjø	Lake, sea	Venstre	Left
Skar	Pass, col	Vidde	Plateau
(snø)Skavl	Cornice	Vik	Bay
Ski	Skis	Vinmonopol	Off-licence
Skog	Forest	Vinter	Winter
Skrå	Slanting	Vår	Spring
Skråning	Face (of mountain)	Øl	Beer

The ability to read, or attempt to listen to, weather forecasts can be an invaluable aid to trip planning once you are in Norway. Below we give a guide to the words most commonly encountered in weather forecasts.

(snø)Skredd	Avalanche	Regn	Rain
Byger	Showers	Skredfare	Avalanche danger
Fin dag	Nice day	Sky	Cloud
Flott	Fine, good	Storm	Storm
Fryser	To freeze	Tåke	Fog, low cloud
Hagl	Hail	Sol	Sun
Iskald	Freezing	Vind	Wind
Kald	Cold	Værmelding	Forecast
Luft	Air, sky		

Appendix I. Ski Touring; Part of the Norwegian Mountain Scene

Ann Quirk

The author in Trollheimen - classic mountain touring terrain   *John Baddeley*

Skiing has been part of Norwegian culture for at least 4000 years. It is thought to have begun with the migratory Sami in the north of what is now Norway, Sweden and Finland, who used it to speed up their travel for hunting. It spread south with the Vikings, and through them was exported around Europe. The word ski comes from the Old Norse word *skith*, a stick of wood.

Nowadays, many Norwegians ski recreationally and it is common to see several generations of the same family group venturing out on ski in the winter, in a similar fashion to a British ramble around the woods on a Sunday afternoon. Just as the popularity of hillwalking and mountaineering has increased over the last 140 years, skiing has developed onto the mountains. In Norway, this has commonly been touring through the valleys, but increasingly people are skiing up and down mountains and exploring new, more difficult areas. The sport now encompasses a wide range of activities from low-level racing to tackling the steepest off-piste descents, and even includes diverse variants such as ski-jumping and biathlon.

Approaching the summit of Rørnestind above Lyngenfjorden   *Espen Nordahl*

In trying to get an impression of mountain touring on ski the first barrier to overcome is one of nomenclature, as there is no single, accepted name that covers this area of activity. Names such as Nordic, free-heel, telemark, ski-mountaineering, cross-country, ski touring, and langlauf are all used, but mean different things to different people. Here we will use the term free-heel, as all variants have one thing in common – the boot is fixed to the ski by the toe only, leaving the heel free to rise. The other features of equipment for this type of skiing vary with the terrain to be covered and are a compromise of design between speed on the flat, downhill turning ease and weight.

For travel through forest and areas of rolling hills the skis of choice are lightweight, thin, long, not edged with metal and have a large "Nordic camber". This camber is seen if the skis are held up with their bases together – in the mid-section they do not meet. When someone stands on the two skis this middle section is clear of the snow. This clearance allows sticky grip wax to be applied to this area (wax pocket). When all of a skier's weight is applied to one ski it flattens onto the snow. This ski grips while the other glides and so forward motion is achieved (kick and glide). This is an efficient method of travel on more gentle terrain with the emphasis on speed and economy of effort, rather than downhill ability. They take a very skilled skier to change direction on anything more than a gentle slope. Boots are very light, like running shoes, and attach to the ski by a small metal bar across the front of the boot. The routes in this book would be unsuitable for this type of ski.

The most commonly used skis in the Norwegian mountains are what are generally termed "mountain touring" ski. These skis have some Nordic camber but this is generally softer, which makes turning easier but holding wax more difficult. They are fitted with metal edges to bite into hard snow and ice. To assist turning, the skis are wider front and back, with the narrowest area under the foot (sidecut). Turning is thus made easier by the shape of the skis, the lack of camber and because they are generally shorter. To give greater grip on steeper ascents, skins (previously animal skins) are applied to the base of the skis with the hair direction pointing to the back of the ski. As the ski glides forward, the hairs lie flat and make it relatively ease to glide, as pressure is applied to the ski the hairs grip the snow and stop the ski moving back wards. The boots are similar to mountain walking boots in leather or low-cut plastic, and attach to the skis via a flattened "duckbill" area at the front of the boot. Three holes in the sole fit onto pins of the ski binding and they are clamped together with a toe bail. This classic design was developed in Norway in 1927 and called the *rottefella* (rat-trap). Skis and boots are now available in a huge variety of styles, to accommodate the very wide range of tours being tackled on mountain touring equipment.

Downhill turns on free-heel skis generally require better technique than on Alpine gear due to some reduced control, but the full range of Alpine turns are possible and widely used. Indeed anyone doubting the downhill heritage of free-heel skiing should note that the "christie" family of turns takes its name from Cristiania, the old name for Oslo, and slalom comes from *Sla* (slope) and *låm* (track). Free-heel equipment also allows the telemark turn, named after a county in southern Norway where it was developed. In it, the skis are parallel through the turn but offset lengthwise, with the outer ski forwards, the inner ski back and the skier centred between the two feet with roughly equal weight on each. It is a satisfying and elegant turn, well suited to open off-piste descents particularly where the snow quality is variable, as it has superb fore-aft stability. These attributes make it well worth the effort of learning.

The telemark turn was born in Norway but almost forgotten until it was reborn in the USA in the 1980's, and it is there that has driven the recent radical change in the free-heel ski scene. Versions of mountain touring skis are now available that are very wide with large sidecut, the Nordic camber has disappeared and skins are necessary to travel even on the flat. These carving skis are superb fun on steeper downhills but their weight and the need for skins can make travel on undulating ground frustrating and slow. The skis are generally chosen for ski-mountaineering outings on steeper ground, where there is a single ascent followed by a long, exhilarating descent. These skis are often used with stiff plastic boots fixed to the skis by a cable which surrounds the heel, giving more control than the three-pin system. With the use of such equipment, there is an on-going expansion in the areas visited by free-heel skiers.

Svein Mortensen cruising down Store Russetind, Balsfjorden   *Espen Nordahl*

Skiing in Norway is possible for a long season and over a wide range of terrain and areas. The duration of the season varies with year, location and altitude but is approximately November to April in the south and March to June in the north. It is worth remembering that the prime season for skiing in Norway is somewhat later than in the European Alps, due to the lack of daylight and the extreme cold, particularly in the far north.

Most of the mountain areas covered in this book are skiable, but obviously this depends on conditions and your ability. We have indicated in the text some routes that are particularly good outings on ski, and one route, the ski traverse of Jostedalsbreen (chapter 18), is described as a ski route. Traditional mountain ski touring in Norway takes place on gently undulating ground. This may be lower-lying hill areas, high mountain plateaux such as the Hardangervidda, or through the valleys of ranges like Jotunheimen and Rondane. Extensive networks of huts in some areas allow multi-day tours with minimal gear to carry. More recently and with the developments in equipment, steeper mountains are being tackled in more extreme ski areas such as the Lofoten, Lyngen and Sunnmøre. In common with other mountaineering activities in winter, the risk of avalanche should always be considered carefully. Snow shovels are considered essential touring equipment, and carrying transceivers and probes (and the knowledge of how to use them) is recommended, especially if visiting the steeper areas.

In addition to enough touring terrain to last a lifetime, Norway has a selection of downhill ski resorts. They are characteristically quiet and friendly, and whilst they are small by Alpine standards they give ideal opportunities to combine some days honing techniques on-piste with day tours in the mountains. Hemsedal and Oppdal are particularly recommended for this kind of holiday, and Geilo, on the edge of the Hardangervidda plateau, is good for less confident ski-tourers. Ski jumps are also widely available for those requiring an extreme way to practice their telemark position.

Skiing is a natural development for many mountaineers. Getting into the sport in Britain is perhaps easier now than ever before, and there are some excellent shops and courses based in the Scottish mountains. Gear can be bought or hired from these specialist retailers, who will give expert advice based on years of experience. Courses in Scotland depend on the unpredictable weather and snow conditions, while the more reliable snow abroad can make learning easier. However, there is a thought that if you can ski in Scotland then you can ski anywhere!

Above all, ski touring is about being out and having fun in snowy mountains, so it's really just a version of what many readers will already aim for. If you haven't tried it, we strongly encourage you to give it a go.

Sources of more information:

Droste, P. & Strotmann, R. "Telemark Skiing". Meyer & Meyer Sport, ISBN 1841260827. *Refreshingly different, photograph-led instructions on how to telemark.*

Gillette, N. & Dostal, J. "Cross-country Skiing". The Mountaineers, ISBN 0898861713. *Comprehensive and humorous guide to the whole range of free-heel skiing, from lycra-clad racing to steep 'n' deep powder and expeditions.*

Parker. P. "Free-heel Skiing". The Mountaineers, ISBN 0898573069. *The authoritative guide to downhill techniques on free-heel equipment.*

Equipment Retailers

www.braemarmountainsports.com	Braemar (and Cairngorm) Mountain Sports, Braemar and Aviemore. Experienced retailers of free-heel ski equipment and Norwegian mountain enthusiasts.
www.mountainspirit.co.uk	Mountain Spirit, Aviemore – together with the above, Britain's best shops for free-heel ski equipment and advice.
www.killinoutdoor.co.uk/Ski.html	Killin Mountain Shop. Free-heel skis for hire and runs courses.

Appendix J. Bibliography – English Books on Norway

A small selection of guide books covering Norway   Anthony Dyer

Walking and Climbing Guidebooks – In Print

The following is a list of guidebooks that are in-print at the time of publication of this book (2006). A web-page has been set up on the Ripping Yarns.com website at:

www.rippingyarns.com/products/Other_Norwegian_guidebooks.htm

This will give links to these books along with a review. Many of these are available at amazon.co.uk, but some are more difficult to find.

Baxter, James. "Hurrungane". Scandinavian Publishing, ISBN 0955049709. *The definitive English guide to the Hurrungane area, giving a good selection of routes of all grades. Well illustrated.*

Den Norske Turistforening. "Norwegian Mountains on Foot". ISBN 8290339356. *English version of the comprehensive guidebook issued to all DNT members. Summary descriptions of all the paths that they maintain and all the DNT (plus many private) huts in the mountains. With a few exceptions, does not contain routes up mountains. Lots of interesting background information.*

Howard, Tony. "Climbs, Scrambles and Walks in Romsdal: Norway". Cordee, ISBN 1904207243. *A detailed English guide to the Romsdal area, giving a good selection of routes of all grades.*

Pollmann Bernhard. "Norway South". Bergverlag Rother, ISBN 3763348077. *A good little pocket book giving a selection of routes in southern Norway.*

Roos, Constance. "Walking in Norway". Cicerone, ISBN 185284230X. *A guidebook with multi-day backpacking and hut-to-hut routes.*

Webster, Ed. "Climbing in the Magic Islands". Nord Norsk Klatreskole, ISBN 8299319900. *A climbing and hiking guidebook to the Lofoten Islands.*

Welle-Strand, Erling. "Mountain Hiking in Norway". Nortrabooks, ISBN 8290103646. *Another guidebook aimed at multi-day backpacking along hut-to-hut routes.*

Weninger, Hans. "Setesdal". Panico Verlag, ISBN 9268072532. *Rock climbing in Setesdalen. Note that this book is mostly in German.*

Walking and climbing guidebooks to Norway tend to get published in small print runs and can go out of print surprisingly quickly. If you see one, don't think twice: buy it while you have the chance.

Guidebooks – Out of Print

The following is a list of guidebooks that are out-of-print at the time of publication of Walks and Scrambles in Norway (2006). These may be reprinted, or alternatively you can try and get a second-hand copy at www.abebooks.com or www.abebooks.co.uk . The British Library is also a good resource and may hold some of the books in stock www.bl.uk

Anon. "Rock Climbs in Arctic Norway". Norway Travel Association.

Anon. "Rock Climbs in Lofoten Norway". Norway Travel Association. *Definitive peak bagging guidebooks from the 1950's and 60's. Hundreds of peaks with summary descriptions. Popular summits have more complete descriptions complete with illustrations. These guide are very difficult to get hold of.*

Lennon, Peter. "Scandinavian Mountains". West Col Productions, ISBN 906227321. *A comprehensive coverage of many mountain areas, but the information on each route is not detailed. We believe that in some cases route descriptions have been taken from third party first ascent notes and may be out of date or inaccurate. Use with caution.*

Prag, Per. "Mountain Holidays in Norway". Norway Travel Association. *A compilation including first two books in this section.*

Travelogues – In Print

The following are not guidebooks but are well worth reading.

Collie, Norman. "From the Himalaya to Skye". Ripping Yarns.com, ISBN 1904466087. *Most of this book is not about Norway, but the chapter on original ascents in Lofoten is well worth reading.*

Lees, J. A. & Clutterbuck, W. J. "Three in Norway: by two of them", ISBN 8276940951. *Original classic text on the adventures of three men in Jotunheimen, which is well known and widely available in Norway as "Tre i Norge".*

Slingsby, Cecil. "Norway: the Northern Playground". Ripping Yarns.com, ISBN 1904466079. *The original, classic text on mountaineering in Norway, highly recommended, even today.*

Wold, Bjørn & Ryvarden, Leif. "Jostedalsbreen". Boksenteret Forlag, ISBN 8276830927. *An excellent coffee table picture book (in English) about the Jostedalsbreen ice-cap and its subsidiaries.*

Travelogues – Out of Print

The following travel literature is now out of print, second hand copies may be available at www.abebooks.co.uk

Fiennes, Ranulph. "Ice Fall in Norway". Mandarin, ISBN 0749319089. *A tale of parachuting onto Jostedalsbreen, traversing it, down-climbing an unknown icefall and rafting down its outflow. Bold, audacious and hugely entertaining.*

le Blond, Mrs Aubrey. "Mountaineering in the Land of the Midnight Sun", Fisher Unwin, London, 1908. *First ascents in the Lyngen Penninsula by one of the pioneering female British climbers (nee Elisabeth Main). Copies of this book are very rare and are priced accordingly.*

Oppenheim, Edwin Camillo. "New Climbs in Norway: an account of some ascents in the Sondmore district", Fisher Unwin, London, 1898. *First ascents in Sunnmøre in 1897. Copies of this book are quite rare.*

Styles, Showell. "Mountains of the Midnight Sun". Hurst and Blackett, London, 1954. *Showell Style's expedition to Lyngen in the 1950s. Not as useful as the Tom Weir book but still a fascinating read.*

Weir, Thomas. "Camps and Climbs in Arctic Norway". Cassell and Company, London, 1953. *An excellent book, describing Tom Weir, Douglas Scott and Adam Watson's expedition to Lofoten and Lyngen in the early 1950s.*

Appendix K. Bibliography – Norse Guidebooks

Walking and Climbing Guidebooks – In Print

There is naturally a greater number of Norse guidebooks in circulation. You should note, however, that these guidebooks are typically twice or even three times as expensive as similar guidebooks covering Britain. A quick search on Google by title or ISBN number will normally reveal plenty of suppliers for Norse guidebooks. However, two worthwhile online stores for Norse guidebook include:

Nordisk Korkhandel	www.scanmaps.dk
Norli Nettbokhandel	www.norli.no

Note that the list given below is by no means exhaustive and generally highlights volumes the authors have found to be useful. There is a large list published on www.dnt-fjellsport.no/oslo/index.php?fo_id=2177

General Guidebooks

Den Norske Turistforening. "Breføreren". *Handbook of DNT glacier group. Contains photographs of just about every significant glacier in Norway, with preferred routes marked. Hard to obtain without joining the group, but online version available (see* "Links").

Den Norske Turistforening. "Til Fots I Norge", ISBN 8290339062. *Previously called "Til Fots i Fjellet", this is the Norwegian version of "Norwegian Mountains on Foot".*

Helgesen, Morten & Helgesen, Julia. "Norges Fjelltopper over 2000 meter". Glittertind Forlag, ISBN 8299701309. *The definitive guidebook to the 2000m summits in Norway. Given its size, with approximately 500 pages & 600 photographs, it is astonishingly good value for money at 499kr.*

Thommessen, Erik W. "Kremen av topper: 40 høge turmål i Sør-Norge". Valdres Forlag, ISBN 8275620546.

Thommessen, Erik W. "Kremen av topper 2", Valdres Forlag, ISBN 8279810013.

Thommessen, Erik W. "Rondslottet – Lodalskåpa: turguide til 2000-metertoppene". Topografisk Forlag, ISBN 8279810226

Ryvarden, Leif. "Norges Nasjonalparker". Damm, ISBN 8204093241.

Ryvarden, L. & Wold, B. "Norges Isbreer". Universitetsforlaget, ISBN 8200374785.

Jotunheimen

Grønvold, Svein *et al.* "Jotunheimen: fra hytte til hytte". Gyldendal, ISBN 8205245215.

Schwarzott, Jan. "Under Storen". Sogn og Fjordane Forlag, ISBN 8290576072.

Thommessen, Erik W. & Skogheim, Tor Harald. "Jotunheimen – turguide Galdhøpiggen – Falketind". Valdres Forlag, ISBN 8275620007.

Thommessen, Erik W. & Skogheim, Tor Harald. "Jotunheimen – turguide Vågåvatnet – Gjende". Valdres Forlag, ISBN 8275620120.

Thommessen, Erik W. & Vigerust, Gunnar. "Jotunheimen – Turguide for fjellene mellom Bygdin og Gjende". Valdres Forlag, ISBN 8275620228.

The above three books are excellent, comprehensive guides to Jotunheimen and cover hut-to-hut routes, mountain walks, climbs and ski ascents.

Sunmøre, Romsdalen & Tafjord

Fylling, John H. "Tafjordfjella - fra fjord til verdens tak". Vista Forlag, ISBN 9299217792.

Gjelstenli, Iver. "Fra topp til topp i Romsdal". Printed in Molde, 1997. www.frusalen.no ISBN 8291883009. *Useful and comprehensive little guide with plenty of photos, sketch maps and English summaries.*

Grimstad, Leiv Arne & Wangen, Gunnar. "Sunnmørsalpane – Tindelandet". Vista Forlag, ISBN 8299217768.

Hagen, Jon & Standal, Helge. "Skiturar i Sunnmørsalpane". Iriss Forlag, ISBN 8299208114.

Hagen, Jon & Standal, Helge. "Molladalen". Iriss Forlag, ISBN 8299208106.

Møllebak, Tor & Bratlie, Espen. "Nordvestlandets fjellverden". Gyldendal, ISBN 8205190682.

Standal, Helge J. *et al.* "Fotturar på Sunnmøre". Iriss Forlag, ISBN 8299208149.

Other Areas

Anon. "Høyt i nord". Tromsø Klatreklubb.

Anon. "Lustrafjell". Luster Turlag, ISBN 8275600022.

Grønvold, Svein *et al.* "Hardangervidda: fra hytte til hytte". Gyldendal, ISBN 8205251983.

Grønvold, Svein *et al.* "Rondane og Femundsmarka: med tilgrensende fjellstrøk. Fra hytte til hytte". Gyldendal, ISBN 8205215464.

Sandvik, Hilde. "Til topps i Nordland". Forlaget Press, ISBN 8275471036.

Walking and Climbing Guidebooks – Out of Print

Johnsen, Ben & Skjerven, Ove. "Lyngsalpene". Universitetsforlaget, ISBN 8200065944.

Johnsen, Ben. "Jotunheimens stortopper". Universitetsforlaget, ISBN 8200226646.

Helberg, Claus *et al.* "Norges Fjellverden". Forlaget Det Beste, ISBN 8270101079.

Appendix L. Links and On-line Information

On-line information is continually changing, so the following is only valid at the time of publication (2006). Ripping Yarns.com will publish updates/addendums to *Walks and Scrambles in Norway* in electronic e-book format. Any major changes to this list can be found in the update at the www.RippingYarns.com website.

Climbs, Route Descriptions and Other Information

English Links

www.RippingYarns.com	Links to Norwegian climbing guidebooks, both published by ourselves and by others
www.mountaineer.plus.com	Anthony Dyer's website
www.scandinavianmountains.com	James Baxter's website, with route descriptions to many mountains over 2000m
www.hordafjell.com	Arnt Flatmo's website gives route descriptions for many mountains, especially in Hordaland
www.tilltopps.com	Bilingual site, describing the tours of three Swedes in many parts of Norway – particularly Jotunheimen
www.ii.uib.no/~petter/mountains/ norway_finest.html	Petter Bjørstad's website of Norway's 100 finest mountains
www.frostisen.com	Alan Law's trip reports include several peak bagging expeditions in the Narvik & Sulitjelma mountains
ari.rdx.net/abc/mountains/ nordic.htm	"Ari's Base Camp" gives information on many different mountain areas, including Norway
home.online.no/~mariusbe/nor/ areas.html	Kristian Martinsen's home page has overall information on the different Norse climbing areas, with many good links
distantpeak.com/web/mountains/ norway	Interesting peak bagging articles on Norwegian mountains
www.lowefoto.com/norway	Vincent Lowe's galleries of numerous Norwegian mountain areas
www.summitpost.org	Under "mountains" menu, search under Norway for relevant articles
www.ntk.no/pages/ NorwegianAlpineClub%20.htm	Norwegian Alpine Club
www.fjords.com	An excellent portal for information about the western fjord district
www.stetind.nu	Climbing information on Stetind
http://www.nomadstravel.co.uk/	Tony Howard's website.

Norse Links

www.fjellforum.net	Discussion forum for Norwegian hillwalking and mountaineering
www.etojm.com	Includes extensive information on tours, the 2000m summits and popular mountain ranges in Norway
www.bergtatt.net	Many articles on summit tours in Norway
www.nfo2000m.no	A site dedicated to facts about the 2000m summits of Norway
www.toppomania.info	Peakbagging site, with some English summaries and plenty of pictures
www.snoskred.no	Avalanche conditions for mountain areas of Norway on the international scale. Detailed accounts of past avalanches
www.tinderangling.net	Two sites dedicated to the summits in
www.sunnmorealps.com	Sunnmøre
www.dnt-fjellsport.no/bergen/ index.php?fo_id=1692	Excellent online version of the Breføreren guide to routes on all major Norwegian glaciers, with maps
www.fjelluft.com	Summit tours for different mountain areas
www.iriss.no	Good site from publishers of "Fotturar på Sunnmøre", with lots of route descriptions and photos with routes drawn on

Web cameras

www.webkameraerinorge.com /webcams.php	Links to web cameras all over Norway

Mountain Guides

www.msmg.org	Midnight Sun Mountain Guides, a very friendly bunch of people based in Tromsø. Orientated towards ski trips but they also do summer work.
www.nordnorskklatreskole.no	Nord Norsk Klatreskole, climbing guides based in Henningsvær, Lofoten. They have also have a pub and basic accommodation
www.telemarkskico.com	The Telemark Ski Company. Wide range of free-heel ski courses, including tours in Norway.
www.adventure-scotland.com	Good free-heel ski courses, but not in Norway.

About the Authors

Anthony Dyer

Anthony was born in West Sussex in 1978. He read Physics at Manchester University before becoming a systems engineer in the aerospace industry. At 23, Anthony climbed all the Scottish Munros after extensive involvement with the Manchester University Hiking Club. Anthony now climbs and makes regular trips to Norway He lives near Preston, Lancashire.

John Baddeley

John's love for the Norwegian mountains began in 1988, when his work as a research biologist took him to northern Scandinavia and Spitzbergen for the first of seven seasons. He walks and climbs in Scotland and abroad, and is an enthusiastic ski-mountaineer in Norway and the Alps. Away from the hills, John races yachts in Scotland, and has skippered boats as far afield as the Caribbean and south-east Asia. He currently lives in Aberdeen, Scotland.

Ian H. Robertson

Ian was born in 1967 in the Scottish Borders. He currently works as a consultant engineer to the North Sea oil and gas industry. In his "spare" time, Ian runs Ripping Yarns.com. As well as walking and mountaineering in Scotland and in Norway; Ian has climbed or walked in the Eastern Alps, Pyrenees, Sierra Nevada, Jordan and Tanzania. He lives near Aberdeen in Scotland.

The authors are happy to be contacted via Ripping Yarns.com.

Acknowledgements

The authors all wish to thank: Ann Baddeley, Mary McCallum and Denis Wilson, for proof-reading.

Ann Baddeley, Nicola Barnfather, James Baxter, Leif-Dan Birkemoe, Petter Bjørstad, Arnt Flatmo, Mike Forrester, Jan Fredrik Frantzen, Øyvind Heen, Tony Howard and Di Taylor, Frode Jenssen, Krystina Lotoczko, Kjell Olav Maldum, Espen Nordahl, John Sundt, Denis Wilson and www.fjords.com for kind permission to use their photographs.

Anthony thanks: Nicola Barnfather and Robert Atkins for helping me reach Stetind, Eric and Inge Frederiksen for supplying old maps and rare literature, Marianne and Michael Dyer for their continued support, and Manchester University Hiking Club for making me what I am today.

John thanks: Ann for all her help and patience through this project, Tone and Svein Birkemoe for providing Oslo basecamp and introductions to some of our guest authors, Lis Cooper for access to her extensive contacts diary, Mike and Morna Forrester for their tolerance, Espen Nordahl for his excellent remote guiding services, John Quirk for some directional inspiration with the maps, and Colin Bruce for his enthusiasm for the Norwegian mountains, which kept me going there when others scoffed.

Ian thanks: Krys for putting up with my time spent on Ripping Yarns.com (and for suggesting we go to Lofoten!) as well as taking some great photos. Anthony and John are due a huge thanks for giving up a year of their spare time to write this book, as are the guest authors who also gave up their spare time. For inspiration, I want to thank Krys, Aberdeen Mountaineering Club, David Durkan, all at Turtagrøs Venner and, last but by no means least, Cecil Slingsby.

All the authors thank the countless unknown Norwegians who have been friendly, helpful and hospitable to us through our travels in their beautiful country.

Updates and Errata

Although the authors have made every effort to ensure that this guidebook is as accurate as possible, conditions do change in the mountains. Rockfall, glacier shrinkage, erosion and forestry plantation can all change a route significantly.

If there are any errors in this book, or if the mountain conditions have changed since it was published, please contact Ripping Yarns.com at the address at the front of this book, or by e-mail at admin@rippingyarns.com.

Any errors or updates that we are aware of will be posted on the website as a free e-book download.

Index of Mountain Names

Names in **bold** are mountain areas in this book, numbers in **bold** refer to descriptions of ascents, numbers in *italics* denote maps. See notes in Appendix H regarding word endings.

303